GUIDE FOR THE CHRISTIAN ASSEMBLY

THIERRY MAERTENS – JEAN FRISQUE

GUIDE FOR THE CHRISTIAN ASSEMBLY

REVISED EDITION

9th to 21st WEEKS

Translated from the French by MOLAISE MEEHAN, O.S.B.

Nihil Obstat: V. Descamps
can. libr. cens.

Imprimatur: J. Thomas, *vic. gen.*
Tournai, February 24, 1970

LCCCN: 72-114245

ISBN: 0-8190-0006-X

2773

Translated from the original French edition,
Guide de l'assemblée chrétienne, Casterman, 1970.
An edition of St. Andrews Abbey, Bruges.

CONTENTS

NINTH WEEK

I. Tobit
1:1-2; 2:1-9
1st reading
1st cycle
Monday

The book of Tobit belongs to a literary genre that was very widespread in the East in the 4th century: tales of edification. The author lived doubtless in the 1st or 2nd century, B.C. His legalism is like that of the Pharisees, and his devotion to angels resembles that of the Jewish apocrypha. His purpose is altogether religious. He wants to show how a particular family, like many others, adapts itself to God's plan, and reveals him to the world. Our passage belongs to the first portion of the book (Tb 1:3-3:17), where we are introduced to the protagonists in the story.

The first scene shows us Tobit's *family* in exile, at the time of the Pentecost celebration. The meal is abundant, as would be expected in a comfortable family, anxious to celebrate the great occasions in salvation history. The father however is troubled above all about the poor (cf. Lk 14:12-14), and tells his son to bring a poor brother, thus training him to have concern for the less fortunate.

But Tobit returns alone because he has found on the road the corpse of a Jew (v. 3), the victim of racial violence. The father alone has the courage to respect the dead in spite of the danger (vv. 4 and 7). He carries out the law of ablutions (vv. 5, 9; cf. Nb 19:11-13) as a scrupulous Pharisee. Surely it was such scrupulous fidelity that gave Jewish families the firm resistance they showed towards challenge.

The whole book of Tobit is a sort of personal journal where family and national events, joy and mourning, observance and devotion are mingled. It is in the ordinary texture of life that God manifests himself: the divine presence is always in proportion to a man's acceptance of the problems and situations with which life confronts him.

II. 2 Peter 1:2-7
1st reading
2nd cycle
Monday

Exegetes in general reject the Petrine authorship of this letter, because of the over-anxiety displayed by the writer to represent himself as Peter (2 P 1:1, 16-18; 3:1-2), and because of some improbable details (2 P 3:16). Furthermore the most ancient Christian communities displayed a similar hesitancy about Petrine authorship.

The author may have been Simon Niger, of Antioch (Ac 13:1). He was part of the delegation sent to Jerusalem to learn James' view about relations between Christians of Jewish and Gentile origin (Ac 15:16). This is of course no more than one among many hypotheses. All agree however that the text is of late redaction.

The author immediately confronts the Christian with the characteristic principles of his life with God, and with the divine *power* he has (v. 3). Power in this context generally indicates God himself in the gift of his graces (Ac 8:10), especially in salvation (Rm 1:16; 1 Co 1:18; 1 Th 1:5) and in the sharing of his knowledge. Philosophers of the time, Stoics in particular, were wont to stress the primacy of knowledge in the conduct of life. The author thus is affirming at the outset that knowledge is found and developed in communion with the divine power.

It cannot thus be a speculative knowledge, but a knowledge that is expressed in action (vv. 5-7). Sharing the divine life is no platonic escape or futile gnosis. It is concretely expressed in seven virtues, which symbolize serious purpose and accomplishment.

III. Mark 12:1-12 *Gospel Monday*

It seems that the primitive version of the parable of the murderous vineyard workers was rather more sober in tone. We can probably recover the original words of Jesus by comparing the synoptic versions with that of the apocryphal gospel of Thomas. Subsequently it was allegorized by the early Christians (Israel-vine, rejected stone) to convey the meaning of Jewish history and the basic tenets of christology.

a) In the original we have the owner of a vineyard (v. 1), who, because he is far away, is obliged to deal with the workers by means of his servants or his son.

The circumstances are those of the contemporary economy. The country was divided into huge *latifundia* which belonged for the most part to foreigners. The Galilean and Judaean peasants who rented these lands, displayed, under the influence of zealot propaganda, a lively opposition towards such owners. It is improbable that Jesus had the vine of Isaiah 5 in mind.

Killing the heir was a way of getting possession of the land. Land left vacant in such a way became by law the property of the first occupant. In the parable though the workers make a mistake. The owner will return to take possession of the vineyard and he will entrust it to others (v. 9).

What was Jesus' purpose in recounting the parable? Conceivably he may have wished to distinguish himself from the Zealots. Injustice might indeed reign in the world; but the kingdom of God would not come through violence and hate. But he was addressing himself principally to the leaders of the people, who readily identified themselves with "vineyard workers." He is telling them that they have not been faithful to their task, that the land in consequence will now be given to others, to the poor above all (cf. Mt 5:4). He has often asserted that the Good News, because it is rejected by the leaders and notables, will be given to the little ones and the forsaken (Lk 14:16-24; Mk 12:41-44).

b) The primitive Church very quickly allegorized the parable. To verse 1 was added an allusion to Isaiah 5:1-5, and to verse 9 reference to 2 Chronicles 24:20-22. The idea was to read into it the *history of the vine-Israel,* her constant rejection of the Messiah (the meaning of "Son" in verse 6; cf. Ps 2:7; Mk 1:11; 9:7), and finally the transference to the apostles of the workers' prerogatives (not now to the poor, as in the primitive version).

c) Mark gives us another kind of allegorization, reading into the parable the outlines of *christology.* There is a gradation in the treatment given to each servant, leading to the theme of the son's death. He calls the son "well-beloved" (v. 6), and borrows verses 10-11 from Psalm 117/118:22-23, which prophesies the resurrection of Christ (cf. Ac 4:11; 1 P 2:7). So he makes the original parable an allegory of the Lord's death and resurrection.

IV. Tobit 2:9-14
1st reading
1st cycle
Tuesday

Here we have a description of the trial undergone by the elder Tobit.

a) The trial is described in quite popular terms. The accident is grotesque, and the doctors despite their skill only succeed in aggravating it (cf. Mk 5:26). The author is demythologizing the ancient theme of trial. It is not the eschatological catastrophe foreseen by the Jewish apocalypses. It is not given the meaning of the Servant's suffering as he expiates for a whole people, or the metaphysical suffering of Job. It is cut down to the proportions of an ordinary accident. The inevitable accompaniment of the pathetic human state.

This is an attitude which actually distinguishes Matthew from Luke. Where the latter, particularly in the beatitudes, concentrates on the eschatological aspect of things, Matthew makes the dimensions of the Kingdom those of ordinary life. The author of Tobit, in like fashion, is consoling his disconcerted contemporaries. The people are not going to find salvation by waiting for some catastrophic trial or a miraculous intervention. They should simply submit humbly to the ambiguity and dreariness of the human lot.

b) An addition by the Vulgate (vv. 12-18) likens Tobit's suffering to Job's. In both cases the suffering puts an end to family happiness. The hero's lot is aggravated by his wife's mockery (v. 11; cf. Jb 2:9), and his patience is emphasized (v. 18; Jb 1:20).

V. 2 Peter 3:12-15, 17-18
1st reading
2nd cycle
Tuesday

These are the author's final recommendations to his readers.

a) He wishes that Christians would live in expectation of the *Day of the Lord* (v. 12; cf. 2 P 3:1-10) and "hasten" its advent by their spiritual preparation and their good works. Far from being something fated, the end of time is determined by spiritual causes like preaching (Mt 24:14), prayer (Mt 6:10; 1 Co 16:22), or practice of the virtues (v. 14).

b) However, the Day of the Lord will be marked by a total *destruction* of the universe (vv. 12-13; cf. 2 P 3:10), in order that the world of God may be manifested. It will be a world of justice (Mt 5:6; 6:33; Is 51:6; 56:1), not necessarily corresponding to Jewish expectation (banquet, rest, etc.), but an altogether new phenomenon (Is 65:17; 66:22; Rev 21:1-5).

VI. Mark 12:13-17
Gospel
Tuesday

This passage is from the section on "temptations" to which Jesus was exposed by Scribes, Pharisees and Sadducees. The herodians make the first assault, ready as they are to detect whatever is damaging to Caesar. They were expecting some such mistake at an early stage from Jesus. His pretensions to Messiahship must inevitably compromise him where the emperor was concerned.

The formula for the question was the classic one among experts in the law: "Is it permissible . . ." Is it permissible to pay tribute (regarded by the Jews as a religious obligation) to Caesar, a foreign prince who does not belong to the line of David and consequently has no divine right to rule over the people? Jesus responds by an argument *ad hominem.* You people accept the authority and advantages of the Roman empire: consequently you should accept its laws and requirements. He does not make any affirmation about the legitimacy of the power; but simply states that it is accepted and thereby requires to be obeyed. By this attitude he desacralizes tributes. It is no longer, as the Jews regarded it, a religious act for the upkeep of the temple, a recognition of the theocracy. It is a profane act, governed by the common good.

The questioners then are put in their place but their pro-Romanism is confirmed. That is the reason for the addition "render to God what is God's." Which is to say: you must so act that your civil obedience does not interfere with your duty to God.

We have then a double teaching. *Civil authority* must be obeyed, above all by people who reap its advantages (Rm 13:1-8; Tt 3:1-3; 1 P 2:13-3:17), but this obedience must never interfere with the higher obedience one owes to God.

The famous contrast between that which is Caesar's and that which is God's accordingly does not indicate any real opposition.

There could not be any question of that of course. The Kingdom of God is not something extraneous to the earthly kingdoms he assumes in Jesus Christ. Wanting to render to God what is God's implies that one is rendering his due to Caesar also. The Kingdom of God is not of this world in the sense that it is not just another earthly kingdom, but it is in this world in the sense that it penetrates all earthly kingdoms. No one can be authentically Christian who opts out of this world, and all such attempts will ultimately locate a style of life that precludes the true God as well.

There is no reason then for the Church to secure herself a reserved space, a center where she can maintain herself as the visible sign of a world reconciled to God. She can no longer make any pretensions to empire over a profane and secularized world. It is not by making the world visibly Christian but by sending her members into the world as dispersed persons that she will bear witness to that world of its salvation in Jesus Christ.

VII. Tobit 3:1-11, 16
1st reading
1st cycle
Wednesday

Here we have two people who are carrying all the suffering and woes of humanity. The generosity of the elder Tobit towards the unfortunate receives poor recompense, because he is stricken blind. And Sarra is the victim of some strange curse that kills her husbands one after the other.

In the lot of both the problem of *evil* makes itself vividly felt. Suffering, in their eyes, comes from God, a chastisement for faults (vv. 3-4). That is why they ask God to take away their life (vv. 6, 10). Is not their suffering without issue? A blind man will never recover sight; the bewitched woman will remain so always. They are destined to have no more happiness on this earth.

We might ask ourselves whether their prayer of resignation and confidence, humble and sincere, is really according to faith. Is it not based on an erroneous concept of retribution? And have Tobit and Sarra a clear understanding about evil?

Is not such a prayer as this a sort of judgment on God, a kind of human logic where God's love is questioned in favor of some ideal we concoct? We think in terms of recovering an earthly paradise rather than of salvation that must be built in hope.

Why do we always feel that God is involved when the matter of evil arises? Does it not have something to do with the somewhat material concept of deity that is still quite prevalent in our Western world? We see him as the "prime mover," the "mechanic" of our universe, directly blaming him for any faults in the mechanism, real or apparent. But such a notion has nothing to do with the God revealed in Jesus Christ.

We should be careful indeed not to lump together so similar phenomena, suffering, catastrophe, war and sin. These are profoundly differentiated when we take man's role into account, direct or indirect. We should never confuse the malady that afflicts with the imperialism that crushes, the selfishness that isolates, the indifference that wounds.

Nevertheless, of course, evil does exist. Our mistake lies mostly in considering the problem in isolation from human liberty. Our attitude should not be one of seeking intellectual justification for a relation between evil, God and love. The hallmark of Christian faith is the discernment of meaning in events and in human existence according to the light of a salvation which makes all history a pilgrimage.

Men no longer believe that the universe is made up of forces which dominate like a fatal destiny. They know on the contrary that it is their business to bend nature to their service and advancement. The achievement of this will come at the end of a history that is punctuated by human liberty.

The solidarity between man and the universe shines forth in the person of Jesus Christ. Saint Paul saw in him the one who unites in himself the totality of creation, now brought to its perfection, a creation in which man holds the central place. The great unity will only become apparent fully at the glorious return of Christ as conqueror. But even now "the sufferings of the present time are not to be compared with the glory which will be revealed in us" (Rm 8:18-21). Whenever we feel tempted like Tobit and Sarra to regard God as responsible for the evil that is a constant in life, we should recall the other truth. In Jesus Christ God came to share our predicament, accompanying us on all the roads we must travel, bearing with us the burden of a struggle that leads gradually to liberation. His exigent mercy strips us of all the subterfuges we resort to in the struggle against sickness, war and selfishness. He leads us towards an ever-growing mastery over nature that will contribute to the service of mankind. Because we recoil from the temporal challenge, we take refuge in a multitude of excuses and pretexts. The example of Jesus, who precedes us in the struggle, shows how paltry they are.

God is with us. He knows the sinner's state. Sinless himself, he passed through the crucible of our physical and moral suffering. Since that we are never alone.

If evil, suffering and death are certain facts, as indeed they are, our faith challenges us to take a new look at situations that seem sometimes intolerable. They become possible in the light of our hope in Jesus Christ. What this will one day bring us we must now live despite obscurity. We are risking our total existence on the promise of a salvation that has already begun, but is yet to be actualized.

VIII. 2 Timothy 1:1-3, 6-12
1st reading
2nd cycle
Wednesday

Some critics reject the Pauline authorship of the letters to Timothy. None of the arguments they put forward are convincing however. It is of course true that things have changed since Paul wrote his first letters. New problems have arisen. Is not this sufficient to explain the difference in style? The apostle moreover has aged. He is more serious, more disturbed about the outcome of his work. The teaching of 2 Timothy however, and indeed the style, are sufficiently similar to the Pauline letters generally to allay doubts about authenticity.

a) When the letter was written, the Church was scarcely institutionalized as yet. Paul had full authority over the communities he had founded, and over some others to which he delegated disciples, especially Timothy. Such "legates" had full power over local authorities, and were invested with a special grace as a result of imposition of hands (v. 6; cf. 1 Tm 1:18; 4:14). The celebration was conducted by a college of "presbyters" (1 Tm 4:14), presided over doubtless by Paul himself (v. 6, more exclusive than 1 Tm 4:14). In today's passage Paul is not very explicit concerning Timothy's powers. He merely insists on the grace that has been given of not being ashamed of the gospel (vv. 7-9). In some not very fully explained way Timothy is to be his "successor" (2 Tm 4:5-7); he is commissioned to teach (2 Tm 2:15); to decide certain problems (1 Tm 5:19); to determine the liturgy (1 Tm 1:1-12); to recruit ministers in the Church (1 Tm 3:1-13; 5:22).

Are we then to regard Timothy as bishop? What are his relations with presbyters? The pastoral letters do not enable us to answer these questions. All we can say is that Paul's letters to Timothy reflect the transition through which the primitive Church was passing as the apostles begin to disappear. Precise relations had to be established between the communities and their *hierarchy*.

b) The hierarchy is defined as *service of the gospel* (vv. 10-11). A member of it, that is to say, who exercises authority over a particular community, can only do so insofar as he takes on responsibility (and has a mandate to this affect) for proclaiming the gospel to the world. He must moreover be a prolongation in some way of the manifestation to humanity of the man-God, who destroyed the alienation of death and provided unhoped-for access to the life of plenitude (v. 10).

In other words the leader of a community is more than just the capable administrator, who presides over the liturgy and catechesis. He is the one who has the proclamation of the gospel most at heart. Hierarchy is not concerned with internal matters only, but first of all with external mission.

We can ask ourselves what is the function now of the hierarchy in the people of God, and what service it should render. Basic in our approach should be humanity itself as it happens to be here and now. We must take man himself seriously. He is the builder of history, the shaper of all those functions—social, economic, political, scientific, technological—that go to make it up. We must understand humanity, not as a given, static entity, but as something that is constantly remolding itself.

Human history has a meaning. Moved by the Spirit of God it is en route towards the future reassembly in a kingdom of life (v. 10), under the aegis of that "symbolic" community which is the Church. That is what the gospel means (vv. 10-11). To give this direction to human history a particular function is necessary, the "priestly" function exercised by Jesus Christ. He has enabled humanity, through himself first of all, then through his brethren, to cooperate in God's plan of absorbing all into his own life. This is what the "manifestation" of Christ means (v. 10).

This priestly function is taken up by the whole people of God, priests and laity. The Church is the symbol of this divine destiny of humanity. She accepts the mission and responsibility of giving a new meaning to this story of the gradual liberation of humanity from every kind of alienation (the forces of nature, the power of money, sin, the sacral world, etc.). Her priesthood consists in the christological dimension she gives to human history, in the manner in which her members live it.

To fulfill all this, she too needs her special functions. Among these is what we call the hierarchy. This ought not to be seen as an assembly of "priestly men," but rather as a college of "pastors of priestly communities." The hierarchy enables the Christian community to exercise its priestly function in the world, by being a constant reminder that the source is Christ, of whom it prolongs the "apparition."

It is not presented, in 1 and 2 Timothy above all, as a "priestly caste," such as the Jewish priests of the Old Testament, or those of pagan religions. Its function on the contrary is one of "desacralization."

We need to study the place of the presbyterate in the Church from two angles: its service in the fold of the Church, making her more priestly, and its involvement with humanity as a whole, giving human destiny a christological dimension.

After such study, perhaps we shall develop insights about new possibilities. Doubtless in the future we are liable to see fewer all-purpose parochial clergy, and more specialized priests. Some will have the charism of celebration, some of mission. Some will follow a profession, some will give their whole time to the community. Some will be married, some celibate. Some will be temporary (not in the sense of "temporary ordination"), some permanent. But all will be for the service of the people of God as a whole.

IX. Mark 12:18-27
Gospel
Wednesday

Jesus continues his discussion with the principal representatives of the Jewish sects. Here the Sadducees are questioning him concerning the resurrection of the body, and bring up an argument designed to show its absurdity (vv. 18-23). His response is ambiguous. The terms in which he mentions marriage in the Kingdom (v. 25) and affirms the resurrection itself (they shall be as angels) are mysterious. The quotation he uses seems at first sight rather unrelated to the Sadducee's argument.

a) We might indeed wonder how Jesus could have regarded the text of Exodus 3:6 as a confirmation of the *resurrection of the body*. The reference to the God of Abraham, Isaac and Jacob (v. 26) is in fact not so much the God the patriarchs adored, but the one who made a covenant with them and protected them. In that he is not a God of the dead but of the living (v. 27), he could have no reason for protecting and forming an alliance with those doomed to die, even belatedly. Why should he aid the patriarchs to triumph over enemies, and then abandon them to die. If Abraham is definitively dead though God proclaims himself his Savior, his salvation would be a mockery. Consequently Abraham and the patriarchs must rise again.

Abraham, Isaac and Jacob were beneficiaries of the covenant because they were founders of the chosen people. This means that the blessings they received will extend to each member of that people. The Jews now enjoy the protection of Yahweh in the land of promise. This would also be illusory, were it not destined to culminate in divine protection against the only real enemy: death.

All this of course is not contained in the single text cited by Jesus. We cannot however fault the use he makes of it. He interprets it in the light of Israel's development in faith.

b) His second affirmation is still more cryptic. Speaking of conjugal relations after the resurrection, he describes the state of resurrected humanity as quasi-angelic, something that scarcely accords with the concept of bodily resurrection.

He does not in fact take any position on the nature of *angels*. Nor does he mean to say that the risen body becomes angelic to the point of losing corporeity. That would be a statement of the problem in terms foreign to Jewish anthropology, for which the angels were "celestial bodies." He is simply affirming that the resurrected state transcends human intelligence. It is remarkable indeed that the gospel always resorts to angels whenever there is question of something that transcends understanding. An angel tells the women of the Lord's resurrection and ascension. "Being as angels" then is not really a description of the resurrected state: it is an affirmation that here is something transcending earthly intelligence.

It is certainly not true that love, conjugal or otherwise, will be suppressed at the resurrection—only the procreative function. It is interesting that this is the only means man has to ensure survival, to give himself the illusion that he is conquering death. Such a function will obviously be no longer necessary when man is living for eternity. Progeny, or towers of Babel, will not be needed for the perpetuation of one's name. The resurrection will be an acceptance from God of a gift, the gift of a life and a name beyond the reach of any human effort.

X. Tobit 6:10-11; 7:1, 9-17; 8:4-10
1st reading
1st cycle
Thursday

Because the original text of the book of Tobit is lost, we are dependent on versions which vary considerably. Thus the marriage service between Tobit and Sarra varies according to the translators, who were more anxious to give the ritual they knew themselves than that of the original text.

a) All the rituals of marriage make a point of the formal request by the spouse to the bride's father for her hand (Greek, v. 7:9). The girl is not present at this interview, nor is her consent officially required. The request may be conveyed by the "friend of the spouse," and this is the case in the ritual given by the Greek versions (v. 7:9) and the Vulgate (v. 7:12). Generally the friend sings the praises of the groom in order to allay any fears on the part of the bride's family (Vulg. v. 7:12). Raphael stresses the fact that Tobit is a relative of the bride, in accordance with an ancient prescription of Jewish law (Nb 36).

If the bride's father is religious, he tries to discern God's will in the events. Raguel performs this priestly function in declaring God's will, confirming that everything is in conformity with the law of Moses (Vulg. v. 7:14), and blessing the wedding night of the young couple (Greek v. 7:12).

Only at this moment, according to the ritual in the Greek versions, is the girl brought to her fiance. Her father takes her right hand and puts it in that of the fiance (Vulg. v. 7:15; Greek v. 7:13). This appears to be the essential marriage gesture. Where the versions vary is in the formula used by the father. The Vulgate gives us a blessing of the God of Abraham, Isaac and Jacob on the couple (the formula with which the nuptial mass of the Roman rite concludes). An old Greek version gives a mutual presentation of the spouses to each other, and a blessing of the wedding night (theme of fecundity). "This girl is given as wife according to the precept of the law of Moses: may the Lord of Heaven be favorable to you this night" (v. 7:12). Other Greek versions have a similar formula of presentations, followed by a general blessing: "May the God of heaven conduct you in peace" (v. 7:13).

Though the law of Moses says nothing of this, the Jews of the Diaspora, under pressure of foreign laws, had developed the practice of signing a contract (Greek v. 7:14; Vulg. 7:16) by which the father of the bride affirmed that he had given his daughter in conformity with the law of Moses. One Greek version indicates that the father must append his seal (v. 7:14) to the contract. The Hebrew version, which is quite late, mentions the presence of two witnesses to the contract signature (v. 7:12).

Doubtless the contract had to mention the sum given by the groom to the bride's parents to compensate them for the loss of their daughter, taking it from her dowry. But we have no mention of this in the book of Tobit. Finally, all the versions indicate that the marriage rite is concluded by a meal (Vulg. v. 7:17; Greek v. 7:14), after which the couple enter the nuptial chamber (Vulg. v. 7:18; Greek v. 7:15).

b) What teaching concerning the rite of marriage is conveyed by the different versions?

The first thing that strikes us is the *inferior position* of the bride. The contract is between the father and the groom. Even though the girl is consulted and has the real love of her prospective husband, as is the case with Tobit, nevertheless she cannot give ritual expression to her consent. She must let herself be led by her father to her husband. Not until the revelation of Christ is the wife destined to receive recognition of her personality.

c) Another notable feature is the *profane* nature of the ritual. It would be wrong indeed to read biblical texts in the light of the modern distinction between sacred and profane, but it is interesting to compare the ancient Jewish ritual with our actual practice. In the former it is sufficient that each protagonist, groom, bride and father fulfill a role in order that God be present to bless. The contract is composed exclusively of profane clauses concerning economic settlements; and the contract is sufficient to seal the validity. The Christian sacrament and ceremony is much more sacralized. We insist on having all the natural elements (as in a civil union under state law) repeated before the priest in order to secure the divine blessing. Do we not run the risk of ignoring the natural, and resorting to a supernaturalism that is foreign to the postexilic Jewish ritual?

d) The purpose of the book of Tobit is to reveal *God's presence* in the events of everyday life and to show that the ideal family life is one that is constantly lived in this presence. The preceding verses show us how anxious Sarra's father is to know the will of God concerning the union between his daughter and Tobit. Likewise the young couple turn towards God at this moment when their destinies are united. The Vulgate actually tells us that they decide to spend the first three nights of their marriage in prayer (vv. 8:4-5). We have here a somewhat Manichean note that is unknown to the other versions. But these do have the young couple make a prayer of thanksgiving, with a blessing (*blessed* may you be . . . , vv. 8:5, Greek; 8:7 Vulg.), an anamnesis of the marvels of God (here, the creation of the first couple: vv. 8:6, Greek; 8.8 Vulg.), an epiclesis calling on God to protect the new couple (which begins with the customary formula, *and now* . . . , vv. 8:7, Greek; 8:9 Vulg.); and the final Amen as ratification (v. 8:8, Greek, not in the Vulgate).

This prayer, which deserves to be included in the corpus of Christian prayers, is strongly marked by the religious tone of pious Jewish families. The Vulgate rightly puts it forward as a contrast to the climate of heightened sexuality that the Jews were encountering in the countries of their dispersion (v. 8:5). Tobit himself, in the epiclesis, actually says that he is not approaching his wife to seek pleasure (vv. 8:7, Greek; 8:9, Vulg.). The only anxiety the couple have is to ensure a posterity who will praise the name of God. Is this something to clinch the discussions about the primary and secondary ends of marriage?

Tobit's and Sarra's marriage is essentially a profane matter. It belongs to the domain of the terrestrial: the parents' consent, discussions about choice of spouse, sealing of a contract, exchange of presents, a meal in common between the families. All these juridical procedures are coupled with moral and psychological data. Egoism and passion (Tb 8:9) are assessed, and modulated by love. Thus the encounter with God becomes possible.

Marriage then has a religious value in itself. The priests' intervention in the ritual (an intervention that did not take place in Israel) is not for the purpose of giving a religious meaning to something that already has that. It is to draw marriage into that great current of "blessing" (vv. 15-17), whereby the Church praises God for his work of salvation.

XI. 2 Timothy 2:8-15
1st reading
2nd cycle
Thursday

Paul has just sketched for Timothy's benefit the story of his apostolic life. It has been exclusively a story of struggles and frequently painful labors. He recalls that he is actually carrying the chains of captivity (2 Tm 2:1-7). However, the memory of Christ's glorious passion (vv. 8-10), and the certainty that his own life will be transfigured (vv. 11-12, which reproduce an early liturgical hymn) ought to encourage the minister of God.

a) The great *leit-motif* of the Pauline gospel is the doctrine of *Christ's resurrection.* It was the risen Christ encountered on the road to Damascus, and this he made the basis of his kerygma. With that he associates the davidic filiation (v. 8), showing that Jesus is not only a heavenly being but altogether a man, sharing the state of apostles.

b) He asserts that there is a relation between Christ's *suffering* and that of the apostle. Both are an accomplishment of God's plan for men in granting them salvation and glory (v. 10). What he is affirming is the value, towards communion, of suffering. It is the source of our relation with Christ, whom we imitate, and with other men, the "elect," in the glorification of whom we collaborate.

c) The principal theme of the hymn that he reproduces (vv. 11-13) is the identification between Christ's suffering and his glory, and between our suffering and our glory. The association arises from *baptism* and from the mystery of Christ's death and resurrection which is symbolized by this sacrament (v. 11b). All postbaptismal life falls into three stages: death already experienced (verb in the aorist; v. 11); sufferings here and now (verbs in the present: v. 12); and the coming kingdom (verbs in the future). This development will not effectively take place unless the Christian remains loyal to baptismal faith (vv. 12b-13). Christ, for his part, will be faithful: he cannot go back on his word.

XII. Mark 12:28-34 *Gospel Thursday*

Jesus, who has been continuously under assault from the Jewish sects, has just dealt with the trap laid by the Sadducees concerning the tribute (Mk 12:13-17). Now a Scribe puts a question concerning the greatest commandment. Whereas Matthew (Mt 22:34-46) puts this incident in a polemic context, Mark, curiously enough, shows us the good dispositions of this man, and his genuine wish for enlightenment. He is the only one to put in Jesus' mouth a eulogy of the Scribe (v. 34). Possibly the synoptics were anxious to gather in a single section a number of polemic episodes, but that Mark did so more awkwardly than the others. The details that he gives are doubtless original, but they fit badly into the desired context.

Jesus replies to the Scribe's question by giving two commandments of love (vv. 29-31), whereas he had only been asked for one. The text of the first is from Deuteronomy 6:4-5, but in the version used in the Jewish morning and evening prayer. The second is from Leviticus 19:18.

Mark reproduces the two precepts, but treats them as of different orders (v. 31). He is adhering to the Jewish practice which juxtaposed the two as a resume of the law. Matthew and Luke mingle the two texts, or speak of one commandment only.

Mark too is alone in reporting the Scribe's commentary. While Matthew however makes love the key to the law, he has the Scribe say that it is above all the key to cult pleasing to God (v. 33; cf. Am 5:21; 1 S 15:22).

Love of God and men is the very core of Christian liturgy. And it is in the eucharistic celebration above all that the indissoluble link between love for God and love for all men is rooted and developed in the Christian soul. This is the heart of Christian initiation. At that very moment when we are called upon to render thanks to the Father for his initiative of love, we are also called upon to be united with all those who are our brothers in Jesus Christ. The thanksgiving is centered round the brotherly sharing of the same bread. It necessarily implies mission, which is the highest expression of love for all men.

Whenever the Church assembles members or future members, she is putting them in relation with God and with all other men. This principle is basic throughout the whole ecclesial institution. Whether it be a eucharistic celebration, a liturgy of the Word, or merely a Catholic Action meeting, it is never a question of assembling now to give thanks to God, and again to turn towards men. The fidelity that is forged on each occasion, that we are asked to deepen, is a single fidelity, a love that includes both God and men.

XIII. Tobit 11:5-17
1st reading
1st cycle
Friday

When the marriage ceremonies have been concluded Tobit and Sarra set out for the house of the elder Tobit. Scarcely have they arrived when the young Tobit applies Raphael's medicine to his father's eyes. The father recovers sight (vv. 11-13) and at once renders thanks to God for his goodness (vv. 14-17).

In the book of Tobit we have the symbolic history of exiled Jewish families. When plunged in darkness, they gradually discover that the only eyes that can remain always clear are those of the heart. A mysterious salve restores *light* to ailing eyes (Rev 3:18), enabling them to see events in God's way, not with man's myopic vision. At the time the Jewish devotion to the angels was so strong that they would not imagine Tobit's healing without Raphael's mediation. The angel's intervention is merely the screen for the very presence of God.

Light, for a Jew, indicated happiness above all. Like life, it is considered a gift of God which gets its true meaning in the covenant. Yahweh is the light of his people because he loves them, and awaits their return to fidelity. Man however is a sinner, and the consequence of sin is the kingdom of darkness or misfortune. Conversion is necessary before Yahweh restores light definitively.

In proportion to the deepening of her insight concerning temporal retribution. Israel begins to realize that light is more than just material happiness. The essential lies at a deeper level. A man's heart must be enlightened if he is to develop proper fidelity; it is he who must reject sin. He cannot reach that point unless God enlightens him. The Father has already brought Jesus through darkness to glory. Anyone that follows Jesus' path can have the same illumination (Jn 8:12).

XIV. 2 Timothy 3:10-17
1st reading
2nd cycle
Friday

Having reminded Timothy of the past marvels of evangelization (2 Tm 1), and shown the present difficulties (2 Tm 2), Saint Paul now considers the future dangers. There will be heresies and perversion of doctrine, apostasies and persecutions, the prelude, as he sees it, to the decisive conflict between good and evil. Anxious to forearm his disciple for the oncoming conflict, he tells him to avoid heretics (2 Tm 3:1-9), to imitate his own example and follow his teaching (vv. 10-14), but also above all to learn constantly from Scripture (vv. 15-17).

a) The example he offers his disciple is that of a spirit molded in the school of *trial*. Because persecution cannot fetter the Word, the interior dynamism of his gospel (Ph 1:13-19), he is convinced that trial is contributing to the salvation of those for whom he works (v. 10) as well as to his own (v. 11). He is glad to see his disciples sharing the same trials. No believer can escape this. On the contrary, here he finds the certainty that his apostolate is succeeding.

b) These verses are among the most explicit in all the New Testament concerning the value of *Scripture*. Paul reminds Timothy in the first place that all his education has been after the Jewish fashion, in the holy writings (v. 15). It is not based on theories or magic formulas like the education of heresiarchs, but on written documents, the "scriptures."

These are in themselves efficacious. They do not give merely a philosophic or cosmic knowledge, but a "wisdom" that is none other than "faith." It is then natural that those who profess to instruct others should base their teaching on the Scriptures (v. 16), whether this is catechetic, apologetic, or ethical. The man of God (v. 17) who uses the various resources of Scripture, and relies on their efficacy, is an "accomplished man" truly equipped for the ministry.

He stresses the fact that the Scriptures are inspired (v. 16). Their language differs from human language, because it was formulated with the power of the Spirit who directed the prophets. For this reason are they useful to the preacher, and it is important that he be impregnated with them.

The presence of God in the salvation-history which the Scriptures record for us, above all in the Word *par excellence* which is Jesus Christ, is the best guarantee of the Christian's faith and hope. But scriptural knowledge will only be full, when it is the possession of a man who is also anxious to discern the presence of God in the event and in his involvement. Scripture is the rule of faith, but faith must also see the world as a gift of God, invariably modern.

We can never in fact dissociate the Bible from the event. Faith is a living reality, by no means a mere ideology, but a manner of encountering God, the Father of Jesus Christ. This is the Jesus of whom the Bible witnesses. The community in the context of which our faith is expressed is that very people of God which first expressed its faith in the Scriptures. Faith is lived in the event, and Scripture is the norm by which the event must be interpreted.

The whole Bible is a book made up of events and reflections, even in its most contemplative areas. When we reflect on the events recorded there we learn to reflect in the same way on our own actual circumstances. It can only become living for us if it turns us to consideration of our own actual lives. The believer can never read it as an ancient document, but as a sort of searchlight on his life. He seeks there the same sort of clarification of what is happening now that was given of what happened then. This is indeed the whole function of the homily which follows the scriptural reading.

It is nevertheless natural to us to turn rather to the real event than to any book, however sacred. Catholic Action movements, after the pattern set by Msgr. Cardijn, have tended to exalt the event over the book in the famous principle of "observing, judging, acting." The review of life begins with observation of life's events, and works towards a discernment of them in the light of Jesus Christ (and thus, implicitly at least, of the gospel). It has the advantage of focusing on the actual and concrete, while "gospel-sharing," where group members help one another to make the Word of God actual, runs the risk of going no further than general considerations about Christian existence.

This sort of development, which emphasizes the event, is in fact in conformity with the evolution of the Church itself. She is quitting the stage when everything was preestablished, and passing into the stage of "diaspora." Believers, scattered in the world, are influenced by the obscurity which envelopes them. Where the "biblical" approach was above all doctrinal, emphasis on the event is above all prophetic. It teaches us to discern the presence of Jesus Christ in the event, and to recognize him as the one who gives meaning to history.

The two approaches are indeed complementary, but the missionary requirements of the Church demand changes of emphasis. If we try to apply these principles in liturgical celebration, we must recognize that domestic liturgies illustrate their application admirably. We could have a structure where the liturgy of the Word comes at the end of a review of actual living and pooled experience. The members would already be alerted to the meaning of the events they are living. The biblical Word would be as it were the final consecration of their study, and the ratification of their decisions. They would the more easily pass to a genuine thanksgiving to the Father, who is present in all things and in all people.

XV. Mark 12:35-37 *Gospel Friday*

This is Jesus' fourth discussion with representatives of Jewish sects. This time it is with the Pharisees. He assumes the direction of the debate at once, concentrating on the question of the origins of the Messiah.

According to the Scribes, the Messiah would be son of David, though David considered himself to be Lord. In the East it was inconceivable that a father would allot the title of Lord to one of his sons. If David made such an affirmation, it could only be under the inspiration of the Spirit. Jesus' argument follows a rabbinic procedure which contrasts two traditions or two biblical texts in order to reach a synthesis. That is the reason indeed for his final question: "If he be Lord, how can he be Son?" The answer evidently could only be that the Messiah could not be at once son of David and Lord, unless he were both man and God (Rm 1:3-4). Christians would discern this, as they contemplated the paschal mystery. They would often cite Psalm 109/110 to show how the son of David is also son of God (Ac 2:34; 7:55-56; 1 P 3:22; Rev 3:21; Col 3:1; He 1:3, 13, etc.)

Jesus' messianic royalty then transcends the nationalist royalty of David. His words however had been assembled with particular care by the primitive community, who discerned in them an affirmation both of resurrection and divine sonship. They understood the word "Lord" in the sense they gave it after the resurrection. Messianic royalty was fulfilled in the lordship of the risen Son of God. Their association of the messianic title with the Lordship of Jesus (cf. further Rm 1:1-5) indicates that God had taken to himself not only humanity in general, but humanity in concrete, contemporary terms, in the social and political Palestine of the time. The Messiah is a gift of God, but also the product of human history.

XVI. Tobit 12:1, 5-15, 20
1st reading
1st cycle
Saturday

At the end of a long journey undertaken by the young Tobit, Raphael, his companion and guide, delivers a discourse which reflects the sapiental ideas about family life, charity and prayer.

The presence of such virtues in a faithful *family* is a proof that God is their protector and guide. The discourse is brief, but very fine.

XVII. 2 Timothy 4:1-8
1st reading
2nd cycle
Saturday

This passage is a sort of farewell discourse. It is a literary genre which requires a number of elements that are stressed in this instance: satisfaction at having accomplished one's mission (vv. 6-7; cf. Jn 17;6-13; Ac 20:20-21); announcement of coming departure (vv. 6-7; cf. Jn 13:33; Ac 20:22-25); solemn blessing of those who remain behind, sometimes coupled with an adjuration (vv. 1-2; cf. Gn 49; Jn 17:17; Ac 20:36); prophecy of future trials (vv. 3-5; cf. Jn 15:18-16:4; Dt 31:21; Tb 14:4. Ac 20:28-32).

a) Into this general context Paul introduces several important ideas. He views the task of bearer of the *Word* under its various aspects (proclamation of the Good News: v. 5): refutation of errors; exhortation; the particular form of preaching for those undergoing trial (Rm 12:8); finally, instruction, which could very well be the function of the teachers who initiated Gentiles to Christian faith. All this activity he sees against a background of struggle against false doctrines (vv. 3-4; 1 Tm 1:3-7; 4:1-16; 6:2-10; 2 Tm 2:14-18), which seek to mingle Christianity with Judaism and gnoses of all kinds.

b) As in 1 Corinthians 1-3 Paul reacts vigorously against such "humanization" of the "Word." This is proclaimed in the name of God, in the sense that it has the actual dynamism of the Kingdom itself. To understand Paul's argumentation in contrasting the Word of the gospel with the words of false teachers, we must remember the biblical theme of struggle against *false prophets* (Jr 23:9-14; 14;13-16; Dt 13:2-6). These latter presumed to attribute to their message the efficacy of the Word of God itself. One has to share Paul's confidence in the efficacy and power of the faith (1 Co 2:5) which is frequently supported by miracles (2 Co 12:12; Ac 4:32; 5:12), to appreciate the vehemence of his adjuration, and the severity with which he condemns error. The more to impress Timothy, he appeals to the power (the name) of the coming Kingdom (v. 1).

XVIII. Mark 12:38-44
Gospel
Saturday

The two episodes in this passage bring to a conclusion the series of discussions between Jesus and the Jewish sects. The episodes are basically associated; a malediction of those Scribes who despoil widows (vv. 38-40) is followed by the blessing of the widow (vv. 41-44), both serving to illustrate the parable of the vineyard workers (Mk 12:1-9). The leaders of the people are going to be deprived of their privileges, and the Kingdom will be offered to the poor.

The *rich-poor* antithesis, or in this case Scribe-widow, is something we frequently find in Christ's eschatological discourses. It is connected with the similar contrast in the beatitudes (Lk 6:20-24), which proclaims the imminence of the Kingdom and the renewal of unjust situations. It is not so much a matter of either defending or condemning a particular social situation. The purpose is to emphasize the upheaval in human structures that will be consequent on the advent of the final times, when life will be a sharing in the very life of God.

For this reason the episode forms a very excellent introduction to the eschatological discourse which follows immediately (Mk 13).

The widow has given from her needed sustenance, by contrast with the rich who give from their power and privilege. She falsifies, that is to say, the proverb about being able to give only what one has. She does not even possess what she gives.

Perhaps, in this, we have an image of God himself. If it was true that he gives only from his abundance, he might be better represented by the rich than by the widow, and it would be hard to understand the importance given by Jesus to the widow's gesture. But what if God also gives from poverty? If we avoid a certain sort of theism and concentrate on the acts of God as revealed in Jesus Christ, we shall realize that godhead means service. It means giving not what one has, but what one is. The poor, enslaved Jesus is more than a mere episode of godhead: it is of the essence of godhead. He did not come on earth as a tourist visits under-developed countries. He was a slave because poverty was essential to his godhead. We begin to see why he takes the side of the poor.

TENTH WEEK

I. 2 Corinthians 1:1-7
1st reading
1st cycle
Monday

The second letter to the Corinthians is made up of a series of fragments from different letters. We have a piece concerning the collection for the Jerusalem Christians (2 Co 9); a harsh letter written by Paul in answer to a movement against him at Corinth (2 Co 10-13); and a piece which reflects the favorable results gained by that letter (2 Co 1:8). This must have been sent some months before the apostle's return to Corinth in 56 or 57.

Paul is disturbed about the repercussions from his previous letter "written in sadness, anguish and tears" (2 Co 2:4). The news reaching him however is good. Accordingly he makes a thanksgiving which is all comfort and *consolation.* It is not possible for us to be certain about the distasteful experiences Paul has had (cf. v. 8), though he gives us a fairly extended list of them (2 Co 11:24-33). Among them certainly was the opposition of the Corinth community. This at least is now removed and some balm is poured on his wounds for the moment.

Misfortune and consolation have a theological emphasis in Pauline language. The word he uses in speaking of misfortunes, *thlipseis,* designates in Jewish apocalypse the trials preliminary to the inauguration of the Kingdom, which guarantee a share in it (the meaning of "temptation" in Mt 6:13; cf. Mk 13). He adds however a christological nuance. Suffering now is more than a preliminary to the Kingdom. It is a way of sharing the Messiah's sufferings (v. 5; Col 1:24) and preparing for his glorious coming.

Consolation (*paraclēsis*) also has a doctrinal emphasis (vv. 4, 6). It arises from the suffering itself, provided that it is lived in Christ. It is a share in the "abundance" of that life which springs from the cross and is an anticipation of eternal life (2 Th 2:16-17). It plays its part in the great Christian conflict with the powers of the universe, that attempt by suffering and persecution

(Lk 21:12-19) to prepare the way of anti-Christ. Christ sends his disciples the Spirit-Paraclete (Jn 8:13-18; 16:5-14), who provides the dynamism of the new world that moves towards glory in spite of opposition and challenge.

The Church must always be pitted against the angelic powers in suffering and misfortune, and against the powers of the universe in persecution and contempt. These repeated assaults however cannot but enable her to recognize in herself that dialogue between God and man which is mediated by the Spirit.

II. 1 Kings 17:1-6
1st reading
2nd cycle
Monday

The career of Elias comprised three complementary traditions, which are reproduced in chapters 17-19, 20, and 20-22. We may have the first appearance of the prophet recounted in chapter 21, and the second in chapter 17. The order of events in his biography then would be that of Scripture.

a) Achab has gone apart from God, who henceforward acts as if the king did not exist. The answer to the king's rejection is God's silence. Elias is in fact speaking in his own name (v. 1): he is not transmitting an oracle of God, or proclaiming a divine action, but dealing with Achab according to his own dialectic. If Yahweh does not exist for the king, Elias will show what the consequences of this nonexistence are, the nonexistence of rain or any prophetic word. He pushes Achab's atheism to the limits of absurdity.

b) Subsequently Elias hides himself and lives a hermit life, in which some people have found the origins of *monasticism* (vv. 2-4). He evades the king's minions, and manages still to bear witness even in his retreat. In the midst of a people who deny God, he continues to be the only one to demonstrate God's existence and solicitude. This eremitic existence indicates some points of resemblance between Elias and Moses that were to be developed by other traditions about the career of Elias. He is just as intransigent as Moses was in the face of Baalist syncretism. Like Moses and the people in the desert (Ex 16:8-12), he receives his nourishment from God, water from the rock and meat from the raven (v. 6).

In today's world, characterized by the silence and the "death" of God, the Church, isolated and challenged, finds herself the only witness of the living Word. In the eucharistic celebration she offers up the agony of her isolation and lack of understanding, just like Elias, and just like Christ at Gethsemani.

III. Matthew 5:1-12a
Gospel
Monday

The beatitudes, as originally delivered by Jesus, were doubtless short formulas in prophetic style. They proclaimed the advent of the Kingdom as foretold by Isaiah, for whom the poor, the hungry and the afflicted would be the beneficiaries of God's salvation (Is 58:6-10; 61-1-3; 49:8-13, etc.). They were an affirmation that the time had come when the privileges of the Kingdom would be accorded, not on the basis of merit or particular conditions fulfilled, but simply because of God's will to save.

a) Luke invested the predominantly prophetic and eschatological tone of these formulas with a sapiental teaching, which offers compensation here below to the afflicted. He interprets them in the light of Jesus' doctrine about poverty and the use of riches. He makes them an apologia for the sociologically poor, the social class to which the first converts belonged (Ac 4:34-5:11).

Matthew's attitude is different. He is concerned to give the gospel a deeper moral dimension, and interprets the beatitudes in the light of the *new justice,* and the spirit of the sermon on the mount. Where Luke distinguishes between a "now" and a "future," he suppresses this distinction. The Kingdom is already present for anyone who wishes to grasp it, by a life in conformity with its justice. Both evangelists have in fact superimposed on the prophetic tone of Jesus' words (God is coming to save), Matthew a moral emphasis, Luke one that is all at once sociological, logical, and eschatological.

b) The *poor,* who are the beneficiaries of the gratuitous salvation of God in the original (Is 61:1-3), become for Luke the sociological poor. For Matthew they are beneficiaries because of their spiritual attitude.

Luke regards as beneficiaries of the future Kingdom the persecuted, the victims that is of events which for the Jews augured the last times. Matthew goes deeper by making the precision that they be persecuted for justice's sake. He has a similar modification of the beatitude of the hungry. They were among the beneficiaries of the future Kingdom for Isaiah (Is 49:6-13). Luke takes them as those who are really hungry for bread (see the parable of the rich man and Lazarus). Matthew, with his moral bias, makes them hunger for justice.

As a further reinforcement of this teaching Matthew adds some further beatitudes to those of Luke, all of them with a similar thrust. Blessed are the "merciful" (charity and pardon); the "meek" (probably a doublet merely for "poor." The Aramaic word for both is the same, and Matthew by the doublet in translation passes from the sociological to the spiritual); the "peace-makers" (or better still: the carriers of peace); and finally the "pure of heart" (a reference to the legal purity that enabled people to "see God in the temple," for which Matthew now substitutes a more spiritual purity, as in Mt 15: 1-20).

The three or four original beatitudes of Jesus were not a proclamation of the conditions necessary for entry to the Kingdom. They were rather an affirmation, in prophetic idiom, that some afflicted folk (the categories usual in prophecy) had finally touched the benevolent concern of God. Very soon, altogether gratuitously, he would inaugurate his Kingdom.

In Luke, this kerygmatic emphasis is profoundly modified. The beatitudes are not now concerned with God's initiative, but with man's predicament (cf. the interpellation "you"). The direct style reinforces this. Luke indeed gives us four maledictions which create the impression that salvation is attainable by some classes, but refused to other. His vocabulary is extremely realistic (have your fill, laugh . . .), the product of social and vengeful eschatological attitudes that were common in some communities ("now" . . . "then" . . .).

Matthew has another view. He, too, doubtless disregards the prophetic emphasis, and concentrates rather on the human conditions for access to the Kingdom than on the divine initiative. He interprets these conditions as an anxious catechist, altogether concerned with the moral improvement of his readers. His whole sermon on the mount revolves around the concept of a new justice. His whole gospel seems to be put forward as a new pentateuch, promulgated by a new Moses.

That is why he introduces concepts like "in spirit," "for justice sake" to the beatitudes and doubles their number. He is altogether a moralizer (gentleness, pure heart, humbleness).

This indicates that there is no absolute, single interpretation of the beatitudes. It indicates too, that while fidelity to Christ's teaching was always unanimous, it was not uniform. The modern Church can learn a lesson from this. Finally, it indicates that the different interpretations of the beatitudes, to be faithful to Christ's teaching, must blend with moralizing, catechetical and eschatological viewpoints the prophetic and kerygmatic emphasis of Jesus himself. God really comes, and he comes gratuitously.

IV. 2 Corinthians 1:18-22
1st reading
1st cycle
Tuesday

Relations between Paul and his Corinthian disciples were not always smooth. In 57, in particular, a grave crisis in the community required the apostle's presence (2 Co 1:23-2:1). During this visit he undertook to return for a longer stay (2 Co 1:15-17). However, so as not to give the impression of "ruling their faith," he canceled this journey, thus drawing on himself the reproach of using a "yes and no" language (vv. 17-18).

He devotes a few verses to a response to this accusation of duplicity. He recalls that he is a minister of Christ, who is altogether "yes" (vv. 19-20), and he concludes the argument with a short trinitarian formula (vv. 21-22).

a) In Christ there is no trace of duplicity. He said yes to the Father without the slightest reservation (v. 19) and because of this obedience God was able to be faithful and accomplish his promises (v. 20a). It also enabled all men who are united with Christ to say yes to the Father in their turn (v. 20b), and thus practice *sincerity*.

Being as he is a minister who proclaims Christ and a Christian who lives by Christ, he himself can have no duplicity in his heart when he makes promises. Every Christian indeed should follow suit; his yes to men should echo his yes to God.

b) In verses 21-22 we have the *trinitarian formula*. To the Father belong anointing and the seal; to the Spirit, the earnest of glory; to the Son the strengthening of faith. This division of functions is literary rather than doctrinal. Unction and the seal probably indicate baptism; earnest of glory the Spirit himself, considered as the pledge of future eternal life. The strengthening given by Christ is the sharing of his yes, in an obedience which brings about fulfillment of the promises.

Sincerity in modern times is valued on an unprecedented scale. Sociology and psychology combine to unmask previous false tabus. Art strives after the greatest simplicity and rejects all ornament to the point of becoming abstract. Public opinion is more tolerant of mistakes and errors in individuals and systems than of falsity or hypocrisy. If a new catalogue of cardinal virtues were possible, sincerity would clearly be placed among them.

The Second Vatican Council made away with a series of ecclesial institutions that hindered sincerity of conscience. This reform however will not be complete until each individual applies it to himself, educates his conscience, and follows it openly and unswervingly.

V. 1 Kings 17:7-16
1st reading
2nd cycle
Tuesday

The career of Elias is full of contrasts. In this passage for instance we have a contrast between the widow of Sarepta and queen Jezebel. The queen imposes her god, Baal, on Israel (1 K 18:19), whereas the widow, in Gentile territory, accepts the god Yahweh, whom the prophet proclaims. Jezebel lives amid riches and luxury (1 K 21), the widow in the greatest destitution. Elias hurls a curse of death against the former (1 K 17-24), but brings blessing and abundance to the widow's life.

a) The episode is principally a chronicle of *faith.* Elias had to have faith in order to demand that the widow give him the little nourishment she had left (vv. 11-13). Like Abraham previously, he does not know the repercussions his action will have, but he trusts in God, the dispenser of all things.

The widow shares the prophet's faith. She accepts the commandment of God that has come through the mouth of his servant, and trusts in his promise without thinking of the possible consequences of her act.

b) The episode also indicates the *universalist* ambit of the prophetic Word. Elias does not address himself exclusively to the members of the chosen people. He offers salvation to the poor of all nations (cf. Lk 4:25-26). Our passage here is indeed an excellent preparation for the fine Pauline passages about access to salvation for the nations by faith alone in the Word of God, without the works of the law.

VI. Matthew 5:13-16
Gospel
Tuesday

This is one of the most composite passages in Matthew's gospel. It combines the themes of salt, light and the city. In order to discern the message properly, it is important to distinguish what Matthew takes from the oral tradition, and what is due to his own rehandling.

a) The logion about salt is understood differently by the synoptics, and placed in three differing contexts. Mark 9:50 gives us the primitive formula, where the logion is linked with other sayings by the key-words salt and fire, and placed in an eschatological context. In Luke 14:34-35 it becomes a parable, the teaching of which is that, where the Kingdom is concerned, one must become totally involved and not fail (cf. the parable of the king who undertakes a war).

Thus, for Mark and Luke, salt stands for the new religion and the demands it imposes. For Matthew on the other hand, the logion is a missionary allegory, and salt stands for the disciples ("you are the salt . . ."). To be the salt of the earth is to be the earth's most precious element. Without it the earth cannot subsist; with it, the earth can carry out its function and destiny. In this sense the apostle who is no longer true to himself not only loses himself, but leaves the world savorless.

b) The logion about *light* (vv. 14-16) was similarly reworked by Matthew. In Mark 4:21, the light taken from the bushel to illuminate the surroundings indicates the teaching of Jesus, as it is gradually discerned and understood. Matthew gives it an allegorizing and moralist interpretation. He adds verse 14a ("you are . . .") to ensure parallelism with salt. Likewise he adds the image of a city on a height (v. 14b), and concludes with a moral application. Each disciple is a light insofar as his actions become signs of God for the world. Christian witness must be visible to all, because it answers a missionary requirement. One can never become sanctified by altogether interior means. But on the other hand one can never be so dispersed in the world that one ceases to bear witness to transcendence.

These two images, salt of the earth and light of the world, have a direct bearing on ecclesiology. The Church can consider herself the light of the world, because she is the body of Christ, who has revealed to humanity the ultimate meaning of human destiny: life with God. Christians in other days were convinced of this. They were reinforced in their conviction by the cultural and educational work of the Church in the countries to whose development she contributed. But now the cultural influence of the Church is yielding to that of the State. Her authority is questioned and the majority of men ignore the light she purports to shed.

A new breed of Christian is beginning to appear. He is not inexorably committed to the hitherto accepted framework of religion and morality. He realizes that his faith is menaced, and he is constantly seeking new answers to the never-ending questions. Very naturally, he wonders what the images of "light" and "salt" will mean in his context.

The way to be a light in our time is precisely this. We must be stripped of all confidence, be content not to know anything else of God beyond the fact that he is faithful to himself and to his love, that he is God just because he can be rejected.

We shall be light and salt on the day when we stand denuded of all our "verities," when we prove our absolute commitment to the search for God by being ready to receive and listen, to pardon and to share.

VII. 2 Corinthians 3:4-11
1st reading
1st cycle
Wednesday

The trouble which arose in the Corinth community seems to have been caused by Judaizing preachers. They questioned Paul's status as an apostle, thus discrediting his positions concerning the law and the old covenant. He immediately justifies his apostolic status and affirms its superiority vis-a-vis Judaism.

a) The Judaizers, who put themselves forward as "disciples of *Moses*," accused Jesus and Paul of wishing to supplant the patriarch. It is to be expected then that Paul, in a commentary which resembles the midrashes on Exodus 34:29-35, will compare his own ministry to that of the great legislator in order to demonstrate its superiority. His first point is the contrast between the letter and the spirit (v. 6). This is an allusion to Jeremiah 31:33, where the prophet foretells a covenant that will no longer be based on the authority of a written text, but on the interior dynamism provided by the Spirit.

The second point is a midrash on the veil of Moses, explaining why the people were unable to discern the glory of his countenance (v. 7, contrary to Exodus 34:29-35). The patriarch was unable to enjoy the glory (an emanation of divine life, according to the Jewish concept) except in a veiled and transitory fashion (v. 7), and he could not communicate it to the people. Paul himself on the other hand can claim a ministry of glory, because he proclaims resurrection and divine life for all those who believe (vv. 8 and 10-11).

Thirdly, whereas the ministry of Moses led only to death and condemnation (vv. 7 and 9) because sin still continued (Rm 7), his own ministry proclaims and actually brings about justification through faith (v. 9; cf. Rm 3-4; Rm 8:2).

b) Paul is confirmed in his *assurance* (v. 4) by this contrast between the ministries of the two covenants. His confidence is not based on personal qualities, but on God's intervention (vv. 5-6). The minister of Jesus Christ can combine the greatest liberty with the keenest sense of service to God, because all that he is he has from God.

Is there any point, in our day, in contrasting the actuality of the new covenant with the passing nature of the old. Is it not enough to know that we are living in the penultimate stage? Why should we keep emphasizing our difference from Israel? Paul's contrast between the two ministries is none the less important. It enables us to grasp the decisive event which brought about the mutation that we now enjoy.

The achievement of Moses was that he confronted the event resolutely and was able to discern the presence of God in history. The one event that he could not challenge was death. He himself perished in tragic circumstances before entering the Land of Promise. Death seemed to him the insurmountable obstacle, the *cul-de-sac* of history. Sinful man could not have any other view. That is why the ministry of Moses continues to be a ministry of death (vv. 7, 9).

Christ was able to absorb death into the Kingdom that he inaugurated. In order to respond to the salvific initiative of his Father he stripped himself of everything. He was saved gratuitously, without raising himself above the human state.

Christians, who are all ministers in the world of the new covenant, can too confront the event with the assurance of Saint Paul. They know that they will encounter there the inevitable weight of death; but they also know the gift of God which directs human destiny. In the Eucharist they relive the death of Christ, opening themselves absolutely to the gratuitous initiative of the Savior-God, buoyed by the certainty that they possess the key to history and to glory.

VIII. 1 Kings 18:20-39
1st reading
2nd cycle
Wednesday

Whenever a conflict arose between two liturgical practices it was the Jewish custom to hold a sort of meeting where God could decide between the rival groups (cf. Gn 4:1-5). Elias resorts to this procedure in order to make the people aware of God's judgment concerning their sacrifices.

a) Mount Carmel, the scene of the meeting, is situated between Palestine and Phoenicia. Possession of it had passed from one kingdom to the other, and consequently there were two sanctuaries on its summit, one dedicated to Yahweh (in ruins), the other to Baal.

The people "hobble on their feet" (v. 21) imitating, in their lack of faith, the ritual dance of the Baal-worshipers (v. 26). The contest, by showing clearly to which God belonged the thunderbolt, made the people abandon their evasions. Faith will not allow any vacillation or any service of two masters (vv. 21 and 24; cf. Mt 6:24).

b) The atmosphere of the meeting is one of *violence.* The prophets of Baal, believing that their God will only manifest himself as a result of human effort, mutilate themselves and fall into trance (v. 28). God reveals himself in the violence of the lightning only (v. 38). Elias applies to the Baal prophets the rigors of the *lex talionis* (v. 40; cf. 1 K 18:4). Soon however he will understand that God is not a God of violence (1 K 19:1-14) but of gentleness and love. To make the world understand this would require the death of Jesus.

IX. Matthew 5:17-20
Gospel
Wednesday

These verses are taken from one of the most composite sections of the sermon on the mount. Matthew's purpose is to analyze here the deep meaning of the new religion, and in these three verses he illustrates the contrast between legal justice and the new justice (Mt 5:21-48). Verse 17 is certainly original and belongs to the tradition which was Matthew's source. It is understood however in the particular context of Matthew's theme of accomplishment.

This theme is basic with him (Mt 24:24-35; 6:26, 56), the fulfillment of the law having more than an ethical significance. Everything that is written in the law has a prophetic meaning. It must be "accomplished" historically during the eschatological era down to the least detail.

In pursuit of his theme he takes the beginning of verse 18 from the synoptic tradition (but from another context, Lk 16:17), the saying, that is, that no detail of the law is without point (Mt 33:23; 15:6). The addition "until all be fulfilled" is Matthew's own, fitting his overall purpose (Mt 1:22; 2:15-17; 4:14; 8:17; 12:17; 13:35, etc.). Jesus has come, not merely to perfect the regime of faith by the gift of whatever was wanting, but to accomplish the law (understood in the Old Testament sense of prophecy). The Christian must not rest content with following the broad outlines of the faith. He must fulfill each detail, because all of the law has the value of a prophecy of Jesus Christ (v. 19). To be a valid prophecy of the final times it must be fulfilled in the life of every Christian.

It is perhaps surprising to find such a eulogy of observance of the law in the New Testament, where we have so many diatribes against it by Jesus and Paul (cf. also: Jr 9:23-24). The explanation lies in Matthew's eschatological theme.

Pharisaic justice was in fact limited to observance of the law. It was not communion with God, and always ran the risk of divinizing the law itself. Christian justice does not depend principally on its observance of the law: it proclaims the presence of Christ, and is somehow a "prophecy" of that. It is important then that Matthew prefaces verses 18-19 by verse 17. From now on there is a mediation between the Christian and the law, the justice given to his own by Christ. When the Christian obeys the law it is not to find there his justice, but to "prophecy" Jesus Christ and the final age of communion with God that he inaugurated.

This affirmation deprives the law of one of its prerogatives, the capacity to justifiy, which is now achieved by communion with God in Jesus Christ. It is the affirmation that was judged blasphemous by the Pharisees, and nailed Christ to the cross. Fulfillment reached its peak in his absolute obedience to the law through total communion with his Father. The Eucharist can bring us this justice of the cross which supplants the justice of the law, by helping us to observe the law in communion with the Father.

X. 2 Corinthians 3:15-4:6
1st reading
1st cycle
Thursday

Paul continues his apologia for his ministry. His chief line of argument is the comparison between the two covenants and their ministries (2 Co 3:11-16). Superiority is based on the principality of Christ, the point of mutation from one covenant to the other (2 Co 3:17-18).

a) The ministers of the old covenant were far from having the assurance and confidence of those of the new. They were under the *veil* of Moses, because they had only an obscure understanding of the Word they proclaimed, and because the people they addressed had themselves a hardened heart.

b) The only means of removing this veil is conversion to Christ (v. 16). He alone, who has fulfilled the Old Testament and revealed the true purpose of the law, is capable of liberating heart and understanding from their blindness (v. 17).

So that the difference between the covenants is that between a journey and its end. If the road seems to have presented itself as an obstacle and a challenge, this was due, not to the old covenant in itself, but to the attitude adopted by the Jewish people. Conversion brings us to see that the covenants, though distinct, are not basically different.

Lord in verse 17 refers to God (as in Ex 34:34, a text which forms a background to all this passage), not Christ. Paul's idea is clear. He is asking the Jews to be converted (v. 16) like Moses to the Lord Yahweh. But he knows that the conversion in question will really be to the *Spirit* foretold by Jeremiah 31:31. The Lord Yahweh of Exodus 34:34 is in fact one with the Spirit of the new covenant. Just as Yahweh transfigured the face of Moses, the Spirit will illuminate all those who turn to him.

c) Verse 18 presents some difficulties. The basic idea is simple. In the Old Testament, the Lord's illumination of Moses was a personal privilege and a passing privilege. Now the same privilege is accorded to all Christians, and accorded permanently.

However, under the new, as under the old, covenant, man cannot have a direct vision of God (Gn 32:30; Dt 4:33; 5:24-25; Is 6:5). He sees God "as in a mirror." The superiority thus of the new covenant does not consist in a more direct vision of God, but in the fact that the vision is now granted to all and granted permanently.

The mirror, by means of which the Christian reaches knowledge of God and is gradually transformed, is none other than Christ himself, through whom we can contemplate the glory of the Lord God.

d) Having made this analysis of the two covenants, Paul now returns to the characteristics of the Christian ministry. He emphasizes above all the *assurance* (v. 1) that comes from the ministry of light, as against the shame and silence of the ministry of Moses. His face had to be veiled for fear of revealing all (v. 2). Paul of course is aware that this assurance is no guarantee of complete success; most of his listeners refused to believe his gospel. On this point his ministry is no better and no worse than that of Moses. The veil does not really lie in the message or the ministry; it consists of the blindness of the listeners' minds (v. 4).

But those who are not blind have the experience that was already described in 2 Corinthians 3:18: a vision of Christ's glory, itself an image of the glory of God (v. 4), or a knowledge of the glory which appeared on the face of Christ (v. 6). Christ reveals the glory of God with open countenance, whereas Moses could only reveal it in veiled and transitory fashion.

e) The whole presentation of Christ and the Christian ministry is clearly inspired by Wisdom 7:25-26. In both texts we find terms associated after a fashion we do not find elsewhere, terms such as splendor, mirror, image and glory. An underlying theme in the 2 Corinthians text is the assimilation of Christ to *Wisdom,* which as image of God reveals the divine mysteries. Because he represents and reveals God, Christ is this image, this wisdom. Anyone who rejects the gospel that Paul discerns clearly on the face of Christ is rejecting God himself.

f) Paul seems to have elaborated his whole doctrine of the covenants by reflecting on certain aspects of his own *vocation,* and interpreting them in a very particular way. The light that shines through the darkness suggests the vision on the road to Damascus (Ac 9:3-8). After his conversion he experienced the veil of blindness (Ac 9:8-17). Light, darkness and glory are indeed a frequent literary motif in ancient conversion accounts (Jr 1:5-8; Ez 2:1-2), particularly in the vocation of the Servant of Yahweh to whom Paul often likens to himself (Is 49:6; Is 42:5-10; cf. Ga 1:15-16). In this way his own conversion leads him to his insights about the covenants, about Christ and the image of God's glory. It is the source of his extraordinary assurance in contemplating the tasks of his apostolic ministry.

XI. 1 Kings 18:41-46
1st reading
2nd cycle
Thursday

After the sacrifice on Mount Carmel, where he called down the divine thunderbolt on the altar of the false god, Elias has a violent semi-ecstatic seizure. It continues throughout the massacre of the prophets of Baal, and under its impulse he runs twenty-five kilometres in front of the king's chariot (v. 46). Finally, in *prayer,* he obtains the rain the people had sought. Both Jewish and Christian traditions emphasized in this episode the power of intercessory prayer (Jm 4:16-18).

XII. Matthew 5:20-26
Gospel
Thursday

This extract from the Lord's discourse on the new justice is concerned chiefly with the fifth commandment. After an introduction in general terms (v. 20) we can distinguish three sections:

Verses 21-22: Jesus transcends the precept about homicide by extending it to simple injury. The style is archaic and the vocabulary typically Jewish. This doubtless is the reason why Luke, in view of his Greek readers, does not give the text.

Verses 23-24: This piece, which is distinct from the preceding, makes charity the essential condition of sacrifice, following the tradition of spiritual sacrifice that had been already developed in the Old Testament. Key-words connect it with the previous piece, suggesting that it too is ancient. Luke does not give it: reference to temple sacrifices had no direct interest for his readers. Mark 11:25 gives us another version.

Verses 25-26: These verses do not seem to be in their original context. Luke's placing of them (Lk 12:58-59) seems to be more primitive.

a) To understand the import of Jesus' teaching, it is necessary to keep in mind the quibblings of the Scribes and commentators concerning the law of homicide. To determine whether or not there had been a homicide the Scribes had a catalogue of conditions, all equally extraneous. Jesus establishes a new criterion: *personal intention.* This could actually be considered more serious than murder, even if the injury were a simple injury.

This piece is in fact composed of two distinct sentences. In the first (vv. 21-22a), Jesus affirms that a simple injury may bring a man to the "tribunal" with the same right as a homicide. Tribunal here indicates the community council which, at the national (Sanhedrin) or local (at Qumran, for instance) level, had the right of excommunicating erring members. It had a sort of life and death jurisdiction, deciding which people were worthy of being community members (Mt 10:17; Jn 16:2). It is certain that the primitive Christian communities exercised a jurisdiction of this nature (Ac 5; 1 Co 5:1-4; 1 Tm 1:20; Mt 18:15-17).

b) The second sentence (v. 22b-c) is not any sort of refinement on the first. It simply states the same thing in different terms. The "tribunal" is neither more nor less grave than the "Sanhedrin" or "gehenna." We are still dealing with a community which casts the guilty from its midst. Where Jewish jurisprudence considered the external only, however, Christians must judge the intention of the individual, as God does.

To achieve this, two preliminary principles must be accepted. First, that God "examines the heart" while man is confined to externals (Jr 11:19-20; 12:1-3; 17:9-11). Second, that more is rightly required from members of the new covenant, because it "changes the heart" (Ez 36:23-30; Jr 31:31-34).

The second piece (vv. 23-24) deals with the necessity of *love in sacrifice*. The Jew, if he suddenly realized before offering his sacrifice that he was unclean (Lv 15-17) was obliged to submit himself to a series of preliminary ablutions. What Jesus is demanding from the Christian is that he have the same reflex if he remembers that he has a dispute with someone. He is no longer referring to the precepts about homicide, but to those concerning ritual purity. The two pieces then have a different inspiration, but they both spring from the desire to establish a new justice. It would be based on interior attitude and opposed to all formalism. It is stressed that the links binding the individual to the Christian assembly are now of the interior order.

When a Christian assembly holds a penance celebration, or presents itself before God in the Eucharist, it should consider whether, even at this moment, there are not numerous accusing voices which could denounce its contrition or its offering. The deep link between the Eucharist and charity is not in general properly understood. Charity is simply made a condition for the individual's sharing of the Eucharist. We fail to realize how co-terminous the Eucharist and charity are, and how charity is a collective obligation too, laid upon the Church herself, and each of her eucharistic assemblies.

The cult to which the priestly people is dedicated is the exercise of charity even to the total gift of self for the salvation of all humanity. When we describe the Church as a priestly people we are seeing it above all as the leaven in the mass. All Christians, dispersed among men, must live out their daily lives in fulfillment of their mission to reassemble the scattered children of God. Though many Christians are unaware of the fact, all this is totally alien to the levitic priesthood of the Old Testament. The priestly people of the new covenant is not a people assembled in a temple for prayer and sacrifice, dedicated exclusively to worship. On the contrary, Christians are a priestly people absorbed in the human mass. They are men and women indistinguishable from other men and women except by their membership of the Body of Christ. They share the great act by which Christ, today as yesterday, builds out of human material the Kingdom of his Father. Their priestly responsibility is exercised by spreading to the very frontiers of humanity the charity of Christ.

The proper fruit of the Mass itself is that the Christian is invested with the power of reconciliation that belongs to Christ alone. It would be wrong to regard the Eucharist as merely the expression of the life of charity lived by Christians. The priority of the dimension of reconciliation, where all human beings are concerned, follows from the absolute priority in the Christian life of Jesus Christ himself.

XIII. 2 Corinthians 4:7-15 *1st reading 1st cycle Friday*

This is a continuation of Paul's apologia for his ministry. This man, whose apostleship had been challenged, dealt first with the glory of the Christian ministry (2 Co 3:4-4:6), and now deals with the shortcomings of his own apostolate. He shows that they do not compromise his titles to glory, but on the contrary are a guarantee of his participation in the paschal mystery.

a) An *antinomy in the apostolic life* arises from the fact that the power given by God and human weakness co-exist side-by-side. Some of his antitheses Paul may have drawn from Stoic literary style, but he makes them serve his own purposes. First we have the antithesis between the weakness of apostleship and the strength of God which cancels this weakness (vv. 7-11). Then comes another, where the weakness of apostleship is contrasted with the supposed strength of the Corinthians (v. 12).

b) The whole antinomy is only a dimension of the basic antinomy which characterizes all Christian life: *the death and resurrection* of Jesus (vv. 10, 11, 14). Like any other Christian, the apostle shares the death of Christ by his failures and sufferings. He shares his resurrection by the success of his mission and the life that his ministry can kindle for others.

This ambiguity which Paul discerned in the apostolic life is found again in the agony of the Church of our time. She is living in a world which has a death-wish, the death of God and the death of man, desacralization and demythologizing. Yet she must proclaim life to this world. To those who are convinced that God cannot be experienced she must show the face of God, and the true face of man in Jesus Christ.

She performs this function inadequately enough, true, when she does not champion sufficiently human beings who are tortured and humiliated. Her grandeur and her weakness are comparable to those of Paul. Her true countenance is so often obscured, or, for that matter, defaced. We yearn for her to be as unchangeable as the God she reflects, but she to be constantly undergoing change. We yearn for her to speak, but she is silent, searching for an idiom that the actual world will understand. So often she discovers that silence is the only means of presence possible for her.

And so a Church, which has known sin and at the same time preaches mercy, presents her ambiguous visage to human kind. She shares men's toil, but manifests the presence of another. She bears witness to the fidelity of God, while her own fidelity has to be precariously constructed from that of men and women who are neither saints nor heroes.

XIV. 1 Kings 19:9-16 *1st reading 2nd cycle Friday*

Elias departs in search of Yahweh to Horeb and Mount Sinai, where for the northern tribes God was present, rather than on Sion where he had recently been installed by David. He hides himself in that very ravine where Moses had retreated to experience the theophany (Ex 33:18-34:9), and at once God's word is addressed to him.

His experience brings him to understand that God is not found in natural phenomena, storm, earthquake or thunderbolt, where the Gentiles would discern him (vv. 11-12). He is not even in the fire, where the Yahwist tradition of the south placed him (Ex 19:18). In the progress toward absolute monotheism, Elias is beginning to desacralize nature, and liberate the idea of God from the Baalist naturism of the Phoenicians and Jezebel.

We are not told that God was present in the gentle breeze of which he heard the murmur (cf. Gn 3:8). In any case it is certainly not a sign of God's gentleness, for God is about to give extremely harsh orders (vv. 15-17). Elias must anoint usurpers who will spread hate and violence throughout the Near-East. The breeze really veils the Absolute, the unknownness and *silence* of God. Only the believer can discern him.

Elias' experience has particular point for the believer in today's world. He desacralized nature so that it no longer could be taken as a sign of God's presence. Insofar as modern atheism has rendered nature and the world "profane," it has really rendered service to the notion of God. He must be the Totally-Other, the great Unknowable so far as human thinking goes. Elias had to pass through a progressive denudation before he ceased searching for God in natural phenomena. But this was dwarfed by the actuality of the encounter. He discerned that which he could not know, encountered that which is hidden.

So it is with the believer. Living in an atheist world, he knows the silent God. He listens to him, covers his face like Elias, and emerges from his retreat to fulfill his mission.

XV. Matthew 5:27-32
Gospel
Friday

This, the second antithesis of the sermon on the mount, determines the attitude of the disciple in conjugal living. Jesus brings to its perfection the ancient prohibition against adultery (vv. 27-28; cf. Ex 20-14), and Matthew adds a sentence about the scandalizing member that must be cut off (vv. 29-30; cf. Mk 9:43-48). Then comes an antithesis which pronounces every marriage contracted after divorce adulterous (vv. 31-32; cf. Mt 19:9). The whole ensemble is coherent. It is Matthew's custom, when he speaks of marriage, to emphasize the sacrifices it entails (cf. Mt 19:10-12).

a) The teaching of Jesus concerning *divorce* is clear (Mt 19:9; Mk 10:10-12; Lk 16:8; 1 Co 7:10-11). The procedure cannot dissolve a union that God has joined. It does not restore liberty to the separated parties, or to anyone who marries either of them. The teaching is new: Jewish doctrine had never been couched in such terms. Doubtless it was to emphasize the newness of the doctrine that Jesus immediately made reference to the position of the divorced woman, and of the man who wished to marry her.

Verse 32 however differs from other gospel texts, in being the only one to mention the responsibility of the husband who divorces his wife, thus exposing her to adultery. The conclusion however is identical: divorce does not cancel the conjugal bond.

b) The phrase "unless it be for fornication" in verse 32 is peculiar to Matthew (cf. also Mt 19:9). It is a reference to Deuteronomy 24:1-4, which must be properly understood. The *divorce* in question is one of fact not law. God has united the couple indissolubly: this is the law. Two facts can put an end to this union, the death of one of the parties, or the spiritual death which is adultery. The law actually forbade a betrayed husband to take back his wife. The stain she had contracted was such that the union could no longer bear witness of God's love for his people (Si 23:24-27; Ho 2:4). It would be a mockery. In law, Deuteronomy did not permit any divorce, but because of pastoral requirements it ordered the deceived husband to relinquish all his rights over his wife, lest she belong to two men at once. Jesus is not reproaching Moses (or Deuteronomy) for this regulation. It is in his eyes just a precept given to combat the hardness of sinners' hearts. These often preferred the ambiguous situation (in this case a sort of bigamy). When the divorce has been brought about through the fault of the woman, the husband who dismisses her is not necessarily adulterous, above all when his purpose is not to acquire another woman, but to obey the law forbidding him to take back his wife. Considering the situation of people under the Mosaic law, Jesus refuses to condemn such a husband. But he does firmly reject any invocation of the Deuteronomic precept against the primordial one.

We do not in fact have this particular case under Christianity, the religion of pardon. It is however interesting to note that Jesus' practical attitude takes account of the human situation. We might well consider the question whether different practical attitudes, inspired by consideration for people, might not be possible sometimes in the Church today.

c) The context from which Matthew borrowed verses 31-32 (Mk 9:42-48) recommends the disciple of the Kingdom to show himself *pitiless* towards himself, whenever he detects a moral failing in himself, if he is to escape the trial of the judgment. The verses probably appear here, in Matthew's expose concerning adultery, to recall the more precise teaching in Matthew 19:9-12. Some decisions, particularly in conjugal life, will prove perhaps highly costly. A divorce may force the spouses to live a eunuch's life.

Adultery and lust, under the Christian regime, are no longer just violations of a sexual prohibition; they are a rupture in communion with God. He is present in the conjugal union. That is why it is better to lose an eye or a member than to lose his presence. It is because he is part of the conjugal union that the precept must be observed to the letter.

In actual practice on the other hand, we might find a better solution for Christians who are shut off from the sacraments. Could not the Roman Church, so much more rigid than other churches in this regard, take a position that would be more indicative of God's love for the afflicted? It is of course never easy to determine what the reason for "fornication" might be, or what sort of spiritual death it is that destroys a household. We might ask ourselves how far the conscience might be clear in a second marriage for one who has not been responsible for the collapse of the first. This could never be regularized in juridical terms, but it would open the way for divorced people to living sacramental communion with the Church. In any case it is on such principles that the problem ought to be examined. Solutions should be sought with all the more intensity, because what is at stake is the love of God for men.

XVI. 2 Corinthians 5:14-21
1st reading
1st cycle
Saturday

This passage is certainly the most important portion of Paul's long apologia at the beginning of 2 Corinthians for the apostolic ministry. It has two important themes: the role of love in the ministry, and the content of the gospel.

a) Basic in his ministry is the *constraining love of Christ* (v. 14). This describes not only Christ's love for him, but his in return for Christ, which has nothing to do with sentimental love, because it is the product of reflection ("thought": v. 14). Once Paul understood the love of Jesus as he died for all on the cross (v. 15), he could not withstand its constraint and dedicated his life to that end (v. 15b).

Liberty is not destroyed by the constraint: he took the time to reflect. But there is some new faculty in man (vv. 16-17), which prevents him from acting with the calculation and reservation of the "flesh": he is a "new creature." It is grace and dynamism which the flesh cannot control (Co 3:14). It yearns for sacrifice, after the pattern of the cross (v. 15). It gives unity and balance to one's life (*sunehô* has this sense in contemporary philosophic writing).

b) In response to Christ's love, he dedicated himself to the "embassy" of *reconciliation* (vv. 18, 20). This is a favorite idea of Paul when he is describing the redemptive work of the cross (Rm 5:10-11; Co 1:20-22; Ep 2:16). It is highly important for modern theology too, in that it defines the doctrine of redemption in terms of personal relation between God and man. The idea should not be extended however beyond a particular significance. Paul guards against this. It is not God who changes sentiment. He does not become reconciled with the world: he reconciles the world to him (v. 18). Paul's own ministry is not confined to reconciling men with God (v. 20): it is first and foremost a proclamation that the reconciliation has been accomplished (Rm 5:10-11). God has actually changed the relationship of humanity to himself. In this way, what we have is truly a new creation (v. 17).

This nuance is rather original. Jewish prayer would petition God for reconciliation (2 M 1:5; 7:33; 8:29), but in the sense that God "be" reconciled, change his sentiments. Divine transcendence is safeguarded in the Pauline doctrine, where no change occurs in God himself. He changes man's condition *vis-a-vis* himself.

The change must be ratified by a personal conversion in the life of each Christian. Such is the task of apostolic ministry. Once people are made aware of the change, they are invited to modify their sentiments accordingly. The very term that Paul uses, embassy (v. 20), suggests an end to hostilities, and the resumption of normal relations (cf. Lk 14:32).

c) Reconciliation is the result of Christ's death, considered above all in its *sacrificial* aspect (v. 21; cf. Rm 5:9-10; Co 1:20-21; Ep 2:16). The most ancient texts of the New Testament had given the death a sacrificial dimension: the sacrifice of the new covenant (1 Co 11:25. Mt 26:28; He 10:29); of the paschal Lamb (1 Co 5:7); of the suffering Servant (Is 53:12 in Rm 4:25; 8:32; Ga 2:20). But this is the first time that it is likened to the "sacrifice for sin," where the victim's blood had expiatory value (Lv 4-5; 6:17-22; 10:16-19; 16; cf. He 9:22). That is why the words blood and sin occur so frequently in the Pauline passages on reconciliation. It is not so much a matter of giving a sanguinary interpretation to the work of Jesus, but of stressing its ritual importance. Reconciliation is accomplished in a liturgical act which definitively supplants the temple economy.

In the Eucharist is fulfilled the embassy of reconciliation through the liturgy of the Word. In the memorial of the cross we have included the world's reconciliation with God. All the members signify by their participation acceptance of a reconciliation that extends to all.

XVII. 1 Kings 19:16,19-21 *1st reading 2nd cycle Saturday*

The account of Eliseus' vocation belongs to the extremely old "Eliseus-cycle" (8th or 9th century). The future prophet is a rich fellah who owns numerous oxen for the cultivation of his lands. Elias chooses him as disciple and covers him with his mantle as a sign that he is taking possession of him (Ruth 3:9; Dt 23:1; 27:20; Ez 16:8). The ancient gesture is accompanied here by a communication of the magic powers attached to the mantle (2 K 2:14).

Such a call could not be denied. It bound the disciple very closely to his master, and we have its echo in the relationship between Christ and the apostles (Lk 9:59-62). The disciple must never look backward towards his own (v. 20). He must abandon his trade or profession (v. 21) and follow his master. The master regarded him as a servant, imposing various tasks on him (cf. Lk 8:3; Jn 4:8). Not until Jesus, would a master make his disciples no longer servants but friends (Jn 15:15).

So demanding was this *master-disciple* relationship that it excluded all romantic attachment. In his choice of disciples Jesus would show himself similarly intransigent, but he was to reward them beyond all expectation. He introduced them into the mystery of his relationship with the Father, and he gave them his friendship. The disciples, for their part, do not come simply for his teaching, or his powers as thaumaturge. They want to share a mission which is accomplished in God's name, and which springs from love (Jn 15:15).

XVIII. Matthew 5:33-37
Gospel
Saturday

This is the third antithesis of the sermon on the mount, which concerns the precept about swearing (vv. 33-37) and the *lex talionis* (vv. 38-42).

Swearing demonstrates the existence of lies. If there were no lie there would be no need to swear. Yes would be yes, and no, no (v. 37). The Old Testament had campaigned against the lie by legislation about oaths, and a prohibition of the lie, at least in oaths (v. 33; cf. Ex 20:7; Nb 20:3). However, a prohibition of the lie in oath amounts to recognition, and tolerance, of it otherwise. When Jesus forbids the lie in any circumstances, he is transcending Jewish law, and rendering the oath superfluous.

The oath of course sacralizes human speech, by placing it in relation with an exterior power, most often divine. By rejecting it, Jesus is rejecting any alienation of human speech. There are many factors, sincerity and accuracy in particular, which can add weight to speech without having recourse to exterior guarantee. If God be present in human speech, this is not so much by invocation of his name as by the fact that he is the source of human sincerity. God does not want man to be a slave; he wants him first of all to be true to himself.

ELEVENTH WEEK

I. 2 Corinthians 6:1-10
1st reading
1st cycle
Monday

This is an extract from the long statement (2 Co 4-6) on the apostolic ministry. Paul is showing how God continues now in his Church, through the medium of his ambassadors the apostles, the work begun by Christ (2 Co 5:19-20).

a) To describe the *apostolic ministry* he has recourse to antitheses which emphasize the contrast between the inner reality and the exterior aspect. He draws upon the portrait of the suffering Servant, whom he takes as his perfect model (Is 53:2-3; cf. Ps 117/118: 17-18).

He has made every effort not to compromise the work of God. Trials have not undermined his fidelity (vv. 3-5); indeed it is through these that his forbearance and charity have been molded (v. 6). Supernatural means, like the Word of truth and the power of miracles, have been generously accorded to him (v. 7). He has not thus modified the message. He wishes that his listeners would welcome it with fidelity (v. 1), so that his embassy can be accomplished without delay, for the "final times" have come (v. 2).

b) By combining the themes of *favorable time* and ministry, he is following the tradition of the great Old Testament prophets, who would proclaim the immanence of the decisive trial and summon the people to repentance (Ez 18:30). Like all Jews, he thought that the final times would be preceded by a particularly arduous trial, of which he discerned the signs in his own sufferings.

To proclaim the "last times" is to affirm that, since Jesus Christ, God is at the center of the physical universe. Paul's training fitted him admirably to be the propounder of this insight. Judaism had never been given to speculations about the after life or the mystery of God, and had clung to an exaggeratedly terrestrial notion of retribution. The Jews loved the earth too much to be satisfied with a God who was celestial only, and this was one of their greatest contributions to humanity.

So God was for them transcendence in terms of the "here below": he had come forth from the mythic and metaphysical heaven. The resurrection doctrine was not the recovery of some life beyond, to the discredit of early life. On the contrary, Paul never ceases to appeal to faith in the resurrection in order to remind his listeners of present demands. He associates passage from death to life with baptism, to indicate that all subsequent earthly life is colored by resurrection.

Christianity did not invent the life beyond; it is always focusing attention on a recreation of the reality offered by God now. It is not based on a dichotomy between the normative and the actual, existence and appearance, God and the world, person and work. Faith links the reality that is God to the realization that is man's task. Believers know that Jesus, who fulfilled the notion of God in the world, and the world in God, has put an end to all those systems which are based on the antithesis between immanence and transcendence.

We still need guidelines which will reveal the presence of God in actual experience. Indeed it is the business of the Church to demonstrate this publicly, just as Paul had the mandate to awaken men's conscience to the actuality of the last times. Christians place high value on the temporal, on God's presence in this world.

II. 1 Kings 21:1-16
1st reading
2nd cycle
Monday

The king wanted the vineyard of his neighbor Naboth, because as a result of centralization and the needs of administration the requirements of the court were growing. He was not however unjust, as he was proposing generous compensation (v. 2).

For hardly adequate reasons Naboth opposed the project. True, the law prescribed that each person should remain on the land of his ancestors, and forbade all transfers of property outside the clan. But this was an agrarian law ill-suited to urbanization and centralization. So he was opposing the king's "modern" request in the name of a law that was outmoded (v. 3; cf. 1 S 8:9-11). Of course, anterior to these inadequate motives there was the person's inalienable right to be happy on the land of his choice. For Naboth his vineyard was the focus of his fidelity to his ancestors and to Yahweh himself, from whom he regarded himself as holding it.

Achab seemed ready to be persuaded despite the resentment he felt (v. 4); but Jezebel had no such scruples. In her home country it was customary to take more radical decisions (v. 7a). Accordingly she plans the murder of Naboth so that Achab can have a free hand. The property of condemned persons automatically became the property of the crown. All that was needed then was to have Naboth condemned on the testimony, required by law, of two or three witnesses (v. 10).

Poverty and injustice are for the most part the result of upheavals or social mutations. And usually the chief victims are those people or those countries whose structures and economy are being changed. It is true that they do not adapt themselves immediately to the change in progress. Other persons or countries better equipped, more powerful, are able to adjust to progress. Some rich nations take this as a disposition of fate for which they are not responsible. So much the worse for the weak if they fail to survive.

Others do indeed pride themselves on bringing the poor to a certain level in progress, but they do so by despoiling them of the resources which in the hands of the poor themselves could lead to technology and advancement. This was exactly what Achab did to Naboth. The man would not die of hunger; he would have adequate recompense in money for his property. But by alienating the property of his fathers, he was relinquishing the right to an independent life as his own master. He would become dependent, and a "vassal."

Nowadays what corresponds to Naboth's vineyard are those natural resources which rich countries purchase from poor in such fashion that they are no longer available for native progress. To sell one's vineyard in our time means that one sells the right to progress and self-development. One sells one's dignity.

III. Matthew 5:38-42a, 43-48
Gospels Monday and Tuesday

In this passage we have the final antitheses of the group of six which Matthew gives in the sermon on the mount (Mt 5:21-48) to describe the "new justice" (v. 20). The conclusion of verse 48 refers to the whole ensemble of antitheses.

The parallel passage in Luke (6:27-36) does not have the antithetic structure. We can regard it as proper to Matthew, who furthermore seems to give us some sayings in a more primitive version. The diatribe by Jesus against publicans and Gentiles (Mt 5:46-47) is in fact replaced in Luke by another against sinners in general (Lk 6:33-34). Doubtless he did not wish to hurt his readers.

In verse 48 we have the Jewish theme of perfection, regarded as the fulfillment of all the precepts of the law, and practiced, according to the rabbis, by God himself. Matthew transcends this formalist notion in his affirmation of perfection as a gratuitous gift, like that which the Father gives men (Mt 5:17, 20; 19:21). Luke goes further still in speaking of goodness and mercy (Lk 6:36).

Matthew's account is just as carefully worked as that of Luke. He gives us the legalist precept, which he takes from both law and rabbinic tradition, and contrasts with it the new commandment of gratuitousness. This he gives in triad form (vv. 44-45, as in Mt 5:22; 34-35 and 39-41). Next come two concrete examples, one Jewish (v. 46), one Gentile (v. 47), which stress the independence of the new morality of any legalist or philanthropic framework.

Luke's exposition is rather more concentric, the same idea repeated several times in different ways (vv. 27-28, 29). We have the triad structure in the examples given ("And if . . . and if . . . and if," vv. 32-34). For his conclusion he turns to antithetic structure ("on the contrary . . ." v. 35), but his antithesis is not so much between Jewish and Christian justice as between interested and gratuitous love.

a) In any case the lesson conveyed in both evangelists is quite similar. *Love* must transcend the boundaries of natural communities, where it arises spontaneously for psychological or sociological reasons, and reach out to the frontiers of all humanity, including enemies. Christ has liberated it from all sacral limits of nation or family. It is sacral in itself, and needs no validation from such preestablished sources. God is not in the family, the race or the nation; he is in the man who loves (Mt 5:48; Lk 6:36). This is what the gospel affirms when it speaks of "imitating" God in love which transcends natural or sacral communities. Instead of the term "imitation" we would nowadays use "communion," but the idea is the same. If God exists, it is the very act of loving that leads us to him, not the sacral quality of the object loved.

Love on such a plane love transcends the natural community and discovers the divine secret of the person himself. It is not just a matter of quantative enlargement in horizon. The process is one of personalization; the faith is finding its proper divine dimension.

b) Verse 48, concerning the duty of *imitating* God, has a very different nuance in the parallel Lucan text: 6:36. A somewhat similar formula was known to the Old Testament in the recommendation of Leviticus 19:2; 11:44-45 about God's holiness. There however, it is not a matter of true imitation ("like") but a consequence ("because") of the covenant. In general, formulas similar to that of Saint Luke about mercy were not unknown to

Judaism. Doubtless it was in continuation of this tradition that we find so many exhortations in the New Testament to a real resemblance to God (1 P 1:15-16; Ep 4:32; 5:1; Col 3:12-13).

When they speak of imitation, Matthew of the perfection Luke of the mercy, of God, they use language which in practice was not subsequently followed.

Matthew's language in speaking of a perfect God is in fact anthropomorphic. A Greek could speak in such terms, not a Jew. It is only man who must strive towards perfection, and Matthew, in insisting on this perfection which is characterized by works, wishes to give it a religious dimension by referring to God's perfection.

In Luke 6:36 the viewpoint is otherwise. God is basically merciful, man not so. He can however clothe himself in this divine quality by the love he shows to others.

The difference then is that, where Matthew is principally interested in human behavior, Luke concentrates on God's goodness to man. He is a theologian where Matthew is a moralist. There is every reason to believe that he preserves the more primitive version. It fits the general context admirably.

IV. 2 Corinthians 8:1-9
1st reading
1st cycle
Tuesday

This is regarded as the conclusion to the letter sent to the Corinthians after their difficulties had been resolved. Chapter 9 is a totally independent section, and chapters 10-13 contain the essential material from an earlier letter sent when the crisis was at its height.

Following his usual custom Paul concludes his letter by practical recommendations, among them the collection which he is undertaking throughout the Gentile churches for the Christians of Jerusalem.

The *collection* apparently had been decided upon by the Corinthians themselves (v. 10; cf. however Ac 11:29), and accepted by the Jerusalem community (Ga 2:10) as an expression of the unity between Greek and Jewish Christians. The chief interest of this passage lies in the arguments put forward by Paul for participating in the collection.

The first argument is the imitation of Jesus Christ (v. 9). For him indeed all Christian moral performance is simply a reproduction of Christ's example. Disciples receive one another mutually because Christ received us (Rm 15:5-7). Men and women, masters and slaves, love one another as Christ loves the Church (Ep 5, etc.). Nor is it just a matter of choosing an ideal model. The individual Christian becomes in turn a sign of salvation, prolonging by his attitude the Lord's incarnation and spreading its benefits to all humanity. The chief value of the collection then resides in its theological and salvific dimension.

The second argument is the need for equality between Greeks and Jews (vv. 5-7). The equality he has in mind is not a social one to be achieved by the adjustment of economic differences, but an equality in the faith. The Jerusalem Christians have not kept to themselves the privileges they enjoyed. Not without hesitancy, they have admitted Gentiles to a share in them, fulfilling the great Gentile emptiness in faith out of their abundance and superfluity. Gentile Christians in return should give from their economic superfluity to the destitute Christians of Jerusalem. Thus will come about, between Jews and Greeks, an unprecedented union and equality.

This gives a new significance then to Christian participation nowadays in movements of solidarity for all humanity. The Christian has just the same reason as other men for seeking solidarity with his brothers, but his efforts in this regard are also a prolongation of the Savior's work. The riches he shares with his brothers become an authentic sign of God's salvation among men. Too often the arguments put forward by collecting preachers are too down-to-earth. Or they may resort to commercial techniques (lotteries, etc.) which obscure the whole theological dimension. Donors will tend to be motivated by the hope of some economic profit. A collection structured in such a way can scarcely be a sign of salvation. It is not sufficient when Christians give their money only. Their gesture must be a sign of the limitless opportunities offered to humanity to transcend themselves and thus reach salvation.

V. 1 Kings 21:17-29
1st reading
2nd cycle
Tuesday

The condemnation of Achab by Elias is like that of David by Nathan (2 S 12). Both prophets reproach the king for contempt of the poor. Both kings *repent* of their fault, and God agrees to transfer the punishment to subsequent generations. It is natural then that the reading should be accompanied by the penitential psalm attributed to David (Ps 50/51).

VI. Matthew 5:43-48
Gospel
Tuesday

This passage was commented on with the Gospel for Monday, p. 57.

VII. 2 Corinthians 9:6-11
1st reading
1st cycle
Wednesday

Here we have an extract from a separate letter (2 Co 9) where Paul is recommending to his audience the collection for the Jerusalem Christians. In a previous passage (2 Co 8:9-15) he had put forward two arguments in favor of this gesture of solidarity between Christians. The present letter gives a third.

The Corinthians are sufficiently wealthy to participate in the *collection.* God has been so generous to them that they in turn should be generous to others (vv. 8-11). The collection is an expression of the spiritual abundance God has showered on his children. The donor is merely an intermediary; giving is the means by which the Christian renders thanks to God and glorifies him for his generosity.

Because it is an acknowledgement of graces received, the collection cannot be made a definite tariff. Each person gives in absolute freedom, with a gesture that is spontaneous and sincere (vv. 6-7; cf. 2 Co 8:3-4; 10-11). It is only in the spontaneity of the gift that God's own gift is made manifest.

Thus Paul makes this collection a religious act, the donor being merely the minister of God's generosity. Too extreme an application of this view carries its dangers of course. Following it, the Church tends to monopolize the exercise of charity in her charitable institutions, as if God could only be present in the good works she mediates.

Nowadays, when Christian charitable enterprises are sometimes executed in common with secular, Christians should be mindful that God is present in every act of love and sharing. But since this presence is humble and concealed, that of his servant, the Church, should avoid ostentation. Individual Christians may wonder whether their alms should be mediated by the Church, or whether they should join any genuine enterprise of sharing and true love. The gospel from Matthew (6:1-6, 16-18, below p. 82) is a good sequel to our present reading. It insists on secrecy in almsgiving.

VIII. 2 Kings 2:1, 6-14
1st reading
2nd cycle
Wednesday

Elias' disappearance took place in mysterious circumstances which the account does not elucidate. All we know is that at the end the prophet betook himself to Bethel, the holy place of Jacob (Gn 28:19) where that patriarch had seen a ladder between heaven and earth. Subsequently he crossed the Jordan and found himself not far from Mount Nebro, where Moses was buried by God himself.

The road he took out of the promised land corresponds curiously with that taken by Joshua and the people to enter it (Jos 4-6). He went from Bethel to Jericho, and from there to Gilgal where he crossed the river, performing a miracle like that of Joshua. There, on the opposite bank, he sees the chariot of Yahweh which Joshua had seen on his entry to Palestine (Jos 5:13-15). It is as if Yahweh, the God of battles, were quitting an unworthy people by the very road of his triumphal entry.

Eliseus was the first beneficiary of this plunge to the sources of ecstasy. What he experienced was the glorification of his master. The account of the assumption is not historical; it belongs to the literary genre of ecstatic visions (as in Gn 28; 1 K 22:19-22; 2 K 6:17; Am 7; Is 6:1-13, etc.). What we have is not so much an account of Elias' disappearance, but rather the ecstatic vision of Eliseus as he sees his master *glorified*. Yahweh appears as the king of the celestial armies, the God of the hosts of Horeb. Eliseus sees him at the head of an army of horses and chariots (2 K 6:17; 1 K 22:19-22). But, instead of coming on earth to manifest himself to his prophet, he summons the prophet to his heavenly court, putting one of his chariots at his disposal (v. 11).

During Eliseus' ecstasy, Elias dies. He is naked as on all occasions when he is seized by God, as Eliseus is able to withdraw the mantle which now becomes the sign of his own mission (v. 13). However the deceased Elias must be honored in the usual way by his disciple, and he begins to rend his garments as a sign of the beginning of mourning (v. 12).

IX. Matthew 6:1-6, 16-18
Gospel
Wednesday

The brief discourse by Jesus concerning the justice that must be done in secret is in fact a separate discourse in the sermon on the mount. Its unity is evident in the vigorous parallelism of phraseology and structure.

"When . . . do not . . . as the hypocrites . . . to appear before men. . . . In truth I tell you they have received their reward. . . . But you when you . . . (your Father) in secret . . . and your Father who sees in secret will reward you."

It is only necessary to fill the spaces with words taken from the sayings concerning almsgiving, prayer and fasting in order to reconstruct with some slight variants the three strophes of the discourse.

The main point of the discourse is that fulfillment of the traditional works of justice must be inspired by a new intention: the desire to please God, and only God. Almsgiving, prayer and fast must never be used as means towards notice; everything should remain in the *secret of God.*

Almsgiving was regarded as the work of justice *par excellence* (vv. 2-4; cf. Si 3:14; 3:30-4:10; 7:10; 12:1-7; Tb 4:11; 12:8-9). It was given a certain publicity, so that donors would be held to their promises, and in order to kindle some emulation (Mk 12:41; Lk 19:8; Si 31:11). Prayer too was generally public. As for fast, while it was not very widespread in official Judaism during Jesus' time, was frequently practiced by sects, who for reasons of propaganda made it ostentatious (Lk 18:12; Mk 2: 19-20). Jesus does not propose to substitute other practices for these observances. When he speaks of perfuming oneself when fasting, or not knowing what the right hand does, he is turning to literary hyperbole. His purpose is to characterize the spirit that should inspire such observance, and to denounce the hypocrisy of people who thought they were serving God while merely advertising themselves. Some prophets had previously tried to bring about a similar spiritualization (Is 58:1-12; Ho 8:11-13; Mi 6:6-8; Am 5:21-25). He follows their tradition, showing that interiorization of this kind gives access to familiar life with the Father.

In our time of secularization, nothing is more necessary perhaps than the moral attitude here described. If we do not let the left hand know what the right hand does, we are renouncing public recognition and turning to a God who sees only in secret. It is a matter of being unaware of the good we do (as in Mt 25:31-40). The measure of good is henceforth hidden for the man who does not presume to judge his acts. The only capable judge is a God who cannot be grasped, who dwells in secret and gives account to no one. Men must not attempt to use the knowledge of good and evil which they stole from paradise.

X. 2 Corinthians 11:1-11
1st reading
1st cycle
Thursday

The Judaeo-Christian missionaries, who had been dispatched by the Twelve, or at least by the brothers of the Lord (James in particular, Ga 2:2), encountered opposition from Paul. They wanted to impose Jewish observances on the Gentiles they converted. They were also bringing discredit on Paul's apostolate and behavior, by undermining the affection felt for him by the communities he founded.

In Paul's defense of his ministry we have a particular concept of the apostolate. He resents the presumption of "arch-apostles" to control of every Church (v. 5). Collegiality with the other apostles he accepts, but he refuses to be in dependence from them, he who holds his mandate from God himself (cf. Ga 1:15; 1 Co 1:1).

In regard to the gospel preached, he reproaches the Judeo-Christians for proclaiming a Christ that is too human, too much the Jewish "messiah," and for their insistence on observance of the law (v. 4). He affirms the liberty of the faith and claims sufficient theological knowledge (v. 6).

Finally, on a personal issue, he rejects once more the criticism that he makes no demands on the communities he visits (vv. 7-9; cf. 1 Co 9:1-18). Such a criticism questions the very nature of his affectionate relations with his disciples (vv. 2-3). He has chosen the way of gratuitous service, so that in his apostolate may be discerned the gratuity of the faith and of God's love.

XI. Sirach 48:1-15 *1st reading 2nd cycle Thursday*

The eulogy of Elias is one of the most important, and one of the finest, of the eulogies compiled by Ben Sirach on prominent figures in the people's history.

a) The figure of the prophet is symbolized by *fire* (v. 1), the element which unites man to God. Fire consumes sacrifices (Lv 1:7; 6:6). It expresses the will of God (Ex 40:38; 13:21-24; 3:2; 19:18; Nb 14:14; Ps 77/78;14, 21; 103/104: 2-4). Deuteronomy associates it with the Word (Dt 4, 12, 15, 33, 36; 5:4). He then who is the bearer of the divine will naturally has a visage of fire, for his God is a "devouring fire" (Dt 4:24; 9:3). Fire will also be the means whereby the last times, the Day of Yahweh will begin (Jl 2:3-5; Dn 10:6; Ps 17/18:9, 13-14; 28/29:7; 96/97:3).

Elias was in a very real sense the prophet of fire. He summoned down drought on the earth (1 K 17:1), lightning on Carmel (1 K 18) and on Achab's armies (2 K 1:10-12). He was borne to heaven on a chariot of fire (2 K 2:1-11).

b) Elias' use of fire corresponds in detail with that of Moses. In the case of the patriarch we have the burning bush (Ex 3:1-6), Sinai smoking as he receives the law (Ex 19:18), the punishment of his adversaries (Lv 10:2; Nb 16:7-35). Nor is the parallel between the two confined to this. Ben Sirach recalls how Elias was a pilgrim to Sinai (v. 7), how he hid himself in the very cave where Moses took refuge in order to receive again the will of God (1 K 19:9; cf. Ex 33:22). He remembers how the death of Moses was mysteriously similar to that of Elias (v. 9).

At verse 10 he borrows a detail from Malachy 3:22-24 and applies it to Elias to strengthen the parallel. "Turning the hearts of fathers to their sons and of sons to their fathers" means bringing the new Jewish generations to observance of the law. Elias' destiny was to safeguard the heritage of Moses.

This throws light on the appearance of Moses and Elias with Jesus at the transfiguration. The Word of the Law, vindicated by the Word of the Prophet, finds its accomplishment in the Word made flesh.

c) Ben Sirach is in fact the first biblical author to envisage an early return of Elias as *precursor* of the Messiah (vv. 10-11). The mysterious circumstances of his disappearance lent probability to the belief that he would return to complete his task at the beginning of the messianic age. He would anoint the Messiah (cf. v. 9; 1 K 19:15-18), exercise his power over life and death, as he had already done in the case of the child at Sarepta (v. 5; cf. 1 K 17:17-24). Above all he seemed to have escaped the law of death. Thereby he becomes the witness of an age when death will be vanquished, when all men will "possess life" (v. 11) by reason of their participation in the Kingdom.

Primitive Christian tradition is unanimous about the fact of Elias' return, but for a considerable time there was hesitancy about whether this should be discerned in John the Baptist or in Jesus himself. Thus, where Matthew 3:1-4; 11:14 and Luke 1:17 associate the Baptist with Elias, in Luke 4:23-30; 7:11-17; Matthew 4:1-5; Luke 9:54-55 and Acts 1:1-11 there is an attempt to find the prophet's traits in Jesus. Might it not be more true that it is to the Church and her witnesses in the world that Elias' role is entrusted? They are the signs that God has come among men to give a new meaning to human history.

XII. Matthew 6:7-15
Gospel
Thursday

The beginning of chapter 6 in Matthew considers the various pious practices of the Pharisees—almsgiving, prayer and fast—as they are to be fitted into Christian observance. We have three paragraphs in the same symmetrical structure. In each instance the wrong manner is contrasted with the right by two phrases introduced by the temporal conjunction: "when you give alms, when you fast, when you pray" (vv. 2, 5, 16) . . . "As for you when you give alms, as for you when you fast, as for you when you pray" (vv. 3, 6, 17). We are dealing then with an original discourse (6:1-6, 16-18), into which has been inserted a long section on prayer (general notions, vv. 7-8; the text of the Our Father, vv. 9-13; a catechesis on pardon, vv 14-15).

In this section Matthew is providing a sort of prayer-catechesis, compiled from different sayings by Jesus and designed for neophytes of Jewish background. These would be already accustomed to prayer, but too often given to routine and formulas. His purpose becomes clear when we compare the parallel section in Luke (11:1-13). Luke too provides, in his fashion, a prayer-catechesis, but it is designed for Gentiles who have everything to learn in this domain, and who need encouragement in the arduous enterprise.

The versions given of the *Our Father* are those in use in their respective communities; but it is extremely difficult to determine which might be the actual prayer of Jesus. Matthew's text seems closer to the Aramaic, at least in those portions he has in common with Luke. It is however difficult to believe that Luke, had he known them, would have suppressed substantial portions of the prayer. We know too that, in the development of the liturgy, prayer-texts underwent gradual accretion. This would suggest that the portions proper to Matthew are later. Such a view however is in the domain of hypothesis.

a) The first part of the catechism concerns the *secret* character of Christian prayer.

To primitive man prayer comes naturally, and the different religions would organize it in a structured pattern of times and styles designed to make it efficacious. It was with this ritual concept that Jesus broke. Prayer is not valued by God because it represents a human achievement. He knows what we need (v. 8), and does not need to be begged in order to give it. Jesus rejects the pseudo-securities with which ritual has surrounded prayer: the contrived publicity (vv. 5-6), the verbosity (v. 7). But then, how should one pray?

The Christian will no longer pray just because he feels the need, but because Christ, who lives in communion with the Father, bids him pray. The conditions for prayer are obedience and faith linking him to the Father (v. 6). There is now no question of attitude or content, but of a confidence. This is independent ultimately of street or chamber, of long or short version of the *Our Father*, of individual or community. It is a conviction that we have a Father who dwells in us by his Spirit, who knows, by the experience of his Son, what man needs (Rm 8:16, 26).

b) We shall take in order the petitions of the *Our Father*.

The invocation of the Father presumes a communion of life and the possibility of imitating the fidelity of Jesus. *Abba,* which is from the Aramaic original, was retained for a long time doubtless in the Greek versions. This would explain the difference of title in Matthew and Luke, and the occurrence of the word in Romans 8:15 and Galatians 4:6.

Next come two wishes: the hallowing of the name and the coming of the kingdom. The name indicates the person. God should be recognized for what he is, holy and transcendent. However this holiness is communicated to a Kingdom; the transcendence becomes immanence (Ez 36:23); the gratuitous gift of God meets human collaboration: "Thy kingdom come."

The third wish may not be original "Thy will be done." It is not in Luke. The will in question is the divine plan for human salvation: a sanctification of man and his admission to the inheritance of the Kingdom (Ep 1:3-8). Thus it would be merely a repetition of the first two.

The petitions follow, for bread, for pardon and for protection. It is impossible to determine whether Jesus was referring to material bread or the bread of life eternal. The two however do not stand in any sort of contrast. Was it not when distributing material bread to the hungry that he revealed the other?

The petition for pardon is further explained in a catechesis at vv. 14-15. We shall deal with it later.

The protection sought is against "temptation" and "evil" (personified). In the Aramaic idiom of the time these referred to the great trial of believers and the final assault by the Evil One before the establishment of the definitive kingdom. The petition then is for God's help lest one apostatize (Mt 24:4-31; Lk 22:53; Jn 12:31).

The whole *Our Father* then is a prayer that the manifestation of God and his Kingdom, and the communication of his life should take place in the context of bread, pardon and protection conceded to the disciples' faith.

c) Matthew returns to the theme of *pardon,* one to which he is particularly prone (Mt 18:11-14; 9:10-13; 11:19; 26:28, etc.). His text of the *Our Father* (v. 12) and its commentary (vv. 14-15) suggest the passage in Sirach 28:1-5. The texts give us a first stage of Christian reflection on the theme of pardon, which was still dominated, like the Sirach passage, by the notion of retribution. God pardons us as we pardon, measuring his by ours (Mt 5:7; 25:31-46). His judgment will be concerned essentially with the mercy we show our neighbor. A later insight will nuance this differently: we pardon because we have been pardoned (Mt 18:23-35; Lk 6:36; Ep 4:32; Col 3:13). Pardon becomes detached from any connection with retribution or merit. It is solely a sign that the Kingdom of God is practically established in the world of sinners.

XIII. 2 Corinthians 11:18-30
1st reading
1st cycle
Friday

This apologia, to which Paul had recourse unwillingly, lifts the veil on his missionary exploits and his life of prayer. It is no part of his intention however to give us an autobiography; he simply wants to ensure the fidelity of his audience to the apostolic ministry. Consequently we should not concentrate on the autobiographical data, extraordinary or otherwise, or on some psychological portrait of the ideal apostle. The essential thing is the teaching concerning the Christian apostolate.

a) We are given considerable *autobiographical data.* Paul is not a Hellenist, but a Jew. Though born in the Diaspora, he was educated in Pharisaic circles at Jerusalem (v. 22). There can consequently be no doubt about his allegiance to the Jewish Palestinian party.

The details concerning the sufferings of his apostolate were meant to impress his readers. His punishments for the most part were those determined by Jewish law for religious fault (whipping: Dt 25:2-3; stoning: Lv 20; Dt 13; 17; 21; 22; cf. Ac 14:19). To these were added the fatigues due to journeys, and dangers due to the hostility of Gentiles and false brethren. The latter were the judaizing Christians, spies and inquisitors (v. 26), who sometimes cost Paul such tragic-comic adventures as the escape from Damascus (vv. 32-33).

b) Paul gives all these details in order to chasten the presumptions of the Corinthians, and to undermine the influence exercised over them by certain false prophets (vv. 19-20). He contrasts the *weakness* of his own apostolate with the power of that of the false apostles. To begin with, he regrets that the Corinthians tolerate false brethren among them (vv. 19-20; cf. 1 Co 1:11; 3:3; 5:1; 10:14; 11:18; 2 Co 6:14). Then he reproaches them. They must indeed be very brave to harbor such people, seeing that he himself cannot abide them. His weakness is no sickness; it arises from the constant obstacles cast in his way by judaizing Christians.

c) Paul is in fact using two well known literary techniques: personal *glorification,* a Greek procedure, and antithesis, a biblical. Even though he boasts and glorifies himself in the Greek manner, he wants this to be controlled by Old Testament wisdom, where "glorifying oneself" means finding one's glory in God alone (Jr 9:22-23; Ps 5:12; 88/89:17-18). At the very moment when he seems to be making a eulogy of himself, he is glorifying God in himself. Trial makes his human frailty more evident, and consequently too the strength of God (Rm 5:3; 2 Co 4:7-11; 12:9). In this fashion he uses the foolish praise of himself as a means toward praise of God and exposes the false prophets to ridicule. Because they are incapable of glorifying God, they turn to glorification of themselves.

It is from God alone that Paul holds his authority and his vocation. Christ provides him with the knowledge and power necessary to discharge his mission properly. He is rendered independent of all human limitation and authority. True, he is aware of the gulf that separates his weak self, him, the one born out of due time, from the great Old Testament figures, Moses, Elias, etc. He even acknowledges his inferiority in charismatic gifts to the false apostles. But he knows that God's power invests the Kingdom that is being founded by the spread of the Word and by love, not by exterior works. Hence his assurance in face of his rivals and accusers.

XIV. 2 Kings 11:1-4, 9-18, 20 *1st reading 2nd cycle Friday* This account of Athalia's death is due probably to two different hands. One has a priestly bias and lays the chief stress on the priests' part in the continuity of the davidic dynasty (vv. 1-12; 18b-20). The other represents the popular view, and emphasizes the revolt by the people themselves, and the responsibility of the Baalist cult for the decadence of Judah (vv. 13-18a).

The whole passage illustrates the solidarity that links Yahweh to his anointed. Once Baal replaces Yahweh in cult the davidic dynasty is massacred, becoming the prey of *violence*. Once the dynasty returns and the cult of Yahweh is restored to the grandeur, the covenant is renewed and the cult of Baal forbidden. We have an important consequence of the covenant between Yahweh and David (cf. 2 S 7:12-16). God wants to establish his lordship over humanity, and allies himself with the king of Judah so that he can commit this project to the descendants of a human dynasty. We have the hint of his own desire to become man.

In the murder of Athalia we are reminded of the role of violence nowadays, as poorer classes and countries combat the political and economic power of the West. With the passing of the Middle Ages humanity was confronted by a new phenomenon. Prior to that the different groups were roughly on an equal footing, and had fairly similar cultures (the Christian world, the Arab, the Chinese). Nineteenth century industrialization and technology however made for the advancement of the West exclusively, and gave it an extraordinary superiority. Present day attempts to industrialize the Third-World continue to be rather pathetic. It is as if capitalism, dominated as it is by the profit motive, were incapable of really helping those countries.

Insofar as Athalia stands for a Baalist sacralization of power (the absolutization of human means, territories or classes) she has counterparts in our world. "Established order" has become an absolute, and is sacralized to the point of abuse. In many instances the question indeed has become rather more urgent than one of determining whether violence is justified in the desacralization of such power. One might argue that we are already confronted by a situation of violence, violence that is by power itself, military and police governments, regimes administered by men of straw, racist and economic discrimination, napalm bombardments. We Christians need very badly to make an accurate analysis of our commitment to violence in the Third World. And we should make our political choices accordingly.

XV. Matthew 6:19-23
Gospel
Friday

In Matthew verses 19-21 serve to introduce a piece concerning detachment from riches (Mt 6:24 ff.) whereas in Luke (12:33-34) they form the conclusion to this topic. Between his introduction and the treatment of the topic strictly speaking, Matthew inserts a few sayings (vv. 22-23 and 24) from other contexts (cf. Lk 11:34-36; 16:13).

a) In verses 19-21 Jesus' actual words are pretty faithfully reproduced. Doubtless he was recommending his disciples to *abandon their goods* in order to follow him. Christian preachers however gave another emphasis to his remarks, associating them above all with the early diatribes against the gods of this world.

b) The saying about the eye, the lamp of the body (vv. 22-23) comes from another context (Lk 11:34-35, who also places it just as arbitrarily in a context where there is mention of a "lamp"). It is quite difficult to determine what exactly Jesus meant, and more difficult still to understand why Matthew places it in a context concerning detachment from goods. Perhaps Jesus was making the point that *simplicity* has the same function in moral life as the eye has in physical? In both cases the whole of one's being has to be mustered towards a single end. Blindness in either domain will prove paralyzing.

If the eye directs attention to several things at the same time it cannot steer the body If the disciple has numerous treasures he can never make the choice and direct his life. By simplicity he bears witness that the presence of his Lord is for him decisive, and that he desires only what will further this communion.

XVI. 2 Corinthians 12:1-10
1st reading
1st cycle
Saturday

Paul's adversaries, in order to discredit him with the Corinthians, had claimed superiority to him in the domain of charisms. An answer which emphasized the action of God in his own weak ministry was not then sufficient (2 Co 11:19-33). He had also to show that even in the domain of charisms he was by no means overwhelmed. He possesses as many as they do, but does not avail himself of them because he is not defending himself personally, but the apostolic ministry as such.

a) In this passage, as in all instances where Paul describes his ministry (1 Co 4:9-13; 2 Co 4:7-15; 6:4-10; 11:23-33; 12-9-10), the dominant theme is *weakness*. His weakness is apparent, but it makes room for the initiative of Christ whose force and power dwell in him. He will not have it that the proof of mandate should be sought in the charismatic phenomena which sometimes accompany apostolic ministry. The inner meaning of mission will be revealed only in exterior weakness. He finds its warranty in the buffets of Satan and the "sting in the flesh" (vv. 7-9), which probably designates the hostility of false brethren (the meaning of the phrase in Nb 33:55; Jos 23:13. Ez 28:24).

b) The charismatic *vision* he mentions (vv. 1-4), to which he accords such little weight where his mission is concerned, is certainly not that of the road to Damascus (Ac 9:4) or at Jerusalem (Ac 22:17). It took place fourteen years prior to the compilation of this letter (v. 2), around 43 that is. Though he will mention with satisfaction the visions that shaped his ministry, Paul is always discrete in his mention of mystic phenomena. Jewish rabbis often described similar visions, but with abundance of detail where Paul speaks simply of ineffable words. Though it is one of the deepest mystic experiences, for Paul it is unimportant by contrast with the persecution which is much more a guarantee of his mission (v. 6).

Thus the criterion for the apostolic ministry is evident: a joyous and patient acceptance of everything that aligns one to the humiliation of the Savior one serves. By this standard the pseudo-apostles of Corinth fall. In fact Paul does no more than apply to the ministry the essential criteria of the Christian life itself. One must initate the wisdom of Christ, who accepted the humiliations of weakness in order to glorify God by revealing divine life to believers (2 Co 13:4; 1 Co 1:18-19; 2:2; Ph 2:6-11), and offering them a share in his resurrection.

XVII. 2 Chronicles 24:17-25
1st reading
2nd cycle
Saturday

The liturgy continues with the history of the kings of Judah, but turns to 2 Chronicles for this reading rather than 2 Kings, because the text is fuller and more explicit. This is the only source to describe the murder of Zachary (cf. Mt 23:35), and to treat the death of Joash as a punishment.

The author of Chronicles wrote in the 3rd century. The priesthood was then in high prestige, and the assassination of a priest's son could not be passed over lightly. In the very person of the king God chastises those who have dared lay hands on a member of a consecrated family in the very precincts of the temple (v. 21). This, for the chronicler, is the heart of Israel.

He is equally convinced that good or evil for the people depends on their fidelity to the temple cult and the levitic priesthood. Thus he wants to fix responsibility for the infidelity of the people and their punishment on the adherents of Baal.

XVIII. Matthew 6:24-34
Gospel
Saturday

This lesson on detachment could well have fitted the conclusion of the parable about the foolish rich man, who amassed treasure in his granaries that death was destined to filch from him (Lk 12:16-20). Luke in fact attaches it to a text rather like the present one, where there is mention of birds who do not "gather in granaries." For him, the antithesis, which is probably original, is between the "unease" of the rich man and the "detachment" of the birds.

Matthew, for his part, joins these counsels on detachment to a saying about the impossibility of serving two masters: God and Mammon. There is a difference of course between "serving

Mammon" and being "worried about what we shall eat." The latter can be a very sensible worry and does not necessarily imply slavery to Mammon. Matthew doubtless was anxious to emphasize the importance of the discourse on the mountain by adding, somewhat haphazardly, a whole series of counsels. However, by placing these in a different context, he creates an impression of harshness and intransigence that were foreign to the purpose of Jesus.

The lesson of our reading consequently is twofold. On the one hand it is emphasized that one cannot serve two masters (v. 24). On the other we have the Christian attitude towards unease (vv. 25-33). In the first instance Jesus is addressing the rich (see Luke's context for the saying: 16:1-9, 13-15). In the second he is speaking to the poor, who run the risk of being disturbed by misfortune and losing their freedom of spirit. The basic lesson however is simple. Whether we are rich or poor, our life is directed towards the Kingdom. This must never be jeopardized by preoccupations or demands that compromise the fundamental option.

a) The service of God is *without sharing* (Dt 6:13; 10:20; 11:13). The option of faith demands interior liberty where everything else is concerned, especially everything that has to do with the world (cf. Do 5:9-16; 1 Tm 6:10).

b) On the other hand if God watches with sollicitude over creatures as frail as birds and flowers which are of no account, what care will he not take over those more worthy creatures, men, who collaborate in his work. Christ frees people from worry (though he does not suggest they imitate the carelessness of birds) so that they can consecrate themselves more fully and more wholeheartedly to the quest of the Kingdom (vv. 31-33). At this point he introduces moreover mention of the "Father," showing that the unease men naturally experience ought to be soothed by consciousness of the filial state. For the benefit of those however who seek to allay their *unease* by mere material membership of the Kingdom, Matthew adds the phrase "and its justice" (as previously in Mt 5:6, 10). He wants to show that the real cure for unease can only be found in observance of the new justice that has been described in the beatitudes and the sermon on the mount.

c) This passage is one of the first to stress the *fatherhood of God*. It is perhaps worthwhile to try to determine the precise sense in which Jesus and Matthew are using this term. In the Old Testament and in Judaism generally it was a theme of only secondary importance (cf. Ex 4:22-23; Is 63:16; Mt 1:31; Jr 4:22; Is 45:10, etc.). In any case it designated only the ethical relations between God and his elect. It was never used in the philosophic sense of relationship between creature and creator. Those Old Testament texts which speak of God's fatherhood do not relate it to his authority and power but to his attributes of love and concern (Ho 11:1; Dt 1:31; Jr 3: 19-22; 31:9-20; Ps 67/68:6; 102/103). The theme appears almost exclusively in prayers.

Matthew places it in the same context. He does not mention fatherhood except in contexts of ethical import (link with Christian perfection: Mt 6:1-6, 16-18) or in prayers (Mt 6:9; 7:7-11; 6:14-15).

Our context here however seems altogether different: the concern of the creator for his creature, as in Matthew 5:45. But in the Jewish categories of thinking the notion of the creator-God is not really of the philosophical order, but belongs to salvation history. The Jews actually made creation the symbol of their election: they would call upon nature to celebrate the happiness they enjoyed under God's promise (Ps 102/103).

Thus, though it may be impossible to exclude from the passage all philosophic notion of fatherhood (v. 34), we must recognize that in verse 26 the notion of election is dominant (man being superior to bird because he is dedicated to the service of God). In verse 32 the attitude towards unease is contrasted with pagan behavior. In general the theme of fatherhood in our passage fits into the covenant context, where God gives his love to his own.

Jesus does not require us to relinquish foresight. We can never foresee everything of course, and be so secure that we can dispense with the Father. But on the other hand we must not believe that taking no thought is a necessary quality of evangelic poverty. Sensible use of goods is more in accord with the concept of "poverty" than total and spectacular renunciation. We must know how to preserve what we have, how to put it at the service of others, while being despoiled ourselves. Foolish detachment is concerned with what we can actually control. True poverty is concerned with the brethren, with being attentive to them, being at their service. Foolish detachment impoverishes the self; poverty loves and welcomes the other, with his family and dependents. One can be detached by oneself; one can only be poor in company with others.

XIX. 2 Corinthians 10:17-11:2 *Alternative reading Liturgy of the Word*

Here we have a fragment from a letter sent to Corinth by Paul when his apostleship was challenged (2 Co 10-13). Criticized for his powerlessness and weakness, he finds himself obliged to reckon the list of works of power he has accomplished.

a) Before seeming to boast, he uses two arguments to convince himself he has the right. First of all he finds support in a text of Jeremiah, which affirms that a man may boast of what God has given to him, not of what he has achieved by his own efforts (Jr 9:22-23). True, he is weak (2 Co 11:30), but it cannot be denied that God has worked powerfully with this weakness (2 Co 11-12).

Next he refers to the jealousy he feels where the Corinthians are concerned. He is prepared to boast, if this boasting will aid them to return to their one and only spouse, the Lord. He is comparing his ministry to the role of the friend of the bridegroom. He is the vindicator of the bridegroom's jealousy, and is specially charged to watch over the integrity of the bride.

b) His imagery then is that of *betrothal* between Christ and the church of Corinth. Christ's jealousy is simply a form of his love (cf. Dt 4:24; 5:9-10; 6:15-18; 32:16-21) and a way of ensuring the spouse's fidelity. But the betrothal theme is eschatological. Paul is thinking of the "Day" when the bride will be presented to the bridegroom for definitive union (cf. Rev 21:2, 9). He considers the heavy responsibility of the friend of the bridegroom, who must ensure the spouse's fidelity until the day of the wedding.

The Church, the assembly of all humanity by God with a view to salvation, appears here under the two aspects. We have humanity as God willed and created it, pure and original, and humanity as it made itself, the crafty Eve, sinful and betrayed (2 Co 11:3). Christ took humanity in its fallen state, out of love for it, and restored it to its purity (v. 2).

So, we see the two faces of the Church: sometimes the pure virgin without spot or wrinkle (Ep 5:21-32), by virtue of the paschal mystery; sometimes the woman seduced by sin, so long as the apostolic ministry fails to achieve the ministry of conversion and pardon.

While still in this sinful life, the Eucharist is at once an anticipation and a celebration of the ultimate union. The leader of the assembly there is the anxious and jealous friend of the bridegroom whose Word must purify, and draw the spouse ever closer to the heavenly model.

TWELFTH WEEK

I. Genesis 12:1-9
1st reading
1st cycle
Monday

Abram came from Ur of the Chaldees (Gn 11:31). His father had been established at Haran, about 1500 kilometers north of Ur. This meant that he grew up in the then most civilized region of the world. There were to be found the earliest tribunals and parliaments known to history, the earliest social legislation. Agriculture had reached the highest point of development hitherto known. Scripture however is reticent about the prodigious influence of Sumerian civilization on Abram. It did not want to give the impression that the patriarch had been under Gentile influence. The principle was that the chosen people had their origins in a complete rupture with the Gentile world.

In the 17th century a great Sumerian movement northwards took place. Prosperous families moved away from territories that were becoming insecure through ceaseless conflict. Among them was the family of Abram. They reached the caravan crossways of Haran. To go farther would mean a change of culture, and the way was barred by the Armenian mountains. Haran was the last settlement to possess lunar religion and civil institutions which resembled somewhat those of Sumeria.

The traditions concerning Abraham's call (vv. 1-4a) and his entry to the promised land (vv. 6-9) are Yahwist in origin. They are connected by another due to a priestly hand (vv. 4b-5).

a) The first two verses seem designed to furnish an etymology for Abram. The word would mean "of whom the father is great." Thus would be explained the promise: if you leave your father who is "great," you will become a "great" people. The theme of *greatness* indeed is the *leitmotiv* of the blessing of Abraham, one of the most imprecise blessings of the whole Bible. The nations will be blessed (will seek after good that is) by using the name of Abraham (v. 3). We may here have an allusion to one of those wish formulas, where the word "ram," "great," would occur. Its occurrence here in the Jewish concept of their father Ab-ram indicates his greatness and the way in which he lives on in everyone.

b) The second portion of our passage tends to make Abraham the founder of two popular sanctuaries. Sichem however does not date from him; it was known for one or two millenia before him, and Elohist documents associate it with Jacob also (Gn 33:18-20). Bethel also is prior to Abraham, and is also associated by Elohist sources with Jacob (Gn 28:11-22). In any case, as verse 7 makes clear, Yahwist sources only preserve the foundation accounts as memories. The real interest is that Abraham's presence at Sichem and Bethel is the first step in total occupation of the country. In order to stress this point, the Yahwist author does not hesitate to insert here the promise of the land, that was not actually formulated until the 9th century.

c) Verses 4b-5 were added at a late stage by a priestly redactor, who was concerned about chronology (v. 4b) and anxious to introduce all the persons who would appear in the subsequent narrative. There is a further, less obvious, motive: the desire to represent Abraham as bringing all the *riches of the Gentiles* for the profit of his own people, just as the people themselves did when they came forth from Egypt (Ex 11:2). Here we discern the Jewish inferiority complex *vis-a-vis* neighboring peoples who were more powerful and civilized. The nations must not be possessors of anything more than the chosen people (cf. further Is 60:1-10).

There is something a little grudging in the scriptural presentation of Abraham. His Gentile origins are passed over in silence. Yet it was in this environment that he lived his experience of God and discerned his vocation. In the texture of events he read the Word of God.

II. 2 Kings 17:5-8, 13-15, 18
1st reading
2nd cycle
Monday

Here we have the account of the fall of Samaria in 721 (vv. 5-6) and a description of the subsequent generations. The author stresses the fact that the fall was a consequence of the *schism* (1 K 12:26-33; cf. v. 7) Writers of deuteronomic bias (vv. 9-15) give opposition to the law and the Jerusalem temple as the cause. Prophets of the school of Jeremiah (vv. 12, 16) reproach Samaria with syncretism and idolatrous cult. Finally (vv. 19 and 20) comes a tradition which includes Judah in the reprobation of Samaria.

Those who quit an institution are always wrong, and the one fatal thing is to have their doings scrutinized for fatal flaws by those who stay. Thus, prior to the ecumenical movement, it was customary for the Roman Church to harp on the shortcomings of Protestantism, either to show it as a work of the devil, or to exonerate herself from responsibility for the break. Similarly defrocked priests or the divorced who remarry are as a class put down, as if we wanted to refuse them the opportunity of working out their destiny in a new manner, however beset by failure.

The same pessimism can be discerned in the authors of this passage. They place reponsibility for the schism on the North, a somewhat simplistic view. The schism is seen as a kind of original sin which almost necessarily entails religious failure and political decadence.

A better way is to have confidence in everyone, on the basis that God may be encountered in any circumstances. As long as liberty remains there is no irretrievable situation. Failure itself can become the way towards communion with God.

III. Matthew 7:1-5
Gospel
Monday

The preceding chapters of the sermon on the mount had reached such a point of moral exigence that they might well take themselves as people "apart." Now that they had their own scale of values and the certitude of an unusual vocation to communion with God and his Christ were they, like the Pharisees, to separate themselves from others, judge others, or exercise authority over them with more or less severity?

The will of Christ here is unequivocal. His disciples cannot *judge* those who do not seem at first sight to share their vocation or their privileges. When a man judges others he is adopting a value system which discovers the beam in the eye of his neighbor (v. 4). There is no law so absolute now as to admit of indiscriminate application. There is only Jesus Christ who summons all men to the same salvation.

The one who judges his neighbor may indeed be charitable when he wants to make the eye clear (v. 4), but such a love is deficient because it is based on the superiority of the one who judges, not on Christ. He is looking into the eye of his neighbor instead of being with him in the Lord. The disciple must realize that when he judges another by a legalist standard, God can judge him too by the same standard. If he can confront the other having a mote in his own eye (vv. 3-4), it is only because God does not apply to him the same standard. God is ready to see all humanity through the medium of his own son.

IV. Genesis 13:2, 5-18
1st reading
1st cycle
Tuesday

The story of the separation between Lot and Abraham is Yahwist in origin. Priestly sources however introduced verses 6 and 11b-12a. The purpose was to indicate that the patriarchs were not separated as a result of a dispute (v. 7; cf. Gn 26:20). God's blessing had rendered their flocks so "numerous" that there was insufficient pasturage for all (cf. Gn 36:7).

The Yahwist purpose is to elaborate accounts that would explain how Abraham by his magnanimity merited the promise (Gn 12:7), whereas Lot who chose the easy way, drew down the curse and his departure from Sodom and Gomorrha (Gn 19). The underlying theme then is that of the *two ways*.

V. 2 Kings 19:9-11, 14-21, 31-36
1st reading
2nd cycle
Tuesday

Sennacherib, the Assyrian king, has just concluded a victorious campaign against the tiny western kingdoms. Jerusalem alone still holds out, convinced as she is that the Lord cannot abandon his holy city. Sennacherib is anxious to break down this resistance as soon as possible because he fears a threat on the part of the Egyptian army. Accordingly he dispatches his cup bearer to Ezechias in order to bring about the early capitulation of the city.

Sennacherib is trying to undermine the Jewish king's confidence in his God: can he be any more powerful than other gods? The prophet responds that Yahweh is superior to other gods because he is unique. The others are but idols of wood incapable of saving their people. Yahweh is sole master of the earth and will prove it by delivering his people.

This confidence is soon to be vindicated. An epidemic, known to Herodotus as well, ravaged Sennacherib's troops, and he was obliged to strike camp at once (vv. 35-39).

The religion put forward here by Ezechias and Isaiah is one of coincidences. This sort of belief in God that is based on coincidences continues indeed to be the attitude of too many Christians. They make faith, which ought to be confidence and complete submission of the self, a matter of calculation, of conditions that must be fulfilled.

VI. Matthew 7:6, 12-14 *Gospel* *Tuesday*

The different sayings that go to make up chapter 7 of Matthew are quite disparate. Occasionally one may be connected with another, but clearly what we are dealing with is an anthology of Jesus' sayings which the other evangelists have retained better in their proper context.

In the original context, which we have in Luke 13:24-27, the theme of the *narrow gate* is in answer to the question whether many will be saved. Jesus is simply advising his listeners so to live that they will be among those who enter the banquet hall before the door is closed (Mt 25:10-12). The idea is clear: the narrow gate is simply the door of the banquet hall.

In Matthew however the theme is different. The gate is not that of a banquet hall, but that of a city. What is more, there are two gates, one broad, one narrow. Two different roads lead to them. What we have is the Jewish theme of the "two ways" (Jr 21:8; Dt 11:16-28; 30:15-20; Ps 117/118:29-30; Pr 4:18-19; Wi 5:6-7). His moralizing tendency is evident: the eschatological emphasis given to the theme in Luke is delegated to second place.

VII. Genesis 15:1-12, 17-18 *1st reading* *1st cycle* *Wednesday*

This chapter, so essential in the doctrine of the covenant, contains a good many obscurities. Furthermore, the Vulgate version of the first three verses is much more an interpretation than a faithful translation.

Recent research however has made it possible to determine with fair accuracy the work of the final redactor. The basic text is undoubtedly Elohist (vv. 1, 2, 6). During his sleep Abram receives a message from God, a warlike message set in the context of chapter 14. He has nothing to fear. God will be his shield in battle and the "booty" will be considerable (v. 1). Abraham replies that nothing enables him to contemplate this combat with hope. He is "denuded" (not, as in the Vulgate, "without child"). He has by him only a single warrior of Damascus, Eliezer (v. 2). But, despite his helpless state, the patriarch has confidence in Yahweh and this "faith" brings him military success (= justice, v. 6).

Into this warlike narrative the redactor has woven a scene of Yahwist origin, set perhaps in the context of chapter 13. Here Yahweh promises Abram and his posterity a country as inheritance (Gn 13:14-16). When he is perturbed by his lack of progeny (v. 3) God calms him by having him read in the multitude of stars the promise of the multitude of his descendants (vv. 4-5). By inserting this before verse 6, which belonged to the original account, the redactor has Abram's faith refer to the promise of posterity.

a) In both accounts Abraham's *faith* entails avowal of human limitations, either with regard to battle (v. 1), paternity (v. 5), or in acceptance of a divine promise that is unattainable humanly speaking. It is a man's acceptance of divine intervention in his destiny, understanding this as life with God. Furthermore it entails the sort of renunciation of self which abdicates any attempt at justification by one's own efforts. This is left to God (v. 6).

Paul (Rm 4; He 11:8-12) and James (Jm 2:14-24) will comment on this text in fashions at once different and complementary. The redactor however, who wrote doubtless during the exile, or some national crisis when the people were losing faith in the promise, had already discerned the essential content of faith and justification by God alone.

b) The Elohist context is one of a contract between a king and a mercenary soldier. As king, Yahweh promises a "shield" to Abram (Gn 15:1), his aid that is to say, and a worthwhile "reward." The word here indicates the pay of the mercenary (as in Jr 46:21; Ez 29:19). In the Near-East this often consisted of some estate (v. 7), here in Abram's case Palestine. Abram, as mercenary, promises fidelity to his master (v. 6). Thus the context of the *covenant* is *military*. However Abram says to Yahweh that he is embarking on the combat without "equerry" (not, "child") other than the native of Damascus (v. 3). Can Yahweh really enter a contract with a mercenary so ill-equipped, and really bind himself? Abram seeks a sign to reassure him (v. 8). The sign consists in a treaty according to the norm: the dismemberment into three portions (a better translation than the "three years" of verse 9a) of a heifer, a goat and a ram.

The treaty concluded, Abram sees in a dream the realization of his wishes. The struggle against the adversaries will be intense (the theme of "prey" in v. 11; cf. Is 46:11), especially against the Egyptians (symbolized by the falcon of Horus, v. 13) and the Canaanites (v. 16). He also sees the passage of Yahweh, symbolized by the firebrand (v. 17) between the dismembered animals. Such a rite of treaty indicated that the contracting parties agreed to be themselves dismembered like the animals if they were false to their word. Yahweh is the only one to pass between the victims, because it is really his fidelity only that is engaged. Nothing similar is required from Abram.

c) The Yahwist tradition about the alliance turns it specifically to Abram's *posterity*. There is now no question of a mercenary's contract, but of a promise of descendants. In this tradition Genesis 15:2 was doubtless interpreted as a complaint of Abram. He is going to death (not, into combat, as in the previous version) without a child (not, without servants, as formerly). Verse 4 is added which foretells a male heir for the patriarch, and his vision of a posterity as numerous as the stars is described (vv. 5-6). At this point Abram asks that Yahweh bind himself by contract. Verse 9 describes the tokens of this. Abram prepares two birds, a turtledove and a pigeon, which are not dismembered (vv. 9b and 10b). Unlike the dismembered animals of the Elohist version (v. 9a), the birds are not sacrificed. Probably they should be regarded as symbolic of the masculine and feminine progeny of the patriarch, placed under the protection of Yahweh (cf. Ps

72/74:19; Dt 32:11). This would explain why Abraham does not sacrifice them like the animals.

The account then represents the patriarch as plunged into a deep slumber (v. 12), like that of Adam before Yahweh gave him Eve and by her his descendants (Gn 2:21). Or like that of Noah before he became the father of a multitude of men (Gn 9:20-29). The culmination of the tradition comes in verse 18. Yahweh reveals the gift of a country to Abraham's descendants. He is no longer seen as a mercenary bound to Yahweh's service, as in the Elohist version.

In combining the two traditions the definitive redactor refrained from any personal additions. With full respect for quite dissimilar data, he manages to give a unified and relatively simple account. Doubtless he was anxious to show that all the tribes, northern (Elohist) as well as southern (Yahwist), depended on a covenant of one and the same patriarch with Yahweh.

VIII. 2 Kings 22:8-13; 23:1-3
1st reading
2nd cycle
Wednesday

The book of Kings presents the reign of Josias exclusively under its religious aspect, giving us only the great deuteronomic reform. In fact his reign, from the political point of view, was one of the most disastrous of Judah's final years, because of the king's bad judgment in his choice of allies.

The discovery, in 621, of the Law in the temple can doubtless be easily explained. After such an impious reign as that of Manasses the Mosaic law could very well have been lost sight of, as well as one or other later collection such as Deuteronomy. Apprised of the discovery, the king feels keenly aware of the maledictions and wants to associate the whole people. A liturgical assembly is devoted to a reading, in the hope of kindling an eleventh hour surge of repentance that will deliver the people yet again from the chastisement.

Probably the most distinctly divine characteristic of the faith is that it can be rediscovered endlessly. People believed they knew it: the precepts seemed clear and precise. But now new demands manifest themselves, a summons to go yet further. Later Jesus will have his listeners make a similar sort of dicovery: "It has been said to you . . . but I say to you." The disciple must go through all his life making discovery after discovery, penetrating always further, and never fully understanding the essence and eternal newness of the faith until the final judgment (Mt 25). Only a law that is divine could disclose such depths. A human law, though more precise and structured, will be tied to the letter and will die because of that.

IX. Matthew 7:15-20
Gospel
Wednesday

In this passage we have three distinct portions:

a) Verse 15: "Beware of false prophets." This was not reproduced by Luke (6:43-44) for reasons we can conjecture. The reference to Jewish history is too direct, and his delicacy is shocked by the harshness of the language. Yet the campaign against false prophets looms large in the history of Israel (Dt 13:2-6; Jr 27-28; 1 K 18:16-40; Ze 11:15-17; Ez 13:22, 23-31). When Jesus likens his own struggle against the Scribes to this, he is affirming that they, like the false prophets, are reducing the religion of salvation to human dimensions.

b) Verses 16-18 and 20 (Lk 6:43-45; Mt 12:33). The central point in the passage is the parable of the *fruits.* This teaching has been preserved in many sources, and variously applied (Matthew refers it to false prophets, Luke to the Pharisees). The formulation is traditional, "fruits" indicating the inner spiritual reality (Jm 3:12; Lk 13:6-9; 23:27-31; Is 5:1-7; Ez 19:10-14; Jn 15: 1-8; Mt 3:7-10).

c) Verse 19: the tree that on *fire*. This is an interpolation by Matthew himself. The preceding verses had only mentioned good and bad fruits, and now there is question of condemning bad fruits. In the parable we have mention of "fruits" (in the plural) whereas verse 19 only gives us "fruit" (in the singular).

X. Genesis 16:1-12
1st reading
1st cycle
Thursday

This tradition is of Yahwist origin, although verses 3, 9, and 10 are priestly. A parallel Elohist tradition is to be found in Genesis 21:8-20. The Yahwist author is interested in the etymology of the Ismaelites' name, and the name of the well (v. 14) where they gathered. The Elohist is more doctrinal and psychological, and introduces the reader to the interior drama between Hagar and Abraham.

According to both traditions, Hagar, driven out by the jealous Sarah (Gn 16:4-5 and 21:9-10), is the recipient of a divine revelation (Gn 16:7-12 and 21:17-19). Both present Ismael as a man of the desert (Gn 16:11 and 21:20-21), who lives exclusively in the environs of the well (Gn 16:14 and 21:19).

There are however important differences. Abraham shows more delicacy in 21:11-14 than in 16:6. The Yahwist tradition makes Hagar an independent figure (Gn 16:4-5, 8) whereas in the Elohist she is entirely dedicated to her son (Gn 21:15-17).

The traditions connect the Moslem world with the covenant and the monotheist faith of Abraham. And Islam indeed has always been just as conscious of descent from Abraham as from Ismael. She also vindicates her right of primogeniture, which no one can ever gainsay, when we remember the family customs of the time.

It required however the second Vatican Council to make Christians, after centuries of war or colonialism, recognize the dignity of Islam. Doubtless it will take many more years to heal her wounds, convince her of Christian sincerity, and have her share with us the same covenant and the same faith. There is very good reason why Christians should strive to give the Arabs who come to work among them a warmer welcome, and better living conditions.

XI. 2 Kings 24:8-17 *1st reading 2nd cycle Thursday*

The king of Babylon had just given Assyria the *coup de grace* (609). The kingdom of Judah, in a reflex defensive gesture that was unfortunate, became the vassal of Egypt and Egypt's outer defense against the growing Babylonian empire.

In spite of prophetic denunciations of this alliance (Is 30-31) the king of Judah remained loyal to the pharaoh, even after he had been defeated by Nabuchadnezzar in 605 and forced to retreat precipitately to Egypt. Jeremiah tried to detach the king from the pharaoh (Jr 36; 46) with no more success than Isaiah. There were swift developments. Nabuchednezzar appeared before Jerusalem, and she was only delivered by becoming Babylon's vassal (2 K 24:1-5). The Jewish king however immediately broke the treaty. Nabuchadnezzar reappeared before the city and sent the army and aristocracy into inexorable exile. In 597 B.C. came the final year of Jerusalem's history (cf. Jr 13:18-22).

With a view to eventual restoration Nabuchadnezzar left a *remnant* at Jerusalem. These were mainly the "poor of the country" (v. 14), who had been exploited by the now exiled aristocrats. They regarded the deportation as a national misfortune, but not as a social catastrophe. The fact that some were now in captivity opened up better economic prospects for others.

As well as these proletarians, there was also in the destroyed capital an ancient dynastic branch. The root of Jesse was not altogether severed. A seed remained (v. 17) in the person of

Sedecias, the uncle of the deposed king. He had been given his name by the victor to remind the people that the situation in which they found themselves was a "judgment of God."

Finally, the last hope, the prophet Jeremiah remained at Jerusalem; though Ezechiel, who doubtless was more identified with the priestly caste, was deported. Thus, though the temple remained deserted, the Word of God was not totally absent.

Everything considered, nothing had been definitively lost. Now keenly conscious of their poverty, with their royal seed however tenuous, with the Word of God always present, the tiny remnant of Sion might yet save itself and endure. . . . The condition would be that their political choices would continue to be as lowly as their social and military condition. Alas, it was not to be so.

XII. Matthew 7:21-29
Gospel Thursday

Even at the stage prior to the redaction as we have it, chapter 7 of the sermon on the mount comprised three warnings (vv. 1-2, 15, and 21), each followed by an illustration (vv. 3-5, 16-20 and 24-27 respectively). Thus the parable of the two houses (vv. 24-27) clarifies the injunction of verse 21 ("put in practice"). Verses 22-23, which are not in Luke's version (Lk 6:46-49) are a needless addition to the original text and come from another context.

The whole piece is given homogeneity of a kind by means of the word "do" or "put in practice." In verse 21 one must "do" the will of the Father: in verses 24 and 26 one must "put in practice" the "words that I have said." Likewise the principle enunciated in verse 21 contrasts "saying" with "doing" (the theme of the parable of the two sons: Mt 21:28-30), while the parable of the two houses (vv. 24-27) contrasts "hearing" with "doing." The structure of verse 21 "it is not . . . but it is" (cf. Mt 5:20; 18:3), and the phrase "Father who is in heaven" (Mt 10:32-33; 12:50; 15:13, etc.) are the result of Matthew's own redactional work.

The parable of the two houses is an excellent example of Matthew's catechetical bias. He concentrates especially on those sayings of Jesus which have an application to life. In this he reflects the mentality of the primitive community. It rejected any formalist concept of membership of the Kingdom or any faith without works (Jm 1:22-25; Mt 5:17).

The later addition of verses 22-23 is to be explained by this *practical, moralizing spirit.* It is Matthew's concern to give Jesus' teaching (Lk 13:26-27) a particular structure. Doubtless he was anxious to influence a certain group in the primitive community who were abundantly endowed with charisms, but devoid of the most elementary moral "practice" (we recall the situation at Corinth: 1 Co 12:13). He is opposing both the legalist formalism of some Jewish groups, and the gnostic speculations of some Gentile groups. There can be no genuine Christianity without involvement. For him the rock is a symbol of this concrete truth.

XIII. Genesis 17:1, 9-12, 15-22
1st reading
1st cycle
Friday

This account of the covenant between Yahweh and Abraham is of priestly origin, and consequently relatively late. The authors compiled it either with the Babylonian exiles in mind, or the little faithful remnant in Jerusalem after the return. They would want to remind the former that God had not abandoned them because his covenant with their ancestor was definitive, or their purpose was to allay the unrest and disillusion of the latter. Throughout the account, the Abraham we encounter is rather the postexilic concept than the historical personage.

a) The notable feature of the covenant is the *promise of the land* (v. 8). We do not have this in the old Yahwist and Elohist traditions concerning the patriarch's life. One is mainly concerned with assembling etymological data or data concerning sanctuaries. The other has the more edifying purpose (theme of a father pathetically frustrated in his affections). The brief reference to the promise of land (Gn 12:7; 13:14-15) is manifestly later than the ancient accounts and appears not to have been inserted until the 9th century, at the time of King Asa, whose precise purpose was to reconstitute the kingdom of David. The promise of land is then relatively recent. We do not find it in Yahweh's discourse to Moses (Ex 3:7-8; 16-17) or in the old patriarchal blessings (Gn 27:27-29; 49:8-12; Nb 24:5-9). We do not even find any reference to it in the prophets prior to Jeremiah and the deuteronomic reform (Dt 6:10, 23; 7:13; 8:1; 10:11, etc. Jr 16:14-15; 23:7-8; 11:3-5). It is really the prophets of the exile who develop it, in proclaiming to the exiles that one day, thanks to the initiative of God, they will recover their land (Is 49:8; 54:2-3). In Isaiah 49:22-23 and 45:14-15 it is the very terms of the promise to Abraham that are used to proclaim the promise to the exiles of "possessing the land." Nor is the promise made to all the people, but only to those who seek Yahweh. A select group, known for their fidelity, will inherit the land (Is 14:20).

It is easy to understand how a promise of land to Abraham would assume such prominence at such a time. By pointing out that the promise had been formerly made to the patriarch, the prophets of the exile would be indicating that its execution depended, not on human resources, so feeble at this time, but on God's gratuitous initiative. Furthermore, as it was addressed to Abraham, the father of believers, the necessity of faith was being emphasized. The land would only be given to the select group of faithful. Verse 8 of our passage is a reference to this doctrine.

b) The second note of the promise in Genesis 17 is the *change of name* from Abram to Abraham. It seems very probable that what we are dealing with is two different representations in writing of one and the same word, meaning "he has a noble father." The priestly redactors however connected Abraham with *ab hamon* meaning "he is father of a multitude," illustrating one of the important themes of the covenant (cf. vv. 4 and 5). Thus would Jerusalem, widowed and abandoned, find herself again the spouse and beloved of God, destined to have an extraordinary posterity (Is 62:1-4; 56:5; 62:12; 44:2-4; 51:2; 49:20-21). When Second-Isaiah proclaims the change of name to the exiles, summoning them to believe in a change of destiny, the basis for this in the life of the patriarch showed Israel that the unique God was present in her history. He would lead her with absolute fidelity along a way that had been fixed for all time.

c) In Genesis 17 we have the priestly version of the prophecy of Isaac's birth (a more ancient version in Gn 18). Isaac however is only mentioned to give concrete form to a more important idea: the *promise of a posterity.* In the priestly view the covenant between Yahweh and Abraham is concerned not so much with the promise of a son's birth, as with a promise of considerable posterity (vv. 2, 5). In no other biblical text do we find so many phrases referring to the future. "Your race after you" recurs six times between verses 7 and 19, and the formula "from generation to generation" three times (vv. 7, 9, 12). The author is concerned to present the patriarch as the model for all those who will walk in the presence of God.

This concern of the priestly documents to represent the encounters between God and Abraham as promises for the future, of land or of posterity, begins a hermeneutic style where a biblical event, above all the event *par excellence,* Jesus Christ, is always seen as the fulfillment of what went before. It is not a matter of inquiring whether God actually did promise something. Rather is it a way of viewing the event, not as something isolated and fortuitous, but as a link, the most important link sometimes in a historical chain which gives it meaning. As Ricoeur says: "The event becomes advent; by getting the dimension of time, it gets meaning."

However we must never see the Christ-event as merely the fulfillment of a history of promise. It too would disappear in history were it not being ceaselessly accomplished in the texture of daily life. It must always be the task of exegesis not only to read the mystery of Jesus in the light of the promise but to relate the event of now to the Christ-event. Thus the meaning of history can be deciphered.

XIV. 2 Kings 25:1-12 *1st reading 2nd cycle Friday*	Scarcely had he been installed on the throne at Jerusalem (cf. 2 K 24, 99, 17) when king Sedecias revolted against Nabuchadnezzar. It was a time of considerable political disturbance, as the frontiers of the new Babylonian empire were being established.

Jeremiah ran through the streets of Jerusalem (Jr 27-29) and even succeeded in convincing the king that Yahweh was not just the God of Judah. He is God of the universe, and if he decides for the moment to give power to Nabuchadnezzar, that is his secret, which must be accepted.

Sedecias however, under continual pressure from the Egyptians, Jerusalem's old allies, very soon casts in his lot with the pharoah Hophra in his new campaign againt the East. Nabuchadnezzar at once embarks on the *siege* of Jerusalem for the third and last time. By reducing this bastion he hopes to dispose of Egyptian aspirations in the East.

Despite the injunctions of Jeremiah (Jr 34:1-7), Sedecias barricades himself in the city for a protracted siege. Some hope was kindled when Nabuchadnezzar temporarily relaxed the siege in order to crush the Egyptian armies. The prophet issued new oracles (Jr 37:1-10), but the king, who was altogether incapable of reading events in the light of God's plan, seized the opportunity of fleeing from the city (v. 4). Overtaken by the Chaldaeans his force was immediately decimated. It was the July of 586.

Nothing now was destined to remain. The dynasty was wiped

out (v. 7), the temple burned (v. 9) and the new captives were sent to join the others at Babylon (v. 11). Only the poor remained (v. 12), with their misery and their hope. Was more than this needed for belief in the future? Jeremiah was cast into prison by the Jewish authorities (Jr 37). He was released by the enemy and given honor. But he chose deliberately to share the life of the poor and foster their hope (Jr 40:1-6).

We are perhaps inclined to accept too casually the story of Jerusalem's fall, thinking that such a disaster could never befall the Church which is built on a rock so much more solid than Sion. It could hardly be expected, however that Christ, whose path towards his own kingdom was that of death, would have placed his Body outside the reach of catastrophe. The Church realizes that death will not have the last word, but she has no guarantee that she herself cannot encounter it.

Some Christians derive an illusory security from the promises, believing themselves dispensed from the pilgrimage that must be made from death to life. That explains the reluctance of some institutions to be superseded, the fear of some people in face of the self-renunciation that becomes necessary for ultimate survival. Jesus did not promise that the Church would not die; he promised that even in death she would have new life.

XV. Matthew 8:1-4
Gospel
Friday

Here we have an extract from a section devoted to miracles by Jesus. Having presented Jesus as teacher (Mt 5-7), Matthew now shows him as healer (Mt 8-9). He gives the miracles in groups of three, concluding each one with a more doctrinal episode. In today's passage we have the first miracle of the first triad. It can only be properly understood in the particular context Mathew gives it, above all as a contrast with the cure of the centurion's servant.

Unlike Mark 1:40-45 and Luke 5:12-16 Matthew gives us the miracle of the leper at once. Lepers were not allowed to live in the city (Lv 13:45-46). Thus it was only before entering a city that Jesus could have met one (v. 5). His healing word is a simple gesture which sufficed to heal. The leper must further demonstrate his faith by fulfilling the regulations required by the law (Lv 13-14). Here we can detect a preoccupation of the first Christians at Jerusalem. Though now of the faith, they still thought it must be manifested in practices that were out-dated. The leper who has been already cleaned by Christ (v. 2) must nevertheless go through the ritual purifications.

In the second miracle Jesus heals the servant of a centurion, who must have been a Gentile. John speaks only of a royal official (who could have been a Jew: Jn 4:46-54). Doubtless Matthew wanted to contrast the attitude of the Jewish leper with that of the Gentile centurion, thereby throwing into relief the doctrinal anxieties of his circle. Were Christians of Jewish origin who continued to observe the law in any better case than Christians of Gentile origin?

The Gentile's profession of faith is much less complicated than the Jew's. He even believes in the efficacity of the word at a distance (cf. Ps 106/107:20). His *faith* is based on the word alone of the Lord, while that of the Jew is lost in innumerable protestations. Because he believes in the power of the word (Mt 28:18; 7:29; 10:1; 21:23; Ac 2:22-27; Lk 4:32) he can dispense with ritual.

The narrative resembles quite closely another passage in Matthew where there is question of a Gentile professing faith (Mt 15:21-28). Having recounted here the two miracles, he adds a personal conclusion which makes his intention clear. By contrasting the Jew's faith with that of the Gentile he wants to provide support for those Christians who rightly regarded themselves as liberated from out-moded observances of the law.

XVI. Genesis 18:1-15
1st reading
1st cycle
Saturday

There are many legends concerning the appearance of divine beings on earth, where they were received by privileged human beings on whom they showered numerous blessings. Doubtless they were far too popular to be ignored by the Jewish religion. Often they were linked with the origin of a sanctuary (in this case Mambre), and, in the ninth or tenth century B.C., the most that Yahwism could do was adapt them to a strict monotheism. So the legend of three divinities who were received by a man at the oak of Mambre becomes a visit by the unique God accompanied by two angels.

However the redactor's adaptation was only made at the cost of considerable awkwardness. In verse 1 we have Yahweh, in verse 2 three men, in verse 3 a personage called "Lord," in verses 4-9 several people, in verse 10 a "quest," in verses 13-14 Yahweh, in verse 15 a person, in verse 16 "men," in verses 17-21 Yahweh, and so on to the end of chapter 19.

The account is manifestly based on several quite obscure traditions, but it is possible to determine some distinct themes. Chapter 18 is divided into two parts. We have the story of the origin of the sanctuary by a theophany (vv. 1-8). Here it is stressed that the meal was taken under the sacred tree, and offered to several people. Then there is the prophecy of the birth of Isaac (vv. 9-15), where there is only one quest, where there is no longer question of a sacred tree, and where the dominant theme is the etymological one (laughter).

a) Abraham is a signal example of *monotheist faith.* He sees three people, but, at least in the final redaction, he realizes that there is only one God among them (v. 3). So it comes about that the legend is incorporated into inspired literature and revelation. This is not only because of its content but because of the Yahwist anxiety to adapt a polytheist interpretation of the universe to monotheism. The world is not given over to divinities or forces who prey upon one another at the expense of humanity. It is subject to a single will; history is made up of events all of which point to a single end. Once Abraham entertains the unique God he is immediately *au courant* with God's view of history. He becomes proximately concerned with the realization of the divine plan, because he is to bring to the world the first fruit of the promise (Gn 18:4-15).

b) Rarely does the Bible show us God on terms of such *familiarity* with men. Even in the account of Paradise, God never sits at table with man, or eats the food prepared by man (Gn 18:4-8). Doubtless it required the reservoir of pagan legends to introduce such a familiar notion of divinity in a book normally so preoccupied with transcendence. But the Bible accepted it and made it its own: God is not far from his servant (v. 3). If he is the God of transcendence, he is also the God of immanence.

c) The name Isaac (Jishaq) means "God will laugh," but the account tries to find here an allusion to the *laughter* of the parents (vv. 10-15). Sarah's laugh at the suggestion of her coming motherhood is harsh and bitter. She recalls her frustrated hopes, and displays the scepticism of a woman who has been too long barren to hope again (v. 12). Only at the birth of Isaac (Gn 21:6) will she laugh for real joy. In the interval God has wrought marvels (v. 14).

d) There is reference to Sarah's *barrenness.* This is a frequent biblical theme. Like Sarah, Lea and Rachel will know barrenness (Gn 29-30) before giving the patriarchs of the tribes to the world. Likewise with the mother of Samson who freed Israel (Jg 13), the mother of Samuel (1 S 1) and the mother of John the Baptist (Lk 1). Doubtless the maternal barrenness became a literary cliche to stress the gratuitousness of the divine act. All the women eventually gave birth of course, but they only achieved this by acquiescing in the divine plan. They had first to accept their child's divine vocation in salvation history before bringing him into the world. Even before the "fiat" of Mary, a "fiat" in all these cases became the source of fertility. And behind the literary cliche itself of course lies the deeper reality: that it is only when she realizes her partnership that a woman becomes a mother (cf. Is 54:1, 49:21).

XVII. Lamentations 2:2, 10-14, 18-19
1st reading
2nd cycle
Saturday

This funereal elegy on the demise of Israel was perhaps part of a liturgy celebrated throughout the period of the exile on the site of the ruined (587) temple by the lesser clergy who remained in Palestine. The lamentations bewail a world that has disappeared: gone is the dynasty and the temple, gone are Israel's pretensions to be God's witness and to play a role in the world. The author is still too close to the dramatic disaster to imagine any other scale of values. His hope, a derisory one, is for a restoration of the past.

Our passage is a sort of invitation to *repentance*. First of all the tragic situation of those left behind by the enemy is described. The elders, once so proud, now cover their head with ashes (v. 10). Children, once the picture of health, now struggle for a morsel of bread (v. 12). The responsibility of the false prophets is great. By speaking of peace and security they have prevented the necessary adjustment and plunged the city in catastrophe. All however is not lost. If only the city listen now to the true prophets, and repent of her sins (vv. 18-19), perhaps she can again hold dialogue with God and make once more a fruitful covenant with him.

XVIII. Matthew 8:5-17
Gospel
Saturday

In the first triad of miracles presented by Matthew in this section we have the cure of those persons hitherto excluded from the liturgical assembly: a leper (Mt 8:1-4), a Gentile and a woman (Mt 8:14-15). Christ by his healing power brings them into his assembly. The cure of the centurion's servant is seen in the context of universal reassembly, irrespective of people's condition.

a) In the account Matthew speaks of a centurion, who must have been *Gentile,* where John mentions a royal official only (who could have been a Jew: Jn 4:46-54). This detail is very revealing where the first gospel is concerned. Jesus comes down from the mount of beatitudes where he had inaugurated his new assembly. Immediately he puts this into effect by convoking both Jews and Gentiles.

Matthew goes further still by drawing a contrast between the attitude of the Jew who was healed (vv. 1-4) and that of the Gentile. The latter it seems can profess his faith more easily than the Jew, who is beset by the various requirements of the Law (Lv 13-14). Even after he is cleansed by Jesus, he goes to present himself to the clergy and fulfill the legal prescriptions. He stands for all those early Judaeo-Christians in Jerusalem, who adhered to both the law and the gospel.

The Gentile on the other hand is free of such complications, and consequently has the more spontaneous faith. He recognizes the efficacy at a distance of Jesus' Word (Ps 106/107), and does not even request that the invalid be touched. This is a faith which accepts the Word as all-powerful and is unconcerned with ritual. It is clearly Matthew's purpose to provide arguments for Christians of Gentile origin against Jewish Christians who criticized them for disregarding legal precepts.

b) Describing the cure of Peter's mother-in-law, Matthew discards the disciples mentioned in Mark 1:29, and has Jesus meet the woman face to face. Attention is directed primarily to Christ's person in his role of "suffering servant." He works a miracle not to please his friends the disciples, nor to kindle belief in the crowd, but to take on himself the suffering of the world (v. 17; cf. Is 53:4). Matthew is discerning Christ's *passion* already at work in his miracles. This interpretation is supported by the use of the term *egeirein* (v. 15; cf. Mt 9:25; 28:6-7) to describe the cure. It is often used to indicate resurrection, especially that of Jesus.

c) Matthew does not mention Jesus' leaving the synagogue (as in Mark 1:29). He seems on the contrary to direct attention to the place where the cure was accomplished, which he describes as the "house of Peter," where the other evangelists have "house of Simon." Is this deliberate? From an evangelist so devoted to this symbol the meaning could be that now it is in the *Church* that the mission of the suffering Servant is exercised. He never ceases to take on himself the suffering of men, in order to make of that the seed of resurrection.

The Jew was frequently universalist, as is evident in Third-Isaiah (cf. Is 66:18-21). But this was a universalism that would annex all to the legalist cultic and moral structures of Israel. Jewish proselytism in the last analysis was always designed to swell the ranks of the chosen people, and increase the temple offerings (cf. Mt 23:15).

With Christ universalism took a totally new turn. Man's response to the universal design of divine love was not now to be based on any cultic or moral criterion, but on adoptive sonship. From a filial "yes" pronounced by man would flow the moral and liturgical principles that would govern his membership.

The Kingdom he inaugurated was truly universal. All men were enabled to be members by virtue of adoptive sonship in him, ever renewed in the Eucharist. In this domain all men are genuinely equal. Ethnic or moral distinctions cease to determine membership. All privileges of race, culture, or learning are abolished.

THIRTEENTH WEEK

I. Genesis 18:16-33
1st reading
1st cycle
Monday

Chapters 18-19 of Genesis form an *ensemble* which is fairly composite in structure. The most ancient material can probably be reconstructed as follows: Genesis 15:1-16, 20-22a, 33b, 19:28, 30-38, etc. Some verses of today's reading would belong to this. At a subsequent date (after the exile?) verses 22a-33b were added. They have literary unity, but fit the context poorly. Abraham's interlocutor is no longer one, or more, angel(s), but Yahweh himself (v. 22b). Lot is saved by the intercession of the patriarch, whereas in the more ancient account he wins salvation by his hospitality (Gn 19:1-16). According to the primitive tradition (cf. v. 21) God comes down to Sodom solely to discover if its bad reputation is justified. According to the other account he has already decided to destroy it.

a) In the narrative we have three doctrinal themes. The first goes to show that according to the promise all *nations* are blessed (Gn 12:3). In Abraham, that is to say, they find the source of happiness. Even Sodom and Gomorrha can benefit by the divine promises to the patriarch if they show a minimum of faith and conversion. If they turn in upon themselves and grow hardened, they will be annihilated.

b) The second theme, that of *intercession,* prepares the people to understand the mediating function of the Messiah. Prophets and men of God were the first to set themselves up as intercessors: Samuel (1 S 7:5; 12:19-23; 15-11; Jr 15:1), Amos (7:1-9), Jeremiah (Jr 7:16; 11:14), Moses surpassing them all in this function. Fairly late witnesses to the tradition like Numbers 11:2, 11-15; 6:20-24; 14:13-19; 21:4-7; Exodus 32:30-34 are a good indication of the manner in which post-exilic reflection became more and more concentrated on the idea of a leader of the people who was dedicated to prayer and a special relation with God. Such an idea went into the portrait of the suffering Servant, the mediator *par excellence* between God and men (Is 53:12).

The older traditions however never made Abraham an intercessor. What we have here is a transference to him of the prerogatives of Moses and the suffering Servant. A leader like them of the people, he enters a personal relationship with God, and becomes through prayer and the life he lives the unique mediator between Yahweh and the people. Jewish thought is transferring to a single person the authority of leader and the priestly office.

c) The final theme affirms that the *merit* of a small number of just men can bring about the salvation of a multitude of sinners. Ancient Israel was convinced of the solidarity in sin and chastisement of all. Exceptions were allowed in the case of a single just man such as Lot (Gn 19:15-16), but the notion of individual responsibility does not seem to have been developed until Jeremiah 31:29-30 and Ezechiel 14:14-15 and 18. At the time of redaction of the account of Abraham's intervention, the notion of individual responsibility had been itself transcended, and the idea had grown that some just persons could save a sinful people. Abraham however does not dare imagine that less than ten could suffice (v. 32). Ezechiel will go further by supposing that a single just man can save a whole city (Ez 22:30). And the Suffering Servant poems, insofar as this personage can be taken as an individual, support him by affirming expiation by a suffering Messiah (Is 53).

As the source of all blessings, even for the sinful nations, as priest and unique intercessor between God and his people, as a just man expiating the sins of all, Abraham is one of the figures who prepares humanity for Christ's universal primacy. This he obtained by his sacrifice and prayer, accomplished once for all in the name of sinful humanity.

It is this primacy of Christ as mediator which gives meaning to the various "mediations" of our modern world, the deaths of Kennedy, King, Guevara, Torres, etc. They come to have intercessory value for a humanity that has grown crass. There are many men who owe their salvation altogether to their solidarity with the heroes and the martyrs. Each Christian, wherever he be, reveals, demonstrates, by his attitude and his choices the solidarity of all men round about the man-God.

II. Amos 2:6-10, 13-16
1st reading
2nd cycle
Monday

The northern kingdom, in the 8th century, saw considerable development under Jeroboam II (783-743). The author of the book of Kings however (2 K 14:23-28) stresses above all the moral weaknesses of this reign based on violence and prevarication. Amos was a Judaean shepherd who had emigrated to the North. We are utterly ignorant about the origins of his vocation, or the circumstances which induced him to bring God's word to the kingdom of Jeroboam.

His oracles are presented in confused order. Our passage today may be made up of three different oracles. Verses 4-7 may be part of a long oracle against Israel and neighboring people (Am 1-2), but they do not seem original. Verses 9-16 certainly constitute an oracle against Israel herself, and verses 7-8 another against sacred prostitution.

Amos' diatribe against Israel is concerned with idolatrous cult (7-8), social injustice (vv. 6-7), and abuse of the privileges of the covenant (vv. 9-12). The style approaches the vulgar, but reveals none the less an important idea of God. He is the judge of conduct, but he is also the God of *history.* He has led the exodus, but can also now direct the chastisement (vv. 13-16). He is no Baal totem who fecundates maidens on the eve of their marriage, but a God who depends on human collaboration.

III. Matthew 8:18-22
Gospel
Monday

Christ uses the occasion of a request by some partisans to determine the conditions necessary for following him. He addresses first a Scribe and then a simple follower.

In both instances he requires *renunciation.* He requires the Scribe to renounce his position, and take up the vocation of an itinerant rabbi who is never sure of sleeping or eating (vv. 18-20). The disciple he requires to break his family ties, even the most sacred, such as caring for a father who is deprived (vv. 21-22).

These quite harsh words should of course be kept to their proper context and literary genre. The context is one where Jesus already sees death looming on the horizon, and wants to be surrounded only by disciples who are capable of living with this destiny. The literary genre is that of a rabbi or master who is recruiting disciples, an environment that is always severe both in the Bible (cf. 1 K 19:19-21) and in Judaism. The master requires a total commitment which admits of no sharing.

We must never forget the context in which Christ makes his demand for renunciation. He is opposing established religion, knowing already that his destiny is the cross. He can no longer escape it, and when he imposes renunciation on his followers, this is not just personal asceticism. It is a necessary state for those who want to be true to themselves.

Renunciation is life in company with the condemned, sharing always the secret of death. It is neither masochist nor sadistic, and is not an apologia for suffering. It guarantees continuity of action and fulfillment of liberty. It is not passivity, but fosters on the contrary the spirit of resistance. It is but one aspect of fidelity to oneself and to Christ. It enables us to live this terrestrial state side by side with him who lived it unto death.

IV. Genesis 19:15-29
1st reading
1st cycle
Tuesday

In chapter 19 of Genesis we have grouped doubtless a series of brief narratives various in provenance. Thus verses 1-11 probably belong to a legend directed against homosexuality (cf. Lv 18:22. 20:13); verses 18-22 to an etymological narrative about the city of Coar ("of little account"); verses 23-26 are an aetiological account of the barrenness of the region and of a rock of unusual shape. Finally, in verses 30-38, we are given an etymology for the names of the ancestors of the Moabites and Ammonites. Verses 12-17 must be from the hand of the final compiler.

All the material is so disposed that it makes a parallel with the scene of chapter 18. In both cases the central protagonist, who is seated at the entrance to his tent or the city, arises to welcome some mysterious persons. He gives them the title of "Lord," invites them to his house and prepares a meal for them. In both cases the wife of the protagonist is censured for her attitude. The protagonist himself, who is incapable of begetting, finally does have children.

Lot's *flight* initiates a theme which will become more and more important in Scripture. In a cultural context where the city has not yet been accepted, seeming to be the center of sin and evil, fleeing a city indicates recognition of its wickedness and assurance of salvation for oneself. It indicates conversion (hence the requirement of not looking behind one: v. 17).

Thus fleeing the cities of Egypt becomes a symbol of salvation, all the more so because the Hebrews there were subjected to heavy tasks in the construction of monstrous cities (Ex 1:11). The flight from perverse Babylon (Is 48:20; Jr 50:8; 51:6, 45; Rev 18:4; 12:6) and that of the disciples from Jerusalem (Mt 24:16-20; Lk 17:28) have the same character.

In our day the problem of the faceless city is scarcely to be solved by the withdrawal of the best. It is our business to confront the difficulties and develop such a network of personal interchanges as will ensure for city dwellers greater love and greater service.

V. Amos 3:1-8; 4:11-12
1st reading
2nd cycle
Tuesday

This passage from Amos combines quite disparate elements. We have, in order, a terse oracle of the ancient type (3:1-2), a poem concerning the prophets' responsibilities (3:3-8), and the conclusion of a solemn oracle about the punishments threatening Israel (4:11-12). Out of all this curiously assembled material, we shall devote our attention at this stage to the central poem (3:3-8).

The *prophet* never acts alone. When he appears among the people it is because God has something to say. It is easy to read the signs of nature. A lion roars because he sights a prey (v. 4): a sparrow alights because bait has been set (v. 5). Amos' argument then is this. You can read the signs of nature and interpret them. Why do you not show the same discernment in reading the message of a prophet?

VI. Matthew 8:23-27
Gospel
Tuesday

In the account of the stilling of the tempest by the synoptics we have some important differences. A proper analysis requires a study of Mark's text (Mk 4:35-41) which appears to be primitive, and of Matthew's, where his qualities as redactor are revealed.

a) In all three the account of the stilling of the tempest comes before the exorcism of the Gerasene (Mk 5:1-20). Tradition combined the two episodes for doctrinal reasons: to demonstrate Jesus' *power* of control over evil forces in nature as well as in hearts. Mark actually (1:23-27) provides an exorcism narrative which corresponds exactly in structure with the stilling of the tempest (compare Mk 1:25 with Mk 3:39: threats; Mk 1:24 with Mk 4:38: Jesus reproached for coming to destroy; Mk 1:27b with Mk 4:41: obedience of elements and spirits to Jesus; Mk 1:27a with Mk 4:41: fear). The stilled tempest is thus the manifestation of Him who is taking under control the work of creation that has been compromised by evil powers (cf. Jb 38: 1-11). What we have is a principle of christology. In Christ God is accomplishing the great cosmogonic task by a decisive victory over evil. Men are transferring to Jesus the fear and admiration reserved for the Creator God (v. 27. cf. Pss 64/65:8-9; 88/89:10; 106/107:28-30).

b) Concerned as he is about catechesis however, Matthew's handling of the account has several original characteristics. His greatest preoccupation is the initiation of the apostles to the faith, and his context for the stilling of the tempest is already an indication of this. The whole emphasis is on the summons, the vocation ("following Jesus"). The Word of Christ is presented in its total aspect (Mt 8:18-22), remitting sins (Mt 9:1-8), exorcising the possessed (Mt 8:28-34), or bringing about the conversion of those who are called (Mt 9:9).

His tempest is a real "upheaval" (v. 24, sometimes rendered too weakly as a "violent agitation"), which is characteristic of the eschatological era (Ag 2:6; Mt 24:7). Jesus' remark (v. 26), which is simply anecdotal in the other accounts, is here central to the narrative. It emphasizes the "little faith" of those who ought to be able to read events and recognize there the signs of God's presence. The apostles become converted (v. 27) and recognize Jesus' divine character. The whole episode then illustrates the process of *catechesis in the faith*. Unbelief is laid aside, and we have the confident expression of a faith that can withstand the buffetings inevitable to life in the Church and life in the world.

The tempest episode is a good illustration of the difficulties presented by the faith and its catechesis in the actual world. In a universe that was sacralized, it was relatively easy to discern God's presence in nature and in events. However, ever since man has taken his destiny into his own hands, and God appears to be silent in face of this presumption, it becomes more agonizing to reconcile one's faith in the divine presence with the whole project that is under way for human advancement. The Christian must always find himself a man of little faith subsisting precariously among brethren whom he evangelizes or with whom he communicates. In this world of the secular and the profane, he too finds himself groping for the avenues of communication with God.

VII. Genesis 21:8-20
1st reading
1st cycle
Wednesday

This passage is simply the Elohist doublet of the Yahwist tradition we have in Genesis 16. A commentary will be found on the Thursday of the twelfth week, p. 91.

VIII. Amos 5:14-15, 21-24
1st reading
2nd cycle
Wednesday

Amos appeared in the northern kingdom about 750, at the end of the reign of Jeroboam II. This had been a time of plenty and prosperity, but the latent seeds of dissension, and above all the threat of Assyria, were far from being dissolved.

a) The period of prosperity had accustomed the people to celebrate the blessings of the covenant with God, and to believe themselves the object of divine benevolence. The prophet is able to read events with greater serenity than his contemporaries. He knows that after Jeroboam the kingdom will lose its stability: he realizes the nature of the threat from the east. That is why he tries to arouse the conscience of the people. Prosperity will last only for a while: the future is by no means reassuring. The *Day of Yahweh,* God's intervention in history, will not be on the side of prosperity but of misfortune (vv. 18-20). Deportation, famine and exile will put an end to happiness. The limits between night and day (Gn 1:17-19) will be violated: darkness will snuff out the light (cf. Am 5:18-20; 2:16; 8:9-13; Is 2:6-21; Jr 30:5-7).

b) And yet, this Day of misfortune is not altogether inevitable: man can still avert it. God follows the trend of a history that is human, and if men agree to be *converted,* they can affect the course of events (vv. 14-15) by the way in which they make these their own.

Conversion can influence the manner of Yahweh's coming. He does not intervene independently of man, his transcendence is not manifested brutally, but adapted to the slow spiritual growth of man. It is only for those who have not cooperated that the Day of Yahweh will be harsh and unexpected. They will be faced by a reckoning for which they have not prepared.

With this emphasis on conversion, Amos is changing the usual notion of the Day of Yahweh. It will be a judgment not so much between Israel and the nations as between good and bad (cf. Ml 3:14-23).

The "Day of Yahweh" indicates the manner in which the event lived by man becomes the advent of God and the sign of his presence. By his involvement in each event, pleasing or harsh, constructive or disintegrating, man can transform it into an advent of God.

Our engagement in the event indeed follows the measure of our transcendence of ourselves. It brings us the dimension of compassion and interpersonal relationship. It is a transcendence which, lived in faith, is stamped with the name of God.

IX. Matthew 8:28-34
Gospel
Wednesday

The cure of the possessed Gerasene is one of the strangest episodes in the gospel. It is recounted by the three synoptics, but with quite different emphasis. In Mark Jesus is encountering the Gentile world (Mk 5:1-20). Luke is mainly concerned with the problem of salvation for one who is a demoniac (Lk 8:26-29). Matthew, principally by his silences, fails to correspond with either, and gives a particular doctrinal emphasis of his own.

a) Like Mark, he is conscious of the significance of Jesus' encounter with the *Gentile world.* In fact he gives us, partially, the stock Jewish imagery concerning Gentiles: "unclean," the mention of swine and tombs (vv. 28, 30). This however, for him, is no more than incidental. He is silent about the chains and fetters of the possessed man (Mk 5:3-6). He makes no mention of a mission among his compatriots for the demoniac (Mk 5:18-20). The missionary emphasis is for him secondary.

b) Other nuances in his account make for a special interpretation and give us a premonition as it were of Christ's *passion.*

In verse 28 he mentions two demoniacs where the others, with greater verisimilitude, speak of one only. He will follow the same procedure concerning the two blind men of Jericho (Mt 20:30), doubtless because of the law of two witnesses, and because he wants to make his readers aware of the solemnity of the event. When he stresses the fact that the demons prevented people from passing their way, he introduces the theme of the road (cf. Mt 7:14). He is showing how the forces of evil prevent men from achieving their destiny of "passage."

Another detail proper to Matthew is the protest by the demons because Jesus comes to attack them "before the time" (v. 29). This is an allusion to the "hour" of suffering when the "Prince of this world" will be definitively overcome (cf. Mt 26:18; Jn 7:6-8).

Jesus has no difficulty in triumphing over demons, who are engulfed by the waters of death like the beast in Revelation (Rev 19:20). He has more difficulty in convincing men, and it is significant that Matthew suppresses any mention of a mission by the demoniac among his compatriots (Mk 5:18-20). He concludes the episode dramatically with an expulsion of Jesus by the local inhabitants. Men have failed to recognize their Savior. The road towards God is open to them and can no longer be barred by demons. They refuse to take it (Jn 1:10-11). One day this rejection will be translated into persecution of Jesus and his condemnation.

X. Genesis 22:1-19
1st reading
1st cycle
Thursday

The author of the account of Abraham's sacrifice mingles quite thoroughly information from Yahwist and above all from Elohist (vv. 1-13) sources.

a) Before being incorporated into the biblical *gesta* of Abraham, the narrative very probably had an independent existence. Like many ancient traditions it was designed to explain the origin of a *high place* by describing the first sacrifice offered there. The mention of the sanctuary should be explicit, but the Elohist tradition had obliterated or concealed it. A later hand tried to remedy the imprecision by speaking of Moriah (v. 2), the old name for the mount of the temple (mount of the "Amorrhaeans").

b) The old redactors of the narrative had also a liturgical purpose: to convince the people that *sacrifices of children* should no longer be offered to God (cf. Jg 11:10-20; 2 K 16:3; 21:6; Dt 12:31. Jr 7:31; 19:5; 32:35). In the 8th and 7th centuries this seems to have been quite prevalent. In view of the fact that all first-born belonged to God (Ex 22:28-30), the law was insistent about the obligation to ransom the first born (Ex 34:19-20; Dt 15:19-23) by substituting another sacrifice.

Our narrative here then inculcates the obligation of ransoming the first-born by the sacrifice of a ram (v. 14).

c) The Elohist narrator however transcends this perspective of the old tradition. He is already affected by the prophetic influence in liturgy, the principle that obedience is better than sacrifice (1 Sm 15:22; Mi 6:6-8). He so disposes his text that verse 12 becomes the peak point. Abraham becomes the promoter of *spiritual sacrifice*.

Frequently the Elohist shows more interest than the Yahwist in the psychology and attitudes of the protagonists. His version is designed to describe in profuse detail Abraham's personal trial, his love for his son, the faith in God he shows by his immediate obedience.

d) We can perhaps discern another element too in the Elohist doctrine. By inserting this account of a sacrifice at the center of a series of traditions about the earliest fulfillment of God's promise of a "multitude" to Abraham; by his insistence on the fact that the sacrificed child is the precise instrument of fulfillment, the narrator is making the *trial of death* integral to the covenant. Man, who is responsible for God's work, cannot garner its fruits until he has experienced in the depths of his own being laceration and sacrifice, the self-emptying that makes place for God's gratuitous gift. In the life of the suffering Servant (Is 50:4-10) we find the same note of access to the multitude by means of the passage through death.

In any case Judaism was destined to make of the episode of Abraham's sacrifice a meditation on the meaning of suffering. Even more indeed, the sacrifice of Isaac, above all in the "Book of Jubilees," will become the standard image for the investiture of the future suffering Messiah. The episode was read in the liturgy of Tabernacles, which is precisely a liturgy of messianic investiture. The most interesting point about the relation seen between the two is the indication of faith in a suffering Messiah. It becomes clear why it was in the context of the Tabernacles feast (Mt 17 and 21) that Jesus revealed his suffering Messiahship, the transfiguration being its fullest illustration.

Abraham has to learn that the promise does not depend on Isaac but on God. The extremely immediate father-son relationship has to be broken in favor of the only ultimately valid relation, that which unites the patriarch with his God. Only thus can he recover his son, but otherwise than formerly, as if God were ceaselessly bestowing him again. There is no true road from man to man that does not pass through God. Between father and son everything is as it was before. Yet everything is new, because God now is implicitly discerned as the mediator of the bond.

XI. Amos 7:10-19
1st reading
2nd cycle
Thursday

It was during the long triumphal reign of Jeroboam II, about 750, that Amos appeared in the northern kingdom. He was a Judaean, coming from Tegoa, south of Jerusalem. He himself affirms his popular origin (v. 14), though this does not mean that he was either ignorant or rustic. He prophesied at Bethel, the principal northern sanctuary, which was opposed to the more artificial cultic center of Samaria. The teaching of his oracles is invariably the same. The northern kingdom must not rest on its laurels. The prestigious reign of Jeroboam is drawing to an end. After him will come the disaster (Am 7:9).

a) Doubtless the oracles were badly interpreted. Amos was classed with the anti-royalist party; he was likened to the anarchist prophets who wanted to overthrow the regime. To avoid embarrassment the priest of Bethel requested him to leave. Bethel was a royal sanctuary and could not subsidize people who defamed the royal institution (v. 13). Amos protested. He was no part of any political plot, and belonged to no school of prophets (v. 14). He holds his *vocation* from God, and nothing had predisposed him towards that (v. 15). One might be reading Saint Paul, as he maintains his independence *vis-a-vis* official Jewry and the college of the Twelve. Amos was not a prophet by profession. He spoke because of a profound compulsion, that took precedence of personal interests.

b) The priest of Bethel confuses him with prophets who exercise a professional ministry and are remunerated for it. The obvious sanction that occurs to him is to deprive Amos of all subsistence. However Amos claims no *recompense*. Because his ministry is gratuitous, the first beneficiary is his freedom of speech. It is an attitude that forces Christians to reflect how far their witness, or their ministry of the Word, might be controlled by the pay they receive.

There can then be no real vocation without freedom. One must be sufficiently detached from the demands of family or profession to be able to respond swiftly to the needs that arise. If one is to be faithful to oneself and to one's basic intuition, one must be independent of salary or any such compromise. Throughout her history the Church must be constantly watchful with regard to restrictions on her liberty arising from this or that concordat, this or that association with power or a dominant class. A good deal remains to be done in this regard. The priest, today particularly, must be constantly in search of closer association with society. But he must be always watchful that integration in these terms does not lead to any alienation where freedom of speech or action is concerned.

XII. Matthew 9:1-8
Gospel
Thursday

The episode of the pardoned paralytic is arranged by Matthew in three stages: the link between pardon and faith (vv. 1-2), the power of the Son of man (vv. 3-7), and the power given to men (v. 8).

a) Christ grants *pardon for sin* to the paralytic because of his own faith and that of the community which surrounds him (Lk 7:48-50; Ac 10:43; 13:38; 26:18). Pardon is one of the most frequent themes of apostolic preaching. The Jews however regarded it as a divine prerogative which was not to be exercised until the "final times," the time of victory over evil and of the new covenant (Is 33:23-24, where the "lame" and the "sinner" are already associated; 35:4-5; Jr 31:34; 33:8; Ez 16:63; 36:25-33).

b) In response to this hope Jesus demonstrates how real his power of pardon is by healing the paralytic and proclaiming himself *Son of Man.* This last indicates that the power of pardon is one of the messianic prerogatives conferred by God on the Son of Man, who is foretold as judge of the nations (Dn 7:13-14). Jesus, possessing such powers, can either punish or absolve.

c) Matthew goes on to widen the perspective. To men, to the apostles in particular, Jesus has transferred his *power of pardon* (v. 8; cf. Mt 16:19; 18:18; 19:28). "Men" are actually recipients of this power of sovereignly judging the nations. They can anticipate the judgment, not to condemn, but to pardon. Because the apostles will be associated with Christ in the judgment of the nations (Dn 7:22; Mt 19:28) they can anticipate the sentence.

So it is that the appearance of the sovereign judge at the end of time is anticipated by the exercise in his name of the power of pardon, and the faith necessary for this pardon is recognition of his presence here and now in the world.

Because the Church, the Body of Christ, is the rooting in the world of Christ's work, she has the power of pardoning sins. Had she not this power, she would not be the Church of Christ, because he would not be truly present in her. She would not be the sacrament of man's salvation. When we affirm that she has the power of pardon, we are affirming that in her the history of pardon is continued. If divine pardon is exercised in this world, that can only be because God's loving initiative finds here below in the Church a fitting response.

Jesus communicated to his apostles his power of pardon, to those, that is to say, who by their ministry would maintain the Church as a Church. When the apostles or their successors pardon in the name of Christ, the whole people of God is engaged in the great divino-human act of pardon that is constituted by the cross. The apostolic ministry makes of all the Church an act of mercy for the whole of mankind. In this sense it can be said that the Christian is a minister of pardon (Mt 18:15-18; Jm 5:16).

All Christians then cooperate in the ecclesial act of pardon.

But they must all too, without exception submit themselves to this ecclesial act. They are all sinners who must implore God's forgiveness. Baptism has marked them with the sign of pardon. But the baptized person is still a sinner who has to submit himself to the power of the keys.

All the Church's sacramental and eucharistic ministry towards her members is one of pardon, but it is in the sacrament of penance particularly that this is exercised. Here God meets the man who admits his sin as the father meets the prodigal son. He thinks only of preparing the family feast, and in this moment all the Church is associated, as she reabsorbs the pentitent into the ecclesial community.

XIII. Genesis 23:1-4, 19; 24:1-8 62-67
1st reading
1st cycle
Friday

The account of Sara's death is of priestly origin, that of Isaac's marriage Yahwist.

a) The first tradition stresses the purchase of a plot of Canaanite land. The nomad Abraham is obliged to take this means of giving dignified burial to his spouse. It is the first step towards possession of the *Promised Land,* a theme of first importance in the priestly tradition. This was developed during an epoch when the Hebrews were dispossessed of their land.

b) The second tradition describes the embassy of Abraham's servant in the East, as he seeks there a wife for Isaac. According to the customs of most Semites he would have to marry a girl from his clan. The servant swears an oath over the patriarch's genital parts (the thighs, v. 24.2), in order to involve his fertility too in the project he is undertaking, and so that the blessing of Yahweh which had made Abraham fertile might ensure its success.

Certain details of the episode and several coincidences show in fact that the God of the promise is himself directing circumstances. It is he who is choosing the wife of Isaac by whom he will bless the *descendants* of Abraham.

XIV. Amos 8:4-6, 9:12
1st reading
2nd cycle
Friday

Frequently Amos indulges in invectives against the injustice of the rich (Am 5:7-13; 8:4-7; 5:11-26; 6:17). The wars of the 8th century and the social changes had in fact multiplied groups of merchants who were selling essential food products at prohibitive prices. They could no longer be restrained even by the practices of cult: festival days became an excuse for despoiling the poor (v. 5).

But God in his anger will apply the law of retaliation to profiteers. Do they await festival days as a means to enrichment? The feasts will be changed into mourning (v. 10). Do they crush the hungry man by making him pay even for the siftings of wheat? Hunger will spread itself throughout the land and become the lot even of the richest (v. 11). It will be a hunger not only for bread, but for God and for prophecy. God will abandon a society that deliberately has cut itself off from the poor.

In our world we no longer invoke God in applying the law of retaliation to profiteers. Economic development and organization have made profiteering ludicrous. The rich nations act as a buffer against hunger, but what is one to say of their culture and their conscience? They still crush the poor countries by buying basic materials from them at a low price, and selling back at a high price the products they could have manufactured themselves. They make people work more in order to produce more, in order to consume more, and in this vicious circle the individual becomes no more than a cipher, the object of pressure by publicity, a creature shorn of all transcendental dimension. The very leisure which ought to take him beyond himself, and nourish his hunger for the word, is consumed in the round of profit and consumption. Man no longer has anything to feed his hunger for the absolute except deceitful sacralizations, or the most outrageous magical procedures.

XV. Matthew 9:9-13
Gospel
Friday

Here is described the meal where Jesus, his disciples and some sinners were gathered immediately after Matthew's call (v. 9). Luke 5:29 and Mark 2:15 tell us that Matthew himself organized the banquet, and Luke tells us that it was sumptuous.

The Pharisees expressed their astonishment to the disciples that their master eat with sinners. Jesus then declares that he has come for the sick and sinners, not for those who are well, or for the just (vv. 12-13).

Doubtless he is thinking of those "just" who cannot transcend their idea of justice and discern the mercy of God. Their attitude resembles that of the workers in the vineyard (Mt 20:1-16) or of the elder son who was jealous of the father's generosity towards the prodigal (Lk 15:11-32). Or again that of the Pharisee who fulfills all justice down to the smallest tithe, but looks askance on the sinner's recourse to divine *mercy* (Lk 18:9-14). To a religion which has been reduced to human justice Jesus is opposing one that is based on divine mercy. By citing Hosea 6:6 (v. 13) he is reminding people that the prophets have already challenged the value of rites, even perfectly executed rites, as inferior to a religion of love and mercy.

The numerous meals taken by Jesus with sinners, and the fact that the father gives a sumptuous repast for the prodigal, are signs of pardon (Lk 15:22-24). Christ's attitude to Judas at the Supper (Mt 26:20-25) and his anxiety to offer the bread and wine for the remission of sins (Mt 26:28) are a clear indication of the desire of the first Christians to see the Eucharist as the sacrament of pardon (cf. further Mt 18:15-18). Too narrow a theology of the Eucharist and penance has tended to ignore the link between the two sacraments, and the manner in which the Eucharist is itself the source of the efficacy of penance. When penance is simply made a purifying rite preparatory to the sacral action, this is a de-ordination which denies to the Eucharist the essential dimension of pardon that it has essentially. If the father of a family communicates to them his life during the course of a meal, does not this include of itself an act of pardon for them? Theology and pastoral practice should begin again to emphasize the eucharistic meal as a "remission of sins."

XVI. Genesis 27:1-5, 15-29
1st reading
1st cycle
Saturday

These are extracts from the Yahwist biography of Jacob. Like many other contemporary biblical traditions, it explains the disappearance of the "huntsman" culture represented by Esau and the Edomites, and the primacy of the "pastoral" culture represented by Jacob.

a) It is characteristic of biblical reflection to discern the presence of God in *cultural mutations*. The Yahwist writer sees this presence in events as a choice by God, something that transcends ordinarily acquired rights, and is often a conflict between a younger and an older son. This is the case in the choice of David (1 S 16:1-13) and of Solomon (1 K 1:28-40). Similarly Ephraim takes precedence of Manasses (Gn 48), Joseph over his brothers (Gn 37:6-12), and Isaac over Ishmael (Gn 21). Saint Paul justifies all this by demonstrating that it shows God's absolute autonomy in the conduct of history, and in the choice of his witnesses on earth (Rm 9:10-13). Such conflicts indeed between younger and older brothers transcend the family context and always indicate a political or social mutation. That between Cain and

Abel (Gn 3) is in fact the conflict between the agricultural world and the nomad tribes. The conflict between Esau and Jacob represents the change between tribes who still live by hunting and those who depend on cattle.

But God, who is present in each change, most frequently manifests himself on the side of change and progress. He belongs to every culture, but never to the point of absolutizing it, and he prefers the growing cultures, those of the younger, to those already established.

Here is something for the classes in possession, who are too apt to monopolize God, to reflect about. Western countries are too inclined generally to believe that God is white. People in power become too convinced that the power they exercise is the best.

b) The transfer of the *right of primogeniture* from Esau to Jacob is described in three parallel accounts. According to one the transfer takes place in the bosom of their mother Rebecca (Gn 25:19-28). Another associates it with a plate of lentils (Gn 25:29-34; He 12:16-17). The third, from which today's passage is taken, associates it with the ceremony of paternal blessing. The context in which the transfer takes place is from the moral point of view quite gross indeed. Nor is there much point in glossing over this by allegorical interpretation. It is better to recognize the fact that God can accomplish his plan in the most equivocal human circumstances, and achieve his end in spite of the frailty of his human instruments.

XVII. Amos 9:11-15
1st reading
2nd cycle
Saturday

Following the five visions which form the essential core of the last part of Amos (Am 7-9), the editors append various oracles that were attributed to the prophet. It is for this reason that we find an oracle of condemnation (vv. 9-10) followed by two others of salvation (vv. 11-12, 13-15).

a) The passage is a figure of God's *judgment.* This is seen in terms of a harvest (a comparison that is to prove enduring), and the image of a sieve, which does not allow the pebble to pass through, indicates that no one can pass through the mesh of judgment without receiving his sentence (v. 9).

The sieve however does not allow the good seed of the "small remnant" to pass. It will prove so fruitful that joy and happiness will again invest Mount Sion (vv. 13-15).

b) To describe the expected happiness, the prophet proclaims that man in future will be delivered from the delays of *time.* The toil of October will coincide with the harvest of May, the seeding of December with the vintage of August. Work will no longer be considered a punishment and alienation (Gn 3:19), but a means of mastering the fruitfulness of nature (v. 14, cf. Gn 1:28).

This human victory over time and the alienation of work can only be regarded as a gift of God. Such is the meaning of verse 15, which associates it with the gift of the Promised Land to the Hebrews, pending the gift of all the earth to humanity.

Oracles such as these of Amos enable us to rediscover lost dimensions of Christian hope. Too often this tends to be individualist, a yearning towards a prefabricated heaven which makes this present life no more than a parenthesis and an accident. The hope of the Old Testament prophets on the other hand embraces the cosmic and political environment. They can only see the coming of God in relation to terrestrial realities which require social and political options.

Christian hope of course must be set in the context of human hope. The resurrection of Christ has opened up a future with which nothing can interfere. Our hope then should welcome and share the efforts others make to organize and shape the future in terms of social and political conditions for humanity.

Christian hope should also be most manifest in circles where human hope is at its peak, where plannings for the future are most intense. It is among the poor rather than the rich that such hope is found alive. That is why Christian hope may be expressed in terms of revolution, as indeed that of the poor of Israel was, if it be a demand for liberation and ransom of the oppressed, and a desire for humanization in the fullest sense.

XVIII. Matthew 9:14-17
Gospel
Saturday

The discipline imposed by Jesus on his disciples scandalized the crowds because it did not at all resemble that of other rabbis. The followers of the Baptist and the Pharisees observed some days of fast, whereas his disciples seemed to dispense themselves. What is posed here is the problem of independence on the part of Jesus and his disciples concerning observances (the Sabbath, rubrics of ablution: cf. Mk 2:23-27). He justifies his attitude by an affirmation concerning the presence of the Spouse, and by two brief parables.

a) In the Old Testament and in Judaism the practice of fast was associated with the wait for the coming of the Messiah. Fasting and refusal to drink wine, which were specific characteristics of the Nazirite state (cf. Lk 22:14-20), indicated dissatisfaction with present time and impatient expectation of the consolation of Israel. The Bapist in particular had made this a fundamental principle of his behavior (cf. Lk 1:15). The disciples of Jesus, by dispensing themselves from prescribed or voluntary fast gave the impression of being disinterested in the coming of the Messiah, of refusing to share messianic hope. The answer of Jesus is clear. They do not fast because the *messianic times* have come. There is no need for them to hasten by ascetic practices the advent of a Messiah in whose intimacy they are already living. The association will of course be interrupted by the passion and death of their master. Then they shall fast (this is to be compared with Luke 22:18) until the day when the Spouse will be given back to them in the resurrection and the definitive kingdom.

b) The parables of the garment and the wine-bottles are a further response to the astonishment of John's disciples and the Pharisees. Because he is the inaugurator of the messianic times, Jesus realizes that what he is bringing into the world has nothing in common with what it previously possessed (cf. Lk 16:16 or the miracle of Cana, Jn 2:10). There is no value judgment in the parables about the superiority of the old to the new (which is true of wine) or the new to the old (which is true of the garment). There is not a comparison really; what is stressed is an *incompatibility*. The new and the old can only be conjoined at the cost of losing both. The patched garment will be ill-matched, and the old bottle will be irretrievably lost, together with the wine. The moral to be drawn is clear. Compromises, where everything is lost, must be rejected.

c) Probably Jesus delivered the parables as proverbs, but they were given the dimension of allegory by the synoptics who placed them immediately after Jesus' affirmation that the presence of the Spouse proved the advent of the messianic times. The garment and the wine are in fact classic symbols for the messianic times (cf. Lk 15:22; Nb 13:23; Pr 9:1-5). Everything that is old has become obsolete, and salvation is dawning in all its *newness*. Thus the original teaching of Jesus about incompatibility is modified by an ecclesial teaching which stresses the radical *newness* of the age that has come.

The passage then reflects two distinct preoccupations of the primitive Church. Their conviction that the messianic age had arrived was ineradicable. But did this entail a totally new approach in life-style? Ought people not perhaps cleave to the legalist prescriptions followed by the Judaeo-Christians? The two parables, by showing the incompatibility between the old and the new, provide the definitive solution. The law must be abandoned. God is on the side of the new.

But, above all in the communities of Gentile origin, the question is no longer one of incompatibility between the two usages. It is the astonishing refusal of Israel to accept the gospel. Christians asked themselves: can we be on the correct path if obedience to the gospel requires separation from the parent trunk of Israel? An allegorizing interpretation of the sayings about the garment and the wine bottles reassured them. Their life is a totally new one, independent of all that is past.

FOURTEENTH WEEK

I. Genesis 28:10-22
1st reading
1st cycle
Monday

Both traditions, the Yahwist and the Elohist, are concerned in this account to explain the origin of the Bethel sanctuary. According to the Elohist (vv. 10-12, 17-18, 20-22), the remarkable character of the site and the erection of the altar are due to Jacob. According to the Yahwist (vv. 13-16, 19) God himself, by means of the promise to Jacob, is the founder of the sanctuary, and the author furnishes us with its etymology.

a) The theophany, for the Yahwist, is set in a quite material context. God comes down to earth and shows himself to Jacob. The Elohist is more spiritual. He speaks only of a dream, in which intermediary beings move between God and his chosen one along a ladder, which might be that of an Egyptian pyramid or a Babylonian ziggurat. The Yahwist vision, material though it is, does have some few spiritualized characteristics. Yahweh now is not the god of a place, but the more personal God of the patriarchs (v. 13). His reign on earth is concerned with a *promise* to which he is faithful (vv. 13-15). Furthermore, Bethel is less a place of cult than a sort of anticipation of entry to the land promised to the patriarchs, a pledge of the divine veracity in promise.

For Jacob, in concrete terms, the promise of land takes on the aspect of a contract by God to have him return "to his soil" (v. 15).

b) In the Elohist rendering the *vow* of Jacob (vv. 20-22) seems like a condition imposed on God by man. It is not the same in the definitive version where the vow follows the promise, and is based on the formal assurance given by God to his interlocutor. The proclamation is not altogether clear, and literary criticism takes great pains to elucidate it. It is suggested that the final redactor reworked it awkwardly in the light of Jeremiah 7:23,

Deuteronomy 29:12, or Hosea 2:25, where we have parallel formulas to express the perfect accord between God and his people. Jacob would then be engaging himself in the life of perfect union between Yahweh and Israel. He would be giving the perfect response to the *divine promise.*

II. Hosea 2:18-25
1st reading
2nd cycle
Monday

Hosea lived in the northern kingdom in the 8th century at a time when world politics were tending towards the eradication of small kingdoms. His role was to reveal the presence of God in the midst of these upheavals.

His deepest intuition was that the disappearance of the northern kingdom was associated with the Canaanization or decadence of its religion. Baalism had been a deleterious influence on the people's vitality and ethos. Only by a return to stable monotheism could they recover confidence, and their proper role in the world.

The passage in today's liturgy is concerned precisely with this theme of return to pristine monotheist fidelity. We can distinguish three distinct oracles, each one introduced by the formula "in that day" (vv. 18, 20, 23).

a) The first oracle is an invective against Baal. Even his name is destined to become so shameful that people will hesitate to use it (particularly doubtless in the composition of proper names). This is a way of affirming that men will free themselves from the tutelage of a *nature God,* in order to dialogue freely with the free God. They will shape history with him, and thus take their proper place in the ebb and flow of events.

b) This free encounter between God and man, now liberated from Baalism, will culminate in a *new alliance.* This is the theme of the second oracle (vv. 20-22). The first effect of the alliance will be the success of efforts for peace (symbolized by the taming of savage animals, cf. Is 2:4; 11:6-8; 65:25. Ze 9:10; Ez 34:25). The alliance itself will be after the manner of an "espousal" where both spouses exchange presents. The bridegroom (God) brings justice and right, fidelity and mercy, pledges that the alliance will be maintained. The bride (Israel), for her part, brings knowledge of God, and a response which indicates willingness to live in communion with God.

c) The third oracle is a reflection on the content of the alliance (vv. 23-25). The parties are compared to persons who never cease to respond mutually to one another. The responses, one notes, take place between natural realities, heaven to earth, earth to wheat, wheat to Israel, etc. This is an affirmation that the personal alliance between God and man will have a *cosmic dimension.* The elements will be set in harmony and placed in the service of man, something that the Baal cult was unable to accomplish.

By using the name of the country Israel, to designate the person, Israel, the author is reminding us that this was at once the richest granary of the promised land, and the scene where the royal house was to play its last card in battle before collapsing into slavery about 733. It is then at the very scene of failure that the fruitfulness of the alliance will burgeon once more. God himself will "fecundate" his spouse in a dialogue of love.

In our time we could take Baal as standing for a certain mastery by man over nature. Mastery could in fact prove just as alienating as the fear-ridden submission to nature that was characteristic of pretechnological man. We can see this very clearly in the unidimensional societies that both capitalism and communism will tend to build.

Hosea can be taken as a prophet of the 20th century to the extent that he shows how mastery of nature must not be the fruit of a spirit of domination and human conquest. It must be a free and gratuitous encounter with the unforeseen and unpredictable, with the divine.

III. Matthew 9:18-26 *Gospel Monday*

In a passage parallel to this (Mk 5:21-43), Mark mentions the ruler of the synagogue by name (Jairus) and gives us the episode in two stages: first the request for healing, then the resuscitation.

Matthew is more modest. He simply seems anxious to gather in a single ensemble different narratives of healing (a leper, the centurion's servant, Peter's mother-in-law, demoniacs, the paralytic, the daughter of Jairus, the woman with the issue of blood, two blind persons, a possessed mute).

This whole section of Matthew (8-9) indeed is a preparation for his doctrinal portion, the mission of the disciples (the kingdom is approaching, go and heal: 10:8). The evangelist seems to have discerned in the cures signs authenticating the Lord's mission of proclaiming the kingdom, a mission to be continued by the Twelve. The expected kingdom had been foretold as a time when men would recover health (Is 29:18-24; 25:5-10; 61:1-3). That is why *healings* were frequent among these missionaries.

However every miracle requires faith on the part of the beneficiary. The woman with the issue of blood, in today's gospel, is saved by her faith. Likewise the daughter of Jairus is resuscitated in secret (v. 24). This is the famous messianic secret (Mk 7:33; 8:23; 4:10-12) which supposes that one enters one's own secret depths, in order to see and hear the wonders wrought by the Lord.

Today, as in apostolic times, the proclamation of the good news should be accompanied by healings. That being so, the first sign of healing that Christians can give the world is the sort of human being they endeavor to produce.

The person who is healed by faith in Jesus Christ, and who, imitating Jesus, becomes himself a healer of others is the man who has made the new commandment his own: "Love one another as I have loved you" (with a love, that is, which goes the length of laying down one's life for others). The whole project is civilization takes on its proper dimension when it is permeated by the healing dynamism of love. Those who work towards it must always display a recognition of the other in the inviolable mystery of his otherness.

Such a lucid exercise of charity is a stumbling block for those who do not have the faith. The non-Christian will only discern the sign of healing, which is offered also to him, insofar as the light of faith begins to dawn for him. When Jesus healed he called for faith: the Church must exercise her healing power in a similar fashion.

It is in the Eucharist above all that believers are put in relation with Jesus, the physician of souls and bodies. Here they become his partners in the work of healing. To demonstrate this, one need only remember two essential dimensions of the eucharistic encounter. There is on the one hand the penitential dimension. It permeates the whole celebration: those who share the body of Christ are conveyors of divine pardon. Then we have the dimension of universal brotherly communion. In the Eucharist the believer accepts all men as his brothers in faith. This makes him an instrument of peace when he returns to ordinary life. In such wise is the Eucharist a medicinal grace.

IV. Genesis 32:23-33
1st reading
1st cycle
Tuesday

The account of Jacob's combat against El is certainly composite. Both Yahwist and Elohist hands can be discerned in it, but exegetes are not agreed about where they begin and end. We are in any case dealing with a very primitive narrative with roots in popular folklore.

a) We often find the theme of combat between a traveler and a local god in ancient Semitic writings. Moses becomes the Jewish protagonist when he wants to reenter Egypt (Ex 4:24). Between his combat and that of Jacob we have a parallel. In both instances a traveler penetrates to a territory that belongs to a certain divinity who opposes his passage. In his flesh he retains the evidence of combat (in Moses' case, circumsion: Ex 4:25-26). Like Moses Jacob tries to know the name of the divinity, in order to adapt himself to his requirements, but in this regard Moses fares better than he does (Ex 3:1-10). Probably the primitive source mentioned, not Yahweh, but a local river spirit. Jewish tradition however suppressed this idolatry, and substituted Yahweh for what was really a Canaanite demon.

b) The Jews used the anecdote to show that their patriarch had fully deserved to enter Canaan. He triumphed over the protecting genius of that country, and had been *blessed* by him to the point of being able to include his name (El) in his own name (Israel). In such fashion did the pagan divinities ratify Yahweh's decision to give Canaan to the Jews. They submit themselves to the hegemony of the only true God and adapt themselves to the fulfillment of his will.

V. Hosea 8:4-7, 11-13
1st reading
2nd cycle
Tuesday

In an extremely rich text which has been frequently retouched, we have here one of the first prophetic diatribes against idolatry. Its principal themes were destined to be taken up frequently again in subsequent prophetic literature (cf. Is 40:20; 41:21). Hosea and the legislative documents of his time (v. 12) declared open war on the current Canaanite religion.

The idolatrous religious practices contemplated by Hosea are principally concerned with the investiture of kings (v. 4) and rites of fecundity (v. 7) connected with the bull, the symbol of vigorous fertility (v. 5). After centuries of coexistence he is the first to challenge such idolatry directly in the name of austere Yahwist monotheism. The struggle is destined to be all the more sharp in that Yahwism had already accommodated itself to many Baalist practices and had endorsed a priesthood that was originally dedicated to the Baalim of the high places. The code of alliance to which doubtless we have an allusion in verse 12 was already known, even if it was frequently a dead letter. Elias had joined issue on the matter, but Hosea was the first to issue accusing oracles.

We could ask the question whether Christianity now ought to adopt towards other religions the attitude taken by Israel towards Canaanite religion. It is to be noted in the first place that in all this matter an evolution has taken place.

To begin with, Christianity was considered the exclusive definitive truth. It was believed that, outside its boundaries, nothing but error, not to say Satanism, was possible. That was Israel's attitude to Canaan.

There was considerable progress when it was realized that in all religions an important element was present: the search for God. Even if this was liable often to go wrong when left to itself, it could serve as starting point for revelation. More than that, it was realized that this yearning of man towards God was an answer to a call directed by God towards all men, whoever they were. Such an answer would not be possible without the action of the Spirit. Ultimately of course the Spirit's action, in God's plan, is directed towards the encounter with Christ, the only Savior of mankind, and can only lead in the last analysis to the sacrament of Jesus Christ which is the Church.

Some go further still and discern in non-Christian religions a certain presence of Christ already, a genuine grace. He is already present by the act of creation, by his will to save all men. Someone who does not know the Church, or who knows it inadequately, can be saved in his own religious framework because of this partial, half-understood, presence. The need to proclaim Christ to non-Christians is all the more urgent because he is already present with them. When Christ is revealed to them they are being led to the proper end of their pilgrimage, to their full religious maturity. To reach that stage it is necessary for them to recognize their own shortcomings and answer the call to conversion.

Such attitudes, relatively new in this domain, as indeed in the whole broad area of Church relations with "the others," are dictated by a deep-laid principle. Negatively it might be expressed as a refusal to understand and live Christianity in terms of difference, divisiveness and opposition. Positively, it is the determination to express our faith with full recognition of what we hold in common with other men, whatever the difference of religion or ideology. This principle, the evidence of a new spirit, is clearly expressed in the documents of Vatican II. It is without doubt one of the most basic insights we owe to the council.

It represents the emergence, at the level of official Church teaching, of the corporate conscience of our time, non-Christian as well as Christian. The desire to cooperate, the yearning for solidarity, the compulsion to be "involved" are not primarily characteristics of Christians. They are the distinguishing traits of all people in our time. We are doing that which all Christian generations did before us, expressing our faith in terms of the culture and ideas we share with all those around us, a framework outside of which we cannot really live or breathe. What is new in our situation is the intensity with which, in a pluralist society, the need for solidarity is felt.

But of course the considerations impelling us towards respect for non-Christian religions are not human merely. The main one is faith in the Risen Christ. We must always maintain unequivocally that there is no salvation other than that in Jesus Christ. This salvation is really universal, and worldwide, in non-Christian religions as well, anterior to any intervention by the Church. Through the paschal event Christ, the only source of salvation, has become present to all generations, to all human communities, in the heart of every man. By his resurrection he has not only "opened the way to heaven," but has effectively wrought the salvation of humanity. In his glorified humanity "in which dwells corporeally all the plenitude of Divinity" (Eph 2:4-6; Col 1:19-20) he remains united with men, simply because once to become a man among men. Thus now as Risen Lord, always united with humanity, his presence in the world is a presence of reconciliation, of peace, of holiness, of salvation.

Every man, in whatever situation he finds himself, especially in his encounters with others, who chooses the way of poverty of spirit, of mercy, of uprightness, of respect and fidelity, of the gift of self, will be meeting Christ. It is in the cut and thrust of human existence that Christ is to be encountered. The man who lives after the pattern set by Jesus in his own life, is, whether he knows it or not, deciding for Christ. "I was hungry and you gave me to eat. . . ." There is no salvation except in alignment with Christ, but if a life is directed after the pattern of his, there is by that fact alignment.

We are dealing here specifically with non-Christian religions. It is worth repeating that it is not so much as religions that we consider them vehicles of salvation, but precisely to the extent that the love and abnegation of the saving Christ are manifested there too. And so we are left with a final question: to what end the Church, if salvation is possible without her intervention? Why continue to preach the gospel?

The divine project is not fully described in the phrase "saving souls." Rather is it a matter of making of all humanity God's people, the body of Christ, the temple of the Spirit. The alignment with Jesus Christ, though it is possible at the personal level, is fully conformed to "God's plan" only under certain conditions. It must be lived in reconciliation, reciprocity, exchange, fraternal sharing, communion and association with a particular group. The group, that is, we call the Church, which sees true human destiny in terms of this divine plan for unity, and has the courage to proclaim this to the world.

The universal presence of Christ among humanity has a thrust towards incarnation, manifestation in some way. It must be actualized, incorporated into history. "The Word was made flesh." The "mission" of the Church is to bear witness to that incarnation here and now. Her catholicity will only be fully exercised when she absorbs all that is individual and inalienable in different cultures, generations and peoples, including their religious differences. Her unity is not achieved by the suppression of differences, but rather by drawing them somehow together. She is the universal sacrament of salvation, the visible sign of Christ's anterior presence. Through her the plan of salvation, fulfilled in him, is authentically revealed and made actual.

Hitherto the need for evangelization has been seen in terms of the need for individual salvation. Now we are coming to view it as the movement rather of the Father's love for men, so that all may come to live more fully with the life of Christ. It is a movement which makes for the unity, here on this earth, of all men in Christ their elder brother. Divisiveness among them is manifested even in their quest for God. Through the revelation of Jesus as the only son of the Father, savior of all men, and only thus can they achieve unity. The love of God will veritably shine among them. The Father's plan to unite them all in his Son will be realized. It will take time to elaborate theological answers for all the issues involved. We can be sure however that certain affirmations have to be simultaneously maintained by the believing Christian:

(a) The necessity of making Christ known to men so that they will have life in abundance;

(b) The radical newness of Christ, salvation being, not the result of human effort, but a gift from God;

(c) The importance of baptism which makes the Christian a co-savior, with Christ, of men;

(d) The actuality of the Spirit's action in all human societies, because God does not limit his love to the "just" only;

(e) The fact that dialogue with people of other religions is, for the Church too, an opportunity for progress and renewal.

VI. Matthew 9:32-38
Gospel Tuesday

The missionary discourse, of which today's passage furnishes the scene and introduction is conserved in different traditions. Mark 6:7-11 gives a very brief account of it, which Luke 9:3-5 adopts to his purposes, integrating it into the despatch of the Twelve on mission. Luke 10:2-16 however gives us a lengthy account of the same discourse and integrates it into his account of the seventy-two disciples. He follows his general principle of avoiding treatments that seem too narrowly confined to the functions of the Twelve.

Matthew chooses to combine the long and short versions, adding some further material, from the eschatological discourse for instance. Such a procedure widens considerably the original perspective of Jesus. We are getting not so much the dispatch of the twelve apostles on a Galillean mission, as a small treatise on missiology in general.

a) The theme of harvest opens the discourse (cf. Mt 9:37-38; Lk 10:2; Jn 4:35-38). Just as he had invited the fishermen to become fishers of men, Jesus now invites the harvesters of wheat to become spiritual harvesters.

The whole image suggests God's action as he puts a term to human history and inaugurates the Kingdom of the final times with his judgment (v. 7; cf. Am 9:13-15; Ps 125/126:5-6; Jl 4:13; Jr 5:17; Mt 13:28-39; Rev 14:15-16). Thus this harvest has a dimension of judgment: the grain and the chaff are separated. Not surprisingly the harvesters become victims of persecution. They will be sheep in the midst of wolves (Mt 10:16).

b) Of greater importance seems to be Jesus' concept of his role as *rabbi*. Unlike contemporary rabbis, who surrounded themselves with some disciples in a school or at the gate of a city, he wishes to be itinerant. Rather than wait for disciples to come to him, he will go to meet them and encounter them in their normal living context. He will not be like the temple priests, who accept material for sacrifice and money from the faithful without worrying about their salvation. Nor does he propose to be like the Pharisees who surround themselves only with the elite. He will go to the "lost sheep" of Israel, those who are lost and forgotten (v. 35). He will have disciples, but not to engage in discussion with them. He will have them share his missionary journeys and turn their attention to the abandoned sheep (vv. 36 and 10:1).

This attitude, which is a totally new one in Israel, automatically makes mission a work of "pity" (v. 36) and mercy towards the poor, the sick and sinners. These are "sheep without shepherds," with whom neither priests, Pharisees nor rabbis deign to concern themselves.

It is the Church, the "people of God" as a whole, which is responsible for the gospel of Jesus Christ. Her mission in the world is the proclamation of the Word. In this common task the priest is not someone set apart; he shares the task with every baptized person.

No consideration arising from mission, the Kingdom or the incarnation of Jesus Christ, should mark the priest off sociologically, politically or culturally on the human level. His ministry in the Christian community carries no implication of privilege, status or living standard other than those determined by Christ for all the baptized. The segregation associated with the priesthood is strictly "theological," not sociological.

Thus everyone, the priest and the baptized Christian, must live out their human lives "in truth," in fidelity to the Word of God. The priest should be altogether a man, fully of the world. He should share the common lot of the men of his time. Like everyone else he should be engaged in the work of renewal and transformation of the world. If he follows this policy, the "missionary" will be truly itinerant and will encounter the "abandoned sheep."

VII. Genesis 41:55-57 42:5-7, 17-24
1st reading 1st cycle Wednesday

This account, almost exclusively Elohist, presents the investiture of Joseph as pro-vizier of Egypt. This was according to an established rule whereby, during periods of misfortune the vizier was relieved of certain important tasks by the pro-vizier (vv. 55:6; cf. Gn 41:37-42).

a) The *agrarian policy* of Joseph was described by the Yahwist in Genesis 47:13-26, but in this passage its marvelous results are proclaimed (vv. 41:56-57; 42:6-7). During the years of abundance Joseph had acquired sufficient corn to supply the lean years. His policy however was not confined exclusively to helping the poor or hungry. On the contrary, it was a service to the pharaoh. He sold to the poor the corn he had on reserve, which meant that in order to subsist they had to alienate their lands or sell their person. Thus at the end of the famine they found themselves reduced to slavery without any personal goods.

While we might be disposed to pass a severe judgment nowadays on this policy, we must excuse Joseph who lived so many centuries ago. How many Joseph's do we not have in the world today? A Christian cannot read this account without thinking of those contemporary powers who are prepared to assist underdeveloped countries to the extent that they can derive profit from this, but who actually make whole populations their economic and political slaves. Such is the case when a military treaty of alliance allows the representative of a great power to intervene in the political structure of a country, or when a whole continent is under the thumb of a series of dictators who can only maintain themselves with the assistance of foreign power. We are certainly not without Joseph's, for whom the power of the king carries more weight than the misery of the poor. However, the greatest misfortune of the world and the Church is that the prophets who arise to denounce this evil are scarcely listened to. Most Christians close their ears, on the pretext that politics has nothing to do with morality. It is easy to understand why some revolutionaries choose not to obey the advice of pharaoh: "Go to Joseph . . ." (v. 55).

b) In the context of this harsh agrarian policy, Joseph is suddenly confronted by ten of his brothers (vv. 5-7, 17-24). The account illustrates the love that Joseph bears his youngest brother, and his anxiety to know whether the elder brethren have treated him perhaps to a fate like his own. He decides to keep Simeon, not Reuben, as hostage, though his right would have been otherwise. Probably this is out of regard for the latter who had enabled him to escape death.

We can consider the nature of the force that renders Joseph capable of such affection and brotherhood, not only for his blood brother, but for all men.

VIII. Hosea 10:1-3, 7-8, 12
1st reading
2nd cycle
Wednesday

Verses 1-3, 7-8 are from a poem where Hosea is once again condemning the Baalist cult of the northern kingdom. Verse 12 belongs to another oracle, which is an appeal to conversion. The first oracle, with its sapiental flavor, may have been addressed to the prophets' disciples, whereas the second is more kerygmatic in tone.

For the first time, Israel is compared to a fruitful vine. But Israel's cult has abused this privilege, and transformed the life-giving presence of Yahweh into a Baalist presence. The falsity of this cult (v. 2) arises from the *hypocrisy* of its followers. While pretending to adore Yahweh, they are in fact rather concerned with the influence of Baal on their lives and their flock. One result of this religious hypocrisy is political instability (the absence of the king: v. 3). Another, very soon, will be the fall of Samaria (v. 7). The sterility of a soil which once produced the vine, and produces nothing now but brambles and thorns (v. 8), will demonstrate to the people their error.

In the time of Jesus this oracle of Hosea will take on a new significance (Lk 23:30; Rev 6:15). The hypocrites will pronounce on themselves the curse called down by the prophet on all those who substitute for fidelity to God political maneuvers or empty cultural pretensions.

IX. Matthew 10:1-7
Gospel
Wednesday

This is the introduction to the apostolic discourse.

a) Unlike the other synoptics who give the list of the Twelve at the time of their calling by Jesus (Mt 3:16-19; Lk 6:14-16) Matthew gives his list when they are dispatched on mission. He is more concerned about their mission than their calling, and by giving us the apostolic college at the beginning of the mission discourse he is stressing the connection between *apostolic collegiality and mission,* something that we find also in Acts 2:14; Mark 1:36 and Luke 9:32.

b) The mission is to be concerned however only with the sheep of *Israel.* Jesus explicitly excludes Gentiles and Samaritans (vv. 5-6). Doubtless his feeling is that his Messiahship is for the chosen people only. At this stage the call of Gentiles to the kingdom is a gratuitous act of God belonging to an eschatological future. So much did Jesus see it as an eschatological initiative of his Father that he did not concern himself with that call during his public life (Lk 13:23-30; Mk 7:24-30). The economy of salvation that he contemplates is "first" for the Jews (Rm 1:16), something that Luke scrupulously respects in his redaction of Acts. The Good News, as he sees it, spreads from Jerusalem and Judaea.

The gradual growth of missionary awareness on the past of the Church and the apostles is an undeniable fact. Texts such as this of Matthew 10, where a theology of mission is being elaborated, are nevertheless still confined to the horizons of Israel. It will take persecution to make Christians go forth from Jerusalem to reach the Diaspora.

The Church is essentially missionary: integral to her vocation is her relation to the non-Christian world. Nor can the Eucharist be properly understood except insofar as we who share it become universalist in outlook.

X. Genesis 44:18-29; 45:1-5
1st reading
1st cycle
Thursday

This is the final stage in Joseph's *reconciliation* with his brothers, when they undertook their second journey to Egypt. The two journeys however we owe to the redactor who made the final compilation. The story of the first voyage he took from the Yahwist tradition, that of the second from the Elohist. The scene of Joseph's recognition by his brothers belongs to both traditions.

XI. Hosea 11:1-9
1st reading
2nd cycle
Thursday

This passage has been called, with good reason, "the ballad of love unregarded." In elegiac and lyrical terms Hosea describes the dramatic aspects of God's love for his people. Having previously compared it to conjugal love (Ho 1-3), he now likens it to paternal love (Ho 11:1). The first strophe celebrates the fatherly education which Yahweh has given to his people (vv. 1-4), the second its apparent failure in the exile (vv. 5-6), the third God's merciful pardon (vv. 7-9). The conclusion envisages a happy future of love between Yahweh and his people.

By her idolatrous syncretism Israel has become guilty before her "Father." God's hand might fall upon her just as heavily as on Sodom, Gomorrha, Adma and Cebojim (v. 8; cf. Gn 10:19; 14:2; 8; 19:24; Dt 29:22). About the same time Amos was threatening the unfaithful people with a chastisement worse than that of the blighted cities (Am 4:11-13), but Hosea is the prophet of

God's faithful love and *pardon.* He knows that in the secret mercy of his heart Yahweh has already decided to spare Ephraim such an irrevocable fate. The fact that the people are chosen leads him to pardon.

But the basic reason why God pardons is precisely the fact that he is God (v. 9). His manner of action differs from that of man, who is vindictive and retributive (v. 9; cf. Nb 23:19; 1 S 15:29). He remains faithful and retains his love despite obstacles and unfaithfulness.

The attitude of pardon is truly divine, because only Yahweh is capable of controlling the immediate event and seeing it in the larger context of salvation history and eternity. Yet the pardon he offers is not a mere return to the affection of childhood, as the earlier verses of the passage might suggest. Childhood of course has its charm. But the Father-God who is rediscovered when the fatal transgression is forgiven is not the father of childhood. He is the father of adulthood, the one we rediscover through experience, when we realize that we have not become all that we might have been.

XII. Matthew 10:7-15
Gospel
Thursday

The evangelists have preserved two different versions of the mission discourse, the short form in Mark 6:8-11 and Luke 9:2-5 (concerned with the special mission of the Twelve) and the long, in Luke 10:2-16 (concerning the seventy-two disciples). Matthew gives us a text which combines both versions, and adds some extraneous elements.

a) In the first place the *coming Kingdom* must be *proclaimed,* the proclamation is formulated in quite primitive terms, similar to those employed by the prophets to describe the messianic reign: the healing of the sick and the resurrection of the dead (v. 8; cf. Mt 11:4-6; Is 26:19; 29:18-20. 35:5-6; 61:1, etc.).

b) The disciple who has the duty of proclaiming the Kingdom must show above all by the style of his life and his *poverty* that this Kingdom is imminent. Conscious of this urgency, the missionary must no longer attach value to riches. The nearness of the Kingdom dispenses him from any concern with his terrestrial future. Poverty is freedom: it has a prophetic meaning in itself (v. 9).

The end of verse 10 however modifies somewhat the prophetic vision of poverty by consideration of the necessary institutional and community organization. Missionary poverty is to be a proclamation of the coming Kingdom. Christians will recognize it as such, and come to the aid of the envoy of God, thus enabling him to pursue his vocation.

e) The second counsel given the missionaries concerns their relations with their hosts (vv. 11-15). They must display the characteristics of the *pilgrim,* the nomad, Christ's disciple, who is never established but always *en route* towards the Kingdom (1 P 2:11; He 11:8-10). He is grateful for the hospitality received, and thinks no more of returning to install himself at Jerusalem. He is already elsewhere, a fact that must be evident.

Jesus is not content to entrust a message to his envoys which they must deliver. He wants their style of life to be the living embodiment of the word they proclaim. This style is not altogether the result of a private decision by missionaries, and the Church now is somewhat disturbed by attitudes noticeable among her priests and religious.

The missionary style of course can change in the course of centuries, according to the culture of the period when the message is proclaimed. Poverty has been understood in many different ways, from the mendicant orders right down to the worker priests. In the Middle Ages, in the West, celibacy took on a particular significance. In the following centuries the motives sustaining it underwent some change.

Today it seems that a new style of life is establishing itself. Characteristic of that are involvement with world amelioration, hospitality and welcome actively profered now rather than accepted, prayer and liturgy, working in teams. Forms change as culture develops. But one thing remains unchanged. Mission is accomplished by personal involvement on the part of the missionary.

XIII. Genesis 46:1-7, 28-30
1st reading
1st cycle
Friday

Chapters 45-47 of Genesis constitute a unity concerned with the establishment of the Jews in Egypt. Each biblical tradition gives an individual nuance to these events.

In the Yahwist tradition it is Joseph who invites his father to establish himself in the land of Goshen with all that he has. Jacob departs from Hebron and sends Judah ahead, and arranges to have Pharaoh receive him with the authorization to sojourn at Goshen. In this tradition the Jews are above all shepherds who install themselves with their flocks in Egypt. Verses 28-30 of our passage belong to the tradition.

In the Elohist tradition it is pharaoh himself who invites Jacob, promising to give him the choice portion of Egyptian territory. Jacob leaves Beersheba with chariots sent by the pharaoh himself. In this version the Jews seem to abandon their pastoral style of life when they enter Egypt. Verses 1-4 of our passage belong to it.

The chief preoccupation of the priestly tradition (vv. 6-7) is the inventory of the displaced persons. We are not told whether the migration is due to Jacob's decision or Pharaoh's initiative. The latter is portrayed as welcoming: he offers the immigrants the land of Ramses. This detail is manifestly an anchronism, as the city of Ramses was constructed only at a later date, and by the Jews themselves (Ex 1:11). At least we can conclude that the Jews gradually penetrated from the land of Goshen in the east to the center of the country.

The only religious note in this account, in verses 2-4, is due to the Elohist tradition. Its purpose is to show that migration on the part of the patriarch, who is the recipient of the *promise of land,* is not contrary to Yahweh's alliance. It is that stage of suffering and trial which necessarily precedes the fulfillment of the promises of abundance.

XIV. Hosea 14:2-10
1st reading
2nd cycle
Friday

The prophetic charism of Hosea was exercised among the northern tribes a little prior to the fall of Samaria (721), at a time when Israel was drifting further and further from Yahwist traditions. His message revolves around two themes: a call for conversion, and a description of the happiness reserved by a loving Yahweh for his unfaithful people, if they return to him.

a) Chastisement is now at the gates: soon Israel will be sent into exile. But she must not forget God's love. If she is *converted,* she is destined yet to have happy days. God chastises only in order to save, and to welcome a repentant people into abundant happiness.

The kind of conversion suggested to Israel consists essentially in recognizing the vanity of human resources if they are put forward as adequate. The alliance with Assur and the recourse to "horses" (v. 4) were such where Israel was concerned. She had adopted such means of salvation despite the denunciations of the prophets. She was mistaken in her reliance on the inadequate horse in political and military associations, but, worse still, she embraced these associations without regarding them as due to God's initiative. She made of them, on the contrary, means towards an absolutization of man.

The alliances had failed sufficiently to make Israel reflect. Her conversion would not consist in changing her policy, but in living every policy in communion with God. The God to whom she must be converted does not dispense with human effort or human politics. The conversion he requires is not capitulation or relinquishment, but acceptance of his initiative and communion with it.

b) The *happiness* that will result is described in imagery that is largely borrowed from the rites of autumn festivals, as practiced in Canaanite religions and incorporated in the Jewish feast of Tabernacles: the theme of winter death and spring resurgence (vv. 6-8), that of harvest and vintage (vv. 8-9).

It should be recognized that the people's conversion is never disinterested. When Israel returns to God, it is because of her passionate search for happiness and abundance. This attitude is certainly a dangerous one when it issues in a morality of retribution and merit. Judaism of course never detached itself sufficiently from such a legalist mentality. That is not to say however that there is not a valid way of contemplating reward for a good action. This can become an affirmation of solidarity between the present and the future, of the constant historic dimension. It is a way of saying that no action is ever isolated, but part of a future that is guided by God's initiative.

Modern man, whether he is Christian or non-Christian, is ill-attuned to the theme of conversion to God. The tasks he has set himself frequently tend to make him wary of easy solutions. The conversion he understands is conversion of man to himself, to what he essentially is. Insofar as conversion to God requires complete openness and total renouncement of self, it finds the man of today unsympathetic or even rebellious. Does not such a conversion make a man concentrate on his own weakness, and sometimes alienate him by turning him from his own resources?

However, between this attitude and that suggested by Hosea to his listeners there does not seem to be any basic difference. He actually changed his compatriot's notion of guilt. As he sees it, the fault does not lie in the violation of ancestral and sacral traditions, a fault to be expiated by penitential rites as in the contemporary pagan cults. The fault lies in refusing to encounter God in the actual event: sin is not seeing God in history. The conversion to which Hosea summons his fellows has a new meaning. There is no question of more or less efficacious ritual ablutions, but of interiorization. It is thus that a man stifles his pride and determines to live the event as an advent of God.

The Christian becomes converted to God, and joins that group of fellow converts which is the Church, in order to have a share in the fulfillment of God's plan for humanity. He will thus be giving full rein to all human resources, relating them to their proper province and their proper source: the presence of God, that is, in all things. Understood thus, we can regard conversion as a basic attitude of the Christian who identifies with the modern world.

XV. Matthew 10:16-23
Gospel
Friday

In chapter 10 of Matthew we have the injunctions given by Jesus to the twelve as he dispatches them on mission. Only the first portion (vv. 5-16) reproduces his exact words, in terms reasonably close to those of the other synoptics. The second portion (vv. 17-42) is composed of material added by Matthew himself, which Mark and Luke place in another context, principally in the eschatological discourse. With regard to today's passage we may take it that Matthew has found verse 16 among the sayings of the original mission discourse, whereas verses 17-22a come from the eschatological discourse (cf. Mk 13:8-13).

Verse 23, which is the most difficult verse of the whole gospel, is considered to be either a fragment from the original mission discourse following logically either verses 12-14 or 5-6; or it may be from the eschatological discourse, following logically verses 17-22.

In any case, by inserting in the mission discourse a text of eschatological import, Matthew's purpose is to raise this discourse concerning the Galilean mission to the level of a general treatise on mission.

a) Jesus resorts to the image of the wolf and the sheep (v. 16) in order to bring home to the Twelve that their mission will encounter opposition and persecution: they who are sent to the sheep (v. 6) can in turn become sheep destined for the wolves (cf. Jn 10:12). The wolf theme indicates the *false prophets* (Mt 7:15-16; Ac 20:29), the doctors of the law who presume to make absolute their interpretations of the sacred text.

The disciples must be careful not to cast themselves into the jaws of the wolf. They must, like serpents, be distrustful before danger, fleeing conflict if necessary. The disciple indeed is like the dove who, because it is simple and above reproach, takes flight at the slightest noise. Consequently it will be their business to avoid yielding to the world, and be devoted simply to the gospel.

b) Matthew cannot avoid contemplating, in this context of Jesus' injunctions to the Twelve, the *persecution* the Church is encountering as he compiles his gospel. That is why he inserts verses 17-22, taken from the eschatological discourse. Persecution is the normal lot of the missionary, because all mission, proclaiming as it does the advent of God's kingdom, thereby rejects any religious pretensions of human empires, synagogues, governors or kings (vv. 17-18).

c) However the presence of the *Spirit* (v. 20) is also normal for the missionary. He transforms the apostle's preaching into witness (v. 18; cf. Is 50:4; Ph 1:19). He has seen that of which the apostle speaks, and gives witness of it throughout the discourse. However he cannot act unless man lays aside "anxiety" which, for Matthew, desginates something which prevents openness to God's action (Mt 6:25).

d) The coming of the *Son of Man* (v. 23) will take place before the missionaries will have exhausted the cities of refuge from persecution. The phrase need not necessarily be understood as the Lord's coming at the end of time. Even in the eschatological discourse this meaning of the "coming of the Son of Man" does not impose itself. It can equally well designate some decisive event of the final times such as Jesus' resurrection (Mt 26:64), or the fall of Jerusalem (Mt 16:28; 24:30). Here the "coming of the Son of Man" expresses Jesus' conviction that requital will follow the passion and suffering of his disciples in the form of a judgment on people hostile to their preaching. Jesus and his followers appear to have had this certitude even prior to the hope they shared of the *Parousia*.

Failure and hostility are not signs of the weak faith of the missionary or a punishment of him. On the contrary, the experience of persecution, for the man who wants to be a sign of God's Word in the world, is the basis for greater communion with the Lord and above all with his Spirit. Yet in a way the counsel of Jesus is somewhat unclear. Who is to distinguish in this context between the wisdom of the servant and the simplicity of the dove? Who is to decide the moment when one should flee and when one should withstand?

Only the Spirit or the Word can train the disciple to have at once both wisdom and simplicity. Where these are present he can function: this must be his norm. Where they are not present he will not risk himself. It is all a matter of purity of heart, clearness of insight, openness to listen, in a word, of grace.

XVI. Genesis 49:29-33; 50:15-24
1st reading
1st cycle
Saturday

This passage, which is altogether by a Yahwist hand, shows how the destiny of the Jewish people henceforward is no longer linked with a single patriarch such as Abraham, Isaac or Jacob. It depends on the collegiality of the twelve brothers, the eponymous ancestors of the tribes.

The people's future then no longer depends on the authority of the "patriarch." It is based on good will, on mutual *pardon* in concrete terms, the pardon shown by the brothers and by the respective tribes.

Joseph was the first to understand the necessity for such collegiality and for mutual pardon. The motives for his attitude are extremely far-reaching. The evil he has suffered at the hands of his brothers is turned to good. His suffering has become a source of uplift for the whole people. How could he take vengeance for an evil that God has used for good?

The theology of pardon in the New Testament follows a similar line in the analysis of motives. The injury sustained or the insult endured are accepted because it is realized that thus God's plan can be furthered. God is present in all things, even the most untoward. Everything can contribute to his reign, and pardon springs from this awareness.

XVII. Isaiah 6:1-8
1st reading
2nd cycle
Saturday

The prophet doubtless is participating in the feast of Expiation in the year 740. From the vestibule of the temple he turns his gaze to the Holy of Holies, accessible for this occasion to the high priest. Two colossal statues are set up there, two cherubim five meters high, whose wings cover and protect the ark. Two guardian figures resemble those of the Asyrian temples. Like them they carry the fire which consumes the sacrifices and reveals the presence of the awesome God.

As he looks on the cherubim and the ark which is regarded as the seat of Yahweh, the prophet believes himself summoned to an audience with the all-powerful God, master of the universe (theme of "armies"). The monarch's entrance is proclaimed by the voice of heralds.

a) The vision of Isaiah is concerned with the *holiness of God.* He connects the presence of Yahweh with the temple of Jerusalem, and consequently must portray a temple and a city worthy of this presence. Because God is holy, that is to say the "Totally Other," anything he touches must also be "totally-other." Thus Isaiah would have himself the prophet of a people of "saints," the small Remnant of those who, in order to share Yahweh's kingdom, agree to be converted and to become "totally-other."

The seraphim proclaim Yahweh's holiness in a triple acclamation (v. 3) that is destined to become a Jewish liturgical formula, and later a Christian one (Rev 4:8). It is not correct of course to discern here a presentiment of the Trinity. The formula appears to have been tripled only at a later stage, for liturgical purposes.

b) Yahweh is the Holy One *par excellence*. His *glory* is communicated to the temple, but also to the *universe*. It is because he is fundamentally monotheist that Yahweh is the prophet of universalism. There being only one God, his glory cannot be limited to the temple of Jerusalem only. It must be manifested in the "armies of the heavens" and cover all the earth. Every event is an item in the history of God's self-revelation: all men and all cultures are manifestations of his unique glory.

Thus, for Isaiah, the discovery of God's holiness and his universal glory cannot be limited to philosophic ideas or definitions. It becomes the origin of a *vocation* (vv. 6-11). It is of little use for man to be able to define God, if his whole life fails to reflect this discovery. In the case of Isaiah himself we can say that he was shaped by the temple vision. His whole message centers round these themes of God's holiness and universal glory. From each and every one he requires the conversion necessary to be associated with God's holiness and universalist plan. One can see God without radiating him.

Isaiah's brand of religion is not mystic, but prophetic. The mystic makes ecstasy an end in itself: the prophet never loses sight of the people towards whom he must turn. Only he however who has experienced the inaccessibility of God can be a true prophet. It is not sufficient to proclaim a new social justice or a better political order. One must clearly realize what concerns the honor of God.

XVIII. Matthew 10:24-33 *Gospel Saturday* This is an extract from the mission discourse. Matthew's purpose is to give here a full treatment of Jesus' teaching on mission, and he inserts a long passage on its eschatological dimension and the persecution it provokes. Verse 23a concludes the eschatological parenthesis.

a) In verse 23b the evangelist takes up again the primitive discourse, but has scarcely done so when he yields again to his general purpose of developing a missionary theology. Verses 24-33 are actually drawn from very different contexts, and assembled here to provide a commentary on verses 17-22.

In verses 24-25 we have two distinct ideas: first, that the servant is not superior to his master and encounters the same treatment (v. 24; Jn 15:20; 13:16); second, how to know when the disciple is properly formed (v. 25a; Lk 6:40). He will be "fulfilled" when he resembles his master. In verse 25b we return again to the first idea, which is probably inspired by the events described in Matthew 9:32-34 or 12:22-24. We discern indeed a curious parallelism between this discourse and that of the Supper: Matthew 10:17 and John 16:1; Matthew 10:19-20 and John 15:26; Matthew 10:21 and John 16:2; Matthew 10:22 and John 15:18-19; Matthew 10:23 and John 15:20b; Matthew 10:24 and John 15:20a. It is as if Matthew were making this a *farewell discourse* by Jesus to the apostles according to the usual laws of this genre. He warns them against the difficulties of the future by tracing in broad outline the general characteristics of his own life, which is one of struggle against persecution and evil.

b) Just as verses 24-25 provide a commentary on verse 17, so do verses 26-27 on verse 19. Here Matthew uses *logia* of Jesus of which doubtless he does not at this stage have quite the original meaning. In Luke 8:17 they are applied to the dynamism of the gospel which cannot remain hidden, and in Luke 12:2-3 to the adversaries of the gospel, whose unworthy discourses will eventually be unmasked.

Matthew however gives us a new interpretation. As he sees it, Jesus wished to say that he himself could not transmit his message with total clarity (Mk 4:22; Jn 16:29-30). This is a task which now devolves upon the missionaries. He is transposing into a missionary context words that were doubtless used by Jesus for a moral purpose.

c) Verses 28-31 are a commentary on verse 19. They determine the attitude required by Jesus from his followers in time of persecution. Two reasons for confidence are put forward: first, that the only real enemy to be feared is Satan who is dealt with by God; second, that God takes care of each of his own (v. 30).

d) Verses 32-33 establish a cause-effect relationship between the Christian's fidelity to Christ, and Christ's to the Christian, at the judgment.

There is then a certain lack of unity about the passage. Matthew is assembling *logia* of Jesus that have been delivered in different circumstances, with something other than the purpose of the mission discourse in view. Connected now by certain keywords, some unity is formed by the evangelist's elaboration of a theology of the difficulties and contradictions of the missionary life. Matthew does not go so far as Paul (Rm 5:1-5; 2 Co 4:16-18), but he does stress some important matters: the solidarity between master and disciple under challenge; the disciple's obligation to go deeper than the master in the revelation of the message; the need for confidence in God's protection; and finally the assurance of reward at the judgment.

For him, as for Paul, the missionary must expect to encounter persecution along his road. The Kingdom of glory and transcendence cannot be built until the heart of man is torn, until a world which presumes to provide its own means of salvation is challenged. Between the wisdom of Christ and the wisdom of the world opposition is inevitable. It may be necessary now for Vatican II to resume dialogue with the world, because such an encounter is essential for her mission. But we must never think that once reconciliation is effected all men will walk hand in hand. We shall always have people who will practice the evangelic beatitudes and be challenged for that.

When we celebrate in the Eucharist the victory of Christ's love over hate, we realize how much our sins and those of others impede the kingdom. We offer our sacrifice in order to be delivered from them.

FIFTEENTH WEEK

I. Exodus 1:8-14, 22
1st reading
1st cycle
Monday

The most plausible hypothesis places the beginning of oppression of the Jews in Egypt about 1260 BC, under the reign of Ramses II, or about 1300 under the reign of Seti the first. The biblical description reflects the procedures of that epoch, when Egypt under the builder kings had great need for manual labor.

The nature of the oppression is the imposition of very harsh tasks (vv. 12-13) and genocide (v. 22). The Yahwist hand concentrates principally on the first, the Elohist on the second. Both however see the measures not only as anti-Jewish, but basically antireligious, because they impede the multiplication of descendants promised by Yahweh to Abraham.

If one people is exploited by another that in itself is an evil. When the victims become aware of their subjugation, when led by one of their number they take measures, including violence, for emancipation, it is evident that the struggle will assume for them a religious character. The basis for the religious campaign is always the fact that the human problem was there, the need for revolt against violence. The time comes when the victim emerges from his chains, and is conscious of something transcendent, something that at once inspires and goes beyond his freedom. His faith leads him to give this the name of God, and it is the dilemma of human liberation which makes the name of God a reality. The true discovery of the savior God is always associated with some successful enterprise for the salvation of the poor. If there is so little sense of God in the modern world, particularly in the world of the poor, perhaps that is because so few Christians are genuinely engaged in movements for human liberation. We should all be involved in the struggle against imperialism, racism and colonialism.

II. Isaiah 1:11-17
1st reading
2nd cycle
Monday

The first chapter of Isaiah is an anthology of original oracles rearranged by a later redactor who wanted to present what he regarded as the essential doctrine of the prophet. Our passage in today's liturgy proclaims the possibility of justification for the people and its conditions.

Isaiah 1:10-17 belongs to that class of oracles that prophets were wont to deliver during liturgical celebrations (cf. Jr 26:12-15; 7:1-23; Is 66:1-4; Sm 4:4-5), inveighing against cult as practiced in their time. These are not antiliturgical, but they denounce a cult that is formal and ritualist. This is too concentrated on victims and formulas to be truly spiritual. The prophets insist that the temple sacrifices must be complemented by an attitude of piety, justice and love in daily life.

Thus Isaiah's *spiritual cult* is not necessarily deritualized (cf. Is 6). But its main value lies in its involvement with social and fraternal life. The prophet really poses the problem of the link between rite and life, cult and moral behavior.

Jewish sacrifice was always liable to formalism. It was more a symbol of moral attitudes than the reality of such attitudes. A bull immolated on an altar cannot carry with him the social justice or the obedience of the worshiper. Though the one carrying them out may live in sin, the ceremonies of sacrifice will retain all their splendor.

This state of affairs was completely changed by Jesus. His sacrifice was devoid of ritual: it was a basic attitude towards God and other men in face of death. When, in the Eucharist, we unite ourselves with his sacrifice, it is not that we are offering him to the Father as a more pure and perfect victim than the bulls of old. We are aligning ourselves with the attitude that was his when confronted by evil and sin, suffering and death.

III. Matthew 10:34-11:1
Gospel
Monday

The final portion of this mission discourse is almost entirely composed of diverse material, freely drawn by Matthew from different contexts. Verses 34-36 we find in Luke 12:51-53; verse 27 in Luke 14:26. Verses 38-39 are a doublet of Matthew 16:24-25, and verses 40-41 are found in both Mark 9:37-41 and Luke 10:16. The passage then is extremely composite.

a) The first verses describe the *ruptures* that the service of Christ will cause in human communities and in the deepest human affections (vv. 34-37; cf. Mi 7:6). In other words, after the appearance of Christ, every human relationship is affected. There is on longer any link between father and son, between husband and wife, that is not mediated by Jesus Christ. From now on friendship, affection and love can only find their true basis as apostolic activity under his inspiration. Mary, Jesus' mother, was the first to appreciate this and follow the painful road that was to lead her to recovery of her Son as the gift of the Father.

b) We may take it that the verses about carrying the *cross* after Jesus (vv. 38-39) were delivered at the moment when he began his last voyage to Jerusalem. He was now convinced that the opposition he had incited was destined to bring about his death. At this point he turns towards his disciples, to see who among them would go with him on this journey that revolutionaries must face to the death of the cross (cf. Mt 16:21-25).

c) The Lord's envoys who imitate him in making the necessary breaks and carrying the cross will ultimately receive an extraordinary reward. Everything that is done to them will in fact be done to Christ (vv. 40-42). Here too the relation between the disciples who welcome, and the envoy who is welcomed, is no longer direct: it is *mediated* by Christ. This is to be expected. If the envoy resembles his master in the severance he had to endure of human ties and the cross he had to bear, he will also resemble him in another dimension. He will receive the same sort of welcome and nourishment from other Christians. He will not have to think of his own needs, but can consecrate himself altogether to the good of the Church.

IV. Exodus 2:1-15
1st reading
1st cycle
Tuesday

The juridical situation concerning abandoned infants and their adoption to which this account, principally of Yahwist origin, makes reference is the normal one in the Near-East in the 9th century BC. Possibly some details are borrowed from the Babylonian story concerning Sargon. He too was exposed in a basket covered with bitumen (as there is no bitumen in Egypt, verse 3 betrays an oriental origin). The redactor seems to be giving an Egyptian background to a tale of Babylonian origin, and a Jewish context to a detail from the annals of the Babylonian imperial dynasty. The details he adds are in fact poorly integrated into the account. We have reference to a supposed sister of Moses (v. 4), whereas verse 2 seems to indicate that Moses is the only child in his family. The intervention by the pharaoh's daughter is quite implausible: members of the royal family were not wont to take their bath in the Nile (v. 5). An Elohist influence is very evident which is concerned with the theme of "humiliation-exaltation," and uses the daughter of the pharaoh as a means of exalting one whom trial had brought low. Finally, though it is natural that the one who adopts should give the child a name, it is highly unlikely that an Egyptian lady would give her protege a Jewish name like "Moses" (v. 10). What we have clearly is an item of near-Eastern folklore, used by the Yahwist author for a doctrinal purpose.

a) The author certainly finds the idea of the *abandoned child* very attractive. It is a fairly common theme in Scripture. Ishmael (Gn 21) and Joseph (Gn 37) were abandoned, and Jerusalem herself is portrayed as an infant deserted in the fields (Ez 16).

Such images stress the generosity of Yahweh as liberator and the gratuity of his salvation. It was important for the redactor that Moses himself should first experience the salvation that he would soon be called on to bring his people.

b) The second theme is that of *abasement-exaltation*. In order to stress it, the author has to ignore the fact that the Egyptian woman is an enemy of the Jewish people and make her the benefactor of the child. In any case, in attempting to provide Moses personally with a history similar to that his people will soon experience, he finds it necessary that the liberator of the people should be himself "liberated." The true leader is the one who has experienced what he proposes to others.

V. Isaiah 7:1-9
1st reading
2nd cycle
Tuesday

A series of political and diplomatic developments were leading Israel to the brink of war (735). The northern kingdom was drawing to an end. In Samaria a puppet king was reigning, whose obvious policy was to arrange the reattachment of the territory to the kingdom of Damascus. With the assistance of Phoenicia and Egypt, Damascus was in fact attempting to consolidate an alliance that would be able to withstand Assyria. King Achaz of Jerusalem would form part of that.

Isaiah takes a different view of the events. He is able to form a lucid estimate of the futility of such efforts at confederation. He tries to discern the presence of God in the catastrophes that are imminent.

Our passage today contrasts King Achaz, in panic at the course of events, who has just offered his son to Moloch (v. 2; cf. 2 K 16:3) with the prophet. The latter is serene, convinced of God's presence in the texture of events. He appears before the king with his own son (v. 3), to persuade him that there is really no urgent necessity for a desperate sacrifice of his children.

He then affirms his conviction that the allies in the north will be crushed, and his faith in God's presence, even in this reversal for Damascus (vv. 7-9). He calls upon the king to adopt this political view (vv. 4-6), and above all to imitate his own faith in *God's presence* in these events.

There is little point in inquiring whether it was not utopian to urge the king to reject every alliance and face the danger from the East. Isaiah is not reading the future; his immediate conviction is firm, that Assyria is about to become mistress of the whole East. There is all the more reason then for rallying to her, finding God in the turn of events and living accordingly. The prophet is not one to preach resistance to the death, or proclaim a semi-miraculous intervention of God. He has the conviction that God is present even in catastrophes and political conflicts. Faith can enter into communion with God. It can find support and comfort in him without feeling obliged to support outmoded structures and ways of life.

VI. Matthew 11:20-24 *Gospel Tuesday*

The malediction of the cities seems to be in a more original context here than in the parallel passage of Luke 10:13-15. It was preserved by memory in a discourse in two stages (vv. 21-22 and 23-24) where the same ideas and words are reiterated.

Malediction of cities is a favorite theme with Old Testament prophets. Their attitude seems to have been determined by two considerations. On the one hand there was the constant anxiety to restore Israel to the nomad spirituality of the desert which had led to the covenant with God (He 11:8-9; Ps 38/39:13). On the other there was the fierce opposition to the pagan atmosphere of the city. Sin for the cities consisted in their perverse pretensions to hegemony (Rev 18:16; Is 13:21; 47:1-10; Jr 50-51), in idolatry and immorality. Page after page of prophetic diatribe and invective is devoted to Sodom, Gomorrha and Babylon.

There came an important turning at the stage when the prophets were no longer content to attack the Gentile cities, but made Jerusalem too, the holy city, a target (Is 3:9; Am 4:11; Jr 23:14; Ez 16:68-53; Dt 23:37). They never foretold the disappearance of the people themselves, but did not fail to prophesy the fall of the capital. This city too, for them, was like others a symbol of assurance and over-weening confidence in self, given to riches and might, presumption and debauchery (Rev 17-18).

Jesus, when he extends the malediction to the little towns on the borders of the lake, seems to endorse the current of protest.

Man is called to live in community; he can only grow in association. Primitive society first discovered and developed the family and clan relationship. With urban society came a special sort of relationship. Concerning such community attitudes the Bible showed unease, and was always reminding people that God alone has the key to communion between men. It is perhaps for this reason that Jesus, immediately after his cursing of the cities, affirms that unity between men is built around the hearing of his word. The only genuine human communion is based on God's message. However this is not to say that he who hears God must for this purpose withdraw himself from modern cities. The Jews in denouncing cities were simply stressing their merely relative value, until the voice of God could be heard. Today God's voice reverberates through all human strivings towards community. It is by such means that the city of God, the fulfillment of history, must come about, when God will be all in all (Rev 21).

VII. Exodus 3:1-6, 9-12
1st reading
1st cycle
Wednesday

At the royal Egyptian school of administration Moses received a formation which certainly equipped him to undertake the direction of the Jews (Ex 2:11-15). His first steps as leader however were not successful. He had to flee precipitately from the pharaoh's vengeance, whose agent he had slain, and from the hatred of the Jews, who did not recognize officials of the pharaoh, even when, like Moses, they were Jewish (Ex 2:14). Thus we find him with the tribe of Madian in the Sinai desert, where he marries the daughter of the chief. Here too doubtless he received a religious and juridical formation in accordance with nomad ancestral traditions. We may take it that it was with Jethro that he discovered even the name of his ancestor's God, and made acquaintance with rites like circumcision (Ex 4:24-26). Such a development must have been profoundly interesting for the patriarch. He was superimposing on his Egyptian formation this new equipment. It was a return to tribal sources, something much more suited to the nomad life he was destined to share with his people.

a) A particularly decisive religious experience took place at this stage. While tending the flocks of his father-in-law, he inadvertently came upon a sacred place of the Madians, perhaps while sheltering from a storm (v. 5). Doubtless as yet he was insufficiently initiated into the tribal religious customs and unacquainted with their shrines. The one he entered was near Horeb (where he would one day return to seal the alliance . . . such premonitions are dear to the redactor). An enclosure surrounded a sacred tree that was suddenly blasted by lightning (vv. 2-3). Moses pondered these mysterious events. A mystic experience led him to the insight that the God of his ancestors is also the *God of the promise* (v. 6).

It all opened his eyes to the unfortunate lot of the Jews in Egypt, and made him realize that this could not be allowed to continue without falsifying the promise. He formed the conviction that Yahweh would soon come to the aid of the descendants of those to whom he had promised land, and a numerous progeny (vv. 7-8).

The encounter between him and God was genuine. But God is to be found not so much in the burning bush as in Moses' heart, as he searches out the meaning of the events he is experiencing.

b) Under Ramses II Egypt knew a period of extraordinary peace and prosperity, under the direction of a highly developed bureaucracy. There were many immigrants, descendants of former prisoners of war or voluntary exiles. Their status was determined by a particular law which accorded them respect, but sought at the same time to use their considerable labor power for the development of land and military structures. The Jews apparently were charged with projects between the eastern branches of the Nile (the land of Goshen), facing the threat from Asia. They had to build a series of fortifications and stores, and maintain the numerous irrigation canals of the region (cf. Ex 1:13-14).

Moses, unable to endure the exactions laid upon his people (Ex 2:11-15), retired to the Sinai desert. His purpose was partly to prepare for revolt. With the family of Jethro he had found pastoral traditions that were purer than those of the Egyptian Jews (Ex 2:16-23). He took the view that a return to the patriarchal land and traditions would restore stability to the tribes.

Obsessed with these two ideas, revolt against the impositions and return to the patriarchal land, one day in the desert he finds himself not far from a shrine, distinguished by its sacred bush (Ex 3:5). Suddenly in front of him the lightning blazes, but to his astonishment leaves him and the sacred bush intact. Lightning is the symbol of God's presence (Ex 9:23-29; Pss 17/18:14; 28/29:3-9). He thus comes to realize that the projects he is contemplating are those of God. His *mission* is determined (vv. 7-15).

The task for which he was preparing himself was that of delivering the tribes from Egyptian domination (vv. 7-10), leading them to the ancient territory of the patriarchs (vv. 8 and 11), a nomad land (the meaning of the phrase "where milk flows" from the flocks "and honey" from the rocks), a country where the cult of the authentic God of the tribes can be reestablished (v. 11).

His mission is in full conformity with the will of God. God "will be with him" (v. 12), he is convinced, as he is with all the prophets (Jr 1:8, 19; Is 40:10; Jos 1:5, 9; 1 S 5:10), and will leave him a sign—the gathering of the people on Sinai to put themselves in the service of God.

VIII. Isaiah 10:5-7, 13-16
1st reading
2nd cycle
Wednesday

We are in the year 701. Doubtless the non-violent Isaiah has approved King Ezechias' submission to the general Sennacherib. But now Sennacherib is breaking the treaty. He reappears before Jerusalem and in order to intimidate further the capital of Judah points to all the cities that have fallen before his armies (vv. 8-9 and 11). This time Isaiah abandons his policy of resignation, and becomes the soul of the people's resistance to the enemy.

In verses 5-7 we have God reproving the attitude of the Assyrian king. He had been a tool in the hands of God. Assyria's policy of unification was *God's* way of being *present* in the new world that was being constructed. However the Assyrian king was exceeding his mandate in seeking on his own account the fusion into one of the whole East. What could such a purpose accomplish? Can a stick or a whip function on its own (v. 5) without a guiding hand? The king's action accordingly is in vain (v. 15).

Verses 8-14 tell us of the proud projects of the king or his general, Sennacherib. Such is their power that nations in their hands are as fledglings in the hand of the nest-robber (v. 14). Then in verse 16 comes God's reply. The furnace will wipe out all the king's pretensions to conquest. God will not have it that the one who serves him serves at the same time his own interests.

If we were to take Isaiah's view literally, we should have to say that God manipulates history and statesmen as marionettes. Does he send Hitler to chastise a Europe that has forgotten him? Proclaim the proximate conversion of Russia? "Permit" the assassination of Kennedy? Very few of our contemporaries would take this view of history. Nor does it seem to be our mission to proclaim and maintain it in season and out of season.

Another, less simplistic, view will have it that the germ of transcendence is in all human activity. Every political ideology implies an ideal that transcends man. The vision of unity among men always demands that we go beyond ourselves, and believe that man is made for something greater than himself. One step further will give the name of God to this "greater something." The Christian mission would be one of affirming and living this truth. Prophetism of this kind however could rather quickly develop into apologetics: there is really no one to decide whether transcendence in these terms ought necessarily be described as God.

A third view sees man's political strivings towards unity or universalism as an ambiguous procedure, where people may be aware of God or not. There is an element of ambiguity in all human things, particularly in political endeavor. The death of Jesus was ambiguous: he was confused with other "resisters." Only the resurrection is clear. It may be indeed that God still dies amid the ambiguity of men's political endeavors and compromises. It is only through their ambiguity that we can discern the hidden divine meaning. Resurrection only will lift the veil. It is not by philosophic-religious inquiry that we can come to see God's presence in the event. It is by faith in the resurrection, that of Christ, that of man, that of the world.

IX. Matthew 11:25-30
Gospel
Wednesday and Thursday

Among exegetes much ink has been spilled concerning the authenticity and unity of doctrine of this passage. The first portion (vv. 25-27) is fairly similar to Luke's version (Lk 10:21-22), but the second is noticeably different Lk-10:23-24 and Mt 11:28-29). Matthew's version however seems to be the primitive one, if we are to judge by the high incidence of Aramaisms.

In the first stage Jesus makes an act of thanksgiving to his

Father (vv. 25-27) for all that they mean to one another and for the mission of revelation to the little ones he has received. In the second he turns towards these little ones (vv. 28-30) and invites them to enter into communion with him.

a) The biblical background of the thanksgiving hymn is very revealing. Jesus is using for his own purposes the hymn of the three boys in Daniel 2:23. These are contrasted with the Babylonian "sages." Thanks to their prayers (Dn 2:18) they have benefitted from the "revelation" of the mystery of the kingdom (a characteristic expression in the book of Daniel which we find too in Lk 10:21), something that has eluded the learned and the sages.

Jesus draws a parallel between the situation as between his disciples and the sages of Judaism, and the boys and the sages in the time of Nabuchadnezzar. By this he signifies his intention of opening the kingdom and offering "revelation" to a very precise category of poor, those poor in intelligence. Here he parts company with certain Jewish doctors who were often without pity for the ignorant people (cf. Is 29:14; 1 Co 1:19-26).

b) In another passage of Daniel (Dn 7:14) the Son of Man finds everything given him by the Ancient of Days—and this is the mystery that is revealed to Daniel. It is in the light of this text that Jesus, who claims the title Son of Man (Mt 24:36) blesses the Ancient of Days, under his new name of Father, for having "transmitted everything" to him. That is to say, for having given him, according to Daniel 7:14, "power over all things" (Mt 28:18; Jn 5:22; 13:3; 17:2), and also a fuller *knowledge* of the Father to reveal to men (v. 27). He is then at once King and Revealer of the kingdom of the little ones. By gathering round him, these can know God and constitute a community distinct from "those who know not God": the Gentiles to begin with (Jr 10:25), but the Jewish sages as well (v. 21; cf. Jn 12:39-50).

c) Those who "labor and are burdened" under the load (v. 28) are identical with the little ones and the ignorant of the preceding verses. In fact the burden or the *yoke* often designates in Jewish idiom the observances of the law (Si 51:26; Jr 2:20; 5:5; Ga 5:1). These had been so surcharged by the Scribes with innumerable prescriptions that the simple and ignorant were constrained to obey without always having the ability to distinguish what was incidental from what was essential (Mt 23:4). Those Jesus has gathered round him then are not so much the afflicted in general as the simple and the ignorant, in bondage to Jewish legalism. He had already taken his stand away from intellectualism, and now does so as against a certain legalism.

d) Nevertheless Jesus presents himself after the manner of those rabbis and sages who recruit disciples for their schools (v. 29; cf. Si 51:31; Is 55:1; Pr 9-5; Si 24:19). He too imposes a yoke. But it is an easy one to carry (1 Jn 5:3-4; Jr 6:6). He himself belongs to the community of the poor foretold in Zephaniah 3:12-13, which embraces the meek and humble of heart. This new master of wisdom is *poor* of heart, because he has freely and willingly accepted this condition.

X. Exodus 3:13-20
1st reading
1st cycle
Thursday

At the moment of his encounter with Yahweh at Sinai Moses is concerned with the lot of his oppressed Jewish brethren in Egypt (Ex 2:11-15), and obsessed with the ancestral pastoral ideal he had rediscovered with Jethro (Ex 2:16-23).

a) His *mission* takes shape in terms of these two considerations. He realizes that his pet projects come from God, because the lightning which struck by his side spared him, and also the bush on which it fell (Ex 3:1-8). God speaks through the lightning (Ex 9:23-29; Ps 17/18:14; Ps 28/29:3-9), and in sparing his life must thereby approve his projects.

The mission was one of delivering the tribes from Egyptian domination (vv. 9-10; 16-17) and leading them to their ancestral land (v. 11), a nomad land (the meaning of the phrase "where milk flows" from the flocks and "honey" from the rocks), where the worship of the authentic God could be reestablished (vv. 11 and 17).

b) An envoy however cannot be accepted unless he says in whose *name* he is fulfilling his mission (v. 13). The name Moses will reveal to his brethren is that of Yhwh-Yahweh (v. 15). We may have here the name of one of the gods of the contemporary pantheon, especially venerated at Sinai. What is important above all is that it designates the somewhat forgotten God of the patriarchs and the promises.

The text however gives a new etymology for the word Yahweh: I am who am (v. 14). There is no question of a metaphysical definition of God's nature: it is an affirmation at two levels. It is evasive in the first sense: God transcends every name and cannot be grasped. But it is historical too. It could be translated more exactly, "I shall be what I shall be." The meaning: "You will know me in what I shall do for you" . . . "it is history that will reveal me."

In this fashion the name of God preserves its mystery and transcendence. Yet it reveals God's immanence in his people's history and the patriarch's mission.

Modern man in attempting to name God is no further advanced than Moses. Indeed he may well have experienced more intensely the emptiness of attempts in myth and metaphysics to give God a meaningful name. Yet it is only in human history that God can be encountered, especially since that history has found its meaning and its purpose in Jesus Christ.

XI. Isaiah 26:7-9, 12-16, 19
1st reading
2nd cycle
Thursday

This poem comes from what people have agreed to term the Apocalypse of Isaiah (Is 24-27), a collection of postexilic poems. In the section we find two distinct strains, apocalyptic poems proper, and lyrical pieces from which our passage is taken.

a) The poem is characteristic of the literature of the poor. The just man remains faithful to Yahweh amid the surrounding paganism, and the succession of political crises which assail the Jewish spirit. It is communion with God that gives him this equanimity (v. 7) and above all the certainty that God has in store for him at a time of happiness and joy. In speaking for God (v. 8) the just man cannot deceive himself. *Hope* is his light. By this means he can see each event as a manifestation of God (v. 9) and become convinced of a future resurrection (v. 19) which is somehow being prepared by the people's struggle on earth for peace (vv. 12-15).

The author's notion of resurrection has high importance in the development of Jewish and Christian eschatology. It is in the first place personal. At the conclusion of a completely faithful life the just man will rise again. But the wicked on the other hand will not (v. 14). Furthermore the resurrection will be due at once to God's initiative (theme of dew in v. 19) and to an expansion of the Spirit. The Spirit of God is placed in a man and burgeons into life "from inside' a man (v. 9), as a child emerges from his mother's womb (v. 19b). Death is but a provisional sleep: the morning dew will awaken the dead. The Spirit which has dwelt in them throughout their long life of faith is the pledge of this new life. The author believes in his own resurrection as God's gift, but also as an expansion of the dynamism he feels within him.

XII. Matthew 11:28-30
Gospel
Thursday

This gospel was commented on with that of Wednesday, p. 168.

XIII. Exodus 11:10-12, 14
1st reading
1st cycle
*Friday**

Here we have a description of the Jewish ceremonial for the paschal meal. It emanates from priestly sources, the latest legislative strata of Scripture that is. The distinguishing mark here is the anxiety to create in the people who have been established in the Promised Land the same openness that characterized their ancestors on the day of delivery from Egypt.

a) By eating in a standing position, with his loins girt while keeping vigil, the Israelite shows that the Pasch concerns him personally and brings about his own deliverance. It is significant that the meal ceremonial is concentrated on the ancient rites of immolation of the lamb and sprinkling of the doors. And the lamb is no longer immolated only but eaten also, so that the participants may be still further involved in the mystery of the feast.

b) The priestly redactors of this ritual inserted it in the perpetual calendar in use among certain strata of the population. According to the new computation the month of *Pasch* (March-April) became the first month of the year, though previously the New-Year festival coincided with that of Tabernacles (September). The arrangement prepared in its way the Christian era, when the Tabernacles feast was totally absorbed by the Pasch.

c) The ritual of *unleavened bread* on the other hand had its origin in an agricultural custom connected with the barley harvest. It was forbidden to mix old leaven with the new grain. One had to wait for the grain to produce its own leaven, and conse-

* See also below, pp. 181, 183, two alternative readings on the paschal ritual.

quently for a time unleavened bread had to be eaten. This custom was associated by the Jews with their nomad religious traditions, and the unleavened bread became a symbol of the haste of their ancestors in fleeing Egypt (Ex 12:33-34). "Haste" became an integral part of the paschal ritual.

The essential part of the ceremony, which was nomad to begin with, consisted in the immolation of the lamb. The blood was considered a safeguard against fluxes and maladies (Ex 12:21-22; 22:14-17; Lv 23:10-12). Perhaps the ritual at one time coincided with a preservation from the Egyptian plagues. Thus the immolated lamb, for people so preserved, would become a symbol of liberation and constitution as a free people (Ex 12:23-29).

During the course of centuries the ceremonial was amplified. It lasted for seven days, in the course of which all work was forbidden, and ultimately it was fused with the agricultural feast of unleavened bread (Dt 16:1-8; 2 K 23:21-23). The most original feature developed was due to the reflection of the early prophets and of Deuteronomy. The father of the family had to explain the rite during the course of the meal. This sort of catechesis made the company feel really involved, and anxious to renew for themselves the liberating ceremony (Ex-12:25-27; 13:7-8; Dt 16:1-8; *it is you who come forth from Egypt*). The note of personal liberation was further stressed by the insistence on the eating of the lamb rather than the immolation or blood-sprinkling (Dt 16:6-7; Ex 12:1-12). Rather than a rite merely commemorating an ancient happening, this became a symbol which directly concerned the participants and brought about their personal deliverance.

The prophets, in proclaiming future delivery from the Babylonian exile, referred to a new Exodus. The paschal feast in which the lamb was immolated and consumed became the sign of future liberation, which would be above all a liberation from sin. Some texts, altogether eschatological in this sense, like Isaiah 10:25-27; 40:1-11; 2 Maccabees 2:7-8; Sirach 36:10-13, may well have been proclaimed or read during the feast. With Ezechiel, the feast becomes essentially that of the people's restoration. Expiation rites are multiplied (Ez 45:18-25; Lv 23:5-14; 2 Ch 30-35) in order to ensure maximum success for the restoration.

John, when he finds in Jesus the true lamb (Jn 13:1; 18:28) and has the immolation of the lambs in the temple coincide with the death of Christ (Jn 19:14, 31, 42; 1 Co 5:6-8), is conveying to his readers that the whole doctrine of the paschal ceremony is fulfilled in Christ's sacrifice. It is this which really sets up the definitive people, achieves true deliverance from the domain of evil, and makes the Christian a pilgrim on the road to the promised land (1 P 1:17), where the Lamb will reign surrounded by the people he has ransomed (Rev 5:6-13; 7:2-17; 12:11; 19:1-9).

XIV. Isaiah 38:1-6, 21-22, 7-8
1st reading 2nd cycle Friday

Isaiah was an enthusiastic partisan of King Ezechias. In the king's birth and accession to the throne he discerned events of a messianic order. Doubtless he was thinking principally of Ezechias when he wrote Isaiah 7-9. Pious though he was however, Ezechias was soon to disillusion the prophet, and for a long time a certain "coolness" separated the two. The grave illness of Ezechias in 706 was destined to reconcile them.

Isaiah tells the king of his approaching death (vv. 1-3), throwing the latter into the most profound despair. At once he turns to prayer, and gets an assurance of recovery from the very man who came to tell of his death (vv. 4-6). We are reminded of the occasion when Nathan before David had to falsify the oracle given a few hours previously (2 S 7). God adds fifteen years to the king's life. The addition is symbolized by a sign that is rather difficult to understand. The shadow on the sundial goes back ten degrees (vv. 7-8).

We are dealing with a theology that is still in process of development. The only way in which God can recompense the just man is to *cure* him and prolong his life by fifteen years. This is a far cry from the faith of the author of Isaiah 20:7-19, who is convinced that the just life will be rewarded by resurrection.

Nevertheless the teaching is an interesting contrast to the platonic and gnostic "other world": the horizon is terrestrial. Our Christian doctrine of the terrestrial will remain faithful to Israel insofar as we discern transcendence, not only in another world, but in the hinterland of terrestrial things and persons.

XV. Matthew 12:1-8
Gospel
Friday

This discussion between Jesus and the Pharisee concerning Sabbath observance is recounted in all the synoptics. Even though he certainly adds verses 5-7 of his own accord, Matthew seems to preserve the most primitive version of the incident. He makes more allusion to classic Jewish polemic than Saint Mark. The latter is adapting the account to the non-Jewish milieu to which he addresses himself. Consequently he is more concerned with universalism, and stresses more than Matthew, the challenge to Jewish institutions.

a) The apostles have been caught by the Pharisees in flagrant violation of the *Sabbath repose* (v. 2). They have not in fact violated any precept of the law proper, but only one of the Mischna regulations (Sabbath 7:2, which gives the thirty-nine activities forbidden on the Sabbath day). Christ's rejoinder is blunt. It is only the commentator's document which forbids plucking ears of corn in the field. The law itself on the contrary clearly authorizes violation when the need of hunger is present (vv. 3-4; cf. 1 S 21:2-7).

b) He goes further however in affirming his awareness of his own role. He is "master of the Sabbath" (v. 8) and, Matthew adds, he is "greater than the temple" (v. 6). Thus he considers that his *messianic* role authorizes him to question Jewish institutions, even those as important as the Sabbath or the temple, if they are no longer in conformity with the will of the legislator, and fail to contribute to the dignity of the person.

When they heard him declare himself "master of the Sabbath" his listeners must have understood him to be substituting himself for Moses, and putting himself forward as a new legislator. But there is no suggestion that Moses has failed in his task. The affirmation must be taken in the context of his polemic with the narrow fanatical partisans of the law. The law had failed to produce the desired fruits because it was stifled by merely human observances. Thus a new legislator was needed to set the Sabbath in in a new perspective. The association between the titles "Son of Man" and "Master of the Sabbath" suggests that Jesus' attitude to the Sabbath flows from his role as eschatological judge. Judaism was actually waiting for the Messiah to modify the legislation, especially Sabbath legislation. We have for instance a question that was posed to the rabbis: "If the Messiah comes, shall a nazier be able to drink the Sabbath wine?" The answer generally given was that it would be part of the Messiah's work to remake ceremonial laws.

When man himself undertakes the achievement of salvation, he tends to make absolute and sacralize the means as he sees them towards salvation. He will excommunicate or suppress those who threaten his security by making these means relative. That is the attitude of the Pharisees towards him who presumes to challenge the Sabbath.

However, when a man accepts the gift of the Father and responds with an unreserved "yes," his salvation no longer depends on exterior means. It depends on the meeting between God's initiative and man's faith. Such a man was the man-God.

Following him, every man who is able to perceive the gift given him by God and tries to respond with unconditional fidelity, shares the mastery of the Sabbath. A desacralized Sabbath loses its absolute value, and becomes no more than the moment of free encounter in the believer's heart.

The Eucharist is that moment where humanity, in the person of Christ, gives the highest testimony of fidelity to God in death, and where God's gift goes to the limit in his resurrection. The Christian who shares it renews the experience of openness and encounter which makes it impossible for him to be ever again a "sabbathizer."

XVI. Exodus 12:37-42
1st reading
1st cycle
Saturday

The primitive account of the departure from Egypt is Yahwist in origin. We find it in verses 38-39. Priestly sources added verses 37, 40-42, chiefly for geographical, chronological and liturgical reasons.

a) The first point in the historian's account is the *haste* that characterized the departure, the dough of the bread being not yet leavened. In fact the Jews in Egypt had become accustomed to eating unleavened bread in spring. Farmers got their leaven from the new grain: they would never mix leaven of the previous year with the new crop. The spirits of different harvests, different fecundities, could not be mingled. The Jews followed this farming custom, but made it a symbol of their own history. They gave an historical interpretation to a detail which had its origin in nature worship. Their God is no longer a God of nature, who controls the seasons and their fruitfulness, but a God who speaks to men in events and attitudes.

b) The second point due to the Yahwist (v. 38) is the *universal* and composite character of the horde which left Egypt. Other Semites accompanied the Jews probably, and perhaps even Egyptians who were victims of the regime (Lv 24:10; Dt 29:10; Jos 8:35). It was then a heterogeneous "rabble" (Nb 11:4). The priestly source is quite euphemistic in portraying an organized army, with 600,000 warriors, and more than three million persons (v. 37).

The exaggeration is understandable. The priestly documents were drawn up at a time when the nation was reduced to a small "remnant," most of the members being in slavery and dispersed throughout the world. The memory of the Egyptian exodus was a beacon of hope. What God had accomplished by gathering such a huge horde of Jews at the departure from Egypt, he could once more accomplish by raising a great people from the tiny shoot of the exile.

c) Verse 42 is a priestly addition. It describes how God kept *vigil* for his people on the famous night of the Exodus, as a mother watches over her sick children, or a sentinal over a city. The paschal feast then, when the Jews keep vigil annually, is a way of sharing God's solicitude for the future of his people.

XVII. Micah 2:1-5
1st reading
2nd cycle
Saturday

Micah exercised his prophetic ministry under Ezechias (716-687) (cf. Jr 26:18-19). He may even have begun it somewhat earlier. The social situation was particularly grave (cf. 1 K 21). The rural economy was in acute crisis, and, in order to survive the peasants had to sell their land and often their person to unscrupulous bourgeois (cf. further 2:8-10; 3; 6:10-12; 7:3).

Social injustice, for Micah, is not only a violation of the rights and person of the poor; it is above all a crime against God and his covenant. For this reason God himself hunts down the sin, because absence of love among the members of his people directly concerns his honor. The matter is larger than mere social duty; a religious obligation binds all those who are associated with God by grace.

XVIII. Matthew 12:14-21
Gospel
Saturday

In verse 15 Matthew gives us a "summary" concerning the cures by Jesus, stressing above all Jesus' wish for secrecy in their regard (v. 16). The victory over evil which the Messiah brings is given only to those who agree to enter the new community of believers (Is 28:16). Secrecy is the only defense Jesus can employ in face of the superficial popular enthusiasm that is unrelated to faith (cf. Mk 3:7-12; Lk 6:17-19). In this discretion Matthew discerns the fulfillment of the oracle of Isaiah 42:1-4 concerning the servant of Yahweh. We shall consider first the doctrinal content of this oracle, and then the evangelist's use of it.

a) The oracle in question is the first poem concerning the *Servant* of Yahweh. These postexilic poems celebrate at once the new Israel, and the person who is found to be its best representative.* The first verse (behold—my elect) is a formula of investiture of the people—and of him who will finally stand for it—in the prophetic ministry (cf. the allusion to the Spirit: Jl 3:1-5; Is 11:1-2, 32, 15) and the task of revealing the law to the nations. Except for Jonah no prophet was entrusted with such a universalist task.

b) Yet it is not the first time that Scripture reminds the people of their mission to bring the law to the nations. But previously, in order to bring this about, people resorted to force and made war (Ex 33:1-3; 1 S 14:47-48; Ps 2). When Israel's contact with the nations was confined to slavery and misery as in the exile, the people could not cry out their message in the streets (v. 2). Still less could they defend it by force of arms (v. 3, where the crushed reed and wavering flame designate Egypt—cf. Is 36:6; 43:17 to which Babylon and Chaldaea are likened).

The author of our poem wants to draw a moral from this situation. Is not *humble* and modest witness borne under these conditions better than the triumphalism of former times (v. 2)? The mission of proclaiming the Kingdom will no longer be accomplished by means of conquest and power, but by a simple and faithful witness borne in the ordinary human condition.*

* The Servant is both collective and individual, and the individual incorporates the people. Likewise in Genesis 3:15; Samuel 7:12-16; Daniel 7:17-23.
* The theme is probably carried on in verse 3, which should be translated: "he will not quench, he will not break."

c) Matthew does not seem to have known the text of Isaiah 42 in the original Hebrew, but through the medium of an anthology of *testimonia* which was already giving a Christian interpretation to the texts included. In verses 1 and 4 the word "right" in the original is replaced by the word *faith,* in order to show that it is not legalism that will accomplish God's plan, but true "religion" which binds a man to the saving God (cf. Is 28:16). The institutions of Judaism were too particular to sustain a universal mission. Only a faith which represented conversion and openness to God—attitudes possible for all—could gather all men in the new Jerusalem.

Thus, in the discretion in which Jesus shrouded his cures and miracles, Matthew sees a fulfillment of the oracle. Doubtless the primary intention of Jesus was to discourage popular manifestations where faith was obscured by enthusiasm. By finding here the attitude of the Servant of Isaiah 42, Matthew is reflecting the mentality of the primitive communities which found the prophecies concerning the *suffering Servant* accomplished in the life of Jesus. His meekness, and the meekness he imposed on his disciples (Mt 13:24-30; Lk 9:54-55) is an aspect of his "*kenosis.*"

XIX. Exodus 12:21-28
Alternate reading Liturgy of the Word

The paschal ritual that we have in this Yahwist tradition has traces of its more or less magical origins. Egypt falls victim to a series of cataclysms where everyone tries to preserve himself by recourse to protection ceremonies common to all religions of the time. The Jews have their own, more efficacious than those of the Egyptians, because God uses them to bring about the delivery of his people.

The rite of the disembowelled lamb whose blood is sprinkled on the doorposts is characteristic of nomad ritual. The sight of the blood is sufficient to put evil spirits to flight, especially the destroying spirit. If the rite is to be efficacious people must not go out during the night (v. 22b). The Yahwist author tries to modify the magic aspect of the ritual, by associating the exterminating angel with Yahweh (v. 23), and integrating the ritual into the context of the feast of *Pasch.* For this purpose he has recourse to an imaginary etymology (v. 23: *to pass before or pass beyond*).

Finally he incorporates the whole in salvation history, and ordains an annual repetition as a memorial of the beginnings of the chosen people (vv. 25-27). He introduces a dialogue between the father of the family and his son, making the efficacity of the rite depend on the Word and the faith it kindles. It is the recollection of the historical event that is important, and the Word which gives it its new meaning.

Just now, at a time when Christians are asking themselves whether their liturgy is not perhaps overladen with "religious" elements that should be phased out, the Yahwist author's remanipulation of an ancient religious rite to make it an expression of his faith is suggestive.

The Yahwist liturgical reform of the ancient ceremony is not so much concerned with the material content. This can be maintained, at the initial stage at least. But the meaning is changed because of the incorporation in salvation history and the dialogue of faith that is included. In our case too, if the reference to salvation history of the event, and the summons to faith which is integral to the event, become obscured, a rite may deteriorate into primitive magic. Of course, when the material of the rite renders it uncontemporary for the participants, this can also lead to decadence. To reform liturgy it is not sufficient to develop a new rite. Faith must inform that rite, and associate it with the original saving act.

XX. Exodus 12:29-34
Alternate reading Liturgy of the Word

We may take it that the plague of the first-born was an epidemic, which in the Near-East was regarded as the greatest scourge of God (Nb 14:37; 17:13; 25:9, 18; 31:16; 1 S 6:4; 2 S 24:21). Here we have the Yahwist version, parallel to Exodus 11:4-8, and just as highly colored. The Yahwist (9th century) is the chief narrator of these famous "plagues of Egypt" (86 of 125 verses), on the number and nature of which popular tradition was fairly varied (Ps 77/78:44-51; Ps 104/105:28-36). The Elohist and priestly traditions are on the whole much more restrained than the Yahwist. But all traditions take great liberties with history.

It does seem likely that biblical tradition preserved a true, but vague, memory of some misfortunes that befell Egypt and helped the Jewish flight. Moses took the death of the pharaoh's eldest son, and the spread of the disease in other Egyptian families, as the occasion counted on by God to deliver his people.

During the last hours of Israel's sojourn in Egypt there is one imperative consideration. The people must be *free* in order to serve God and give him adequate *cult* (v. 31), which would actually be liberating for those who gave it. This emphasis on freedom in relation to God's worship is reflected here in the reinterpretation of an old agricultural rite (vv. 33-34). At harvest time the leaven or grain of the previous harvest ceased to be used. Unleavened bread was eaten until such time as the new grain would produce its own leaven. This "magic" custom, in Jewish ritual, became the symbol of the haste with which the people, freed from all fetters, regained liberty. The Jew, when he ate annually the unleavened bread, was affirming his freedom and its connection with the service of God.

The Jewish pilgrimage in search of a land where they would be free is characterized by a quest of faith that was absolutely unique. Of course all peoples who seek happiness and liberty always place God, or gods, at their side. Very often though the gods are of no more than human stature. They are no more masters of the event than men themselves. They exhibit too often the sentiments that men would have them exhibit, to be truly God.

The Jews on the other hand looked for a God who would not necessarily correspond with their desires, or with what they would wish. They found Yahweh. Throughout their quest for freedom, they agreed to live in communion with this God and this was the covenant. It was the discovery of the Totally-Other God that inspired them to celebrate the Pasch event each year.

To celebrate the Pasch then is to share in all movements for human emancipation (there can be no Pasch without forward movement). A very particular sort of faith is required, a desire to live in communion with a God whose view of history and the world we discover little by little. We become better, more aware, more human.

There is always a risk. So Totally-Other is God that no one can ever be certain of having found him. The search for his will is always long. Catechism definitions or counsel of spiritual directors will not disclose the answer.

We do however have some criteria which will enable us to test the validity of the search for God in the various movements of our modern world. We find them in Jesus Christ. He was ready to die and be raised up during a feast of the Pasch, so that man's quest might find its true level.

The first criterion is that of suffering and death. If we wonder on which side God is to be found, that of the poor or that of the powerful, we can never be wrong in finding him among those who suffer. The cross of Christ is the proof, as against priests or theologians who presume to know more than him about God. When the apostles proclaim the death and resurrection of Jesus, they are telling us that God is to be found at the term of oppression and suffering, not in the projects of power and contempt for the other.

It is for every Christian then today to consider his reasons for participation in this or that movement. To know whether he is really searching for God, and cooperating in God's plan for men, he has only to scrutinize his motives and judgments.

The second criterion is fidelity to the human condition. By dying when he could have escaped death, by suffering where he might not have suffered, Jesus decided to be faithful to the human state to the bitter end. Consequently all movements which attempt to escape human limitations, which reject them or pretend that they are not there, preclude a search for the God of Jesus Christ.

To find modern movements that resemble the Jewish paschal one, or that of Jesus, we shall have to look for those where the relativity of things is understood. There must be a realization of the imperfect, finite character of all human efforts, of their frailty and ambiguity, of the great length of the pilgrimage. Fanatical movements on the other hand, where absolute and relative are confused, the definitive and the merely human; movements whose members are dispensed from effort, from solidarity, from concern for others, never give evidence of the search for God.

The third and most difficult criterion is the total remission to God of self, just as Jesus gave his life into the hands of the Father. It is only people with faith (which all Christians do not automatically have) who can make this jump into the unknown. We must have certainty that God is able to accomplish things unattainable by man. We must have confidence that the very greatest mistake can be always surmounted, that no situation is ever desperate. What is impossible for man now, God can bring to pass. He can even raise the dead to life.

And the final criterion, the most important of all, is that none of the former should ever be made absolute. Man is the sort of creature who is very liable to go wrong in his search for God, to confuse it with violence and hate, just as the Jews did indeed. He can go on for a time believing that because God is all-powerful he must be on the side of power. And so he comes to condemn his fellow men in the very name of God. We should not despair of men who do this. Who is to say whether their quest, from such wrong beginnings, may not one day lead them to conversion and the truth?

XXI. Isaiah 44:1-5 *Alternate reading Liturgy of the Word*

Second-Isaiah brings words of consolation and comfort to the people. God will pardon them and life will recover its meaning. This short poem provides new arguments to reassure exiled or oppressed Jews of their future mission.

To accomplish his purpose, the prophet personifies the peoples. It stands for Jacob, this ancestor whom Yahweh formed in the womb of his mother (Gn 25:19-35): the classic theme of prophetic *vocation* is applied to it. For her prophetic task in the world Israel will receive the Spirit of God (v. 3), as the nabis did formerly, and as did Ezechiel (Ez 2:1). She is called from her mother's womb as was the prophet Jeremiah (v. 2; cf. Jr 1:5). She is termed servant (v. 1) like Moses, and the mysterious "servant" elsewhere mentioned (Is 42:1).

Her prophetic activity among the nations (vv. 4-5 of the poem doubtless refer to the conversion of the Gentiles) will be witnessed in the abundance and fruitfulness of the earth (v. 5). For Scripture generally the sign of the presence of the Spirit of God among men is in the fruitfulness of men and of all things (cf. Am 8:18-25).

In most biblical accounts of prophetic (Is 6; Jr 1; Is 44; 1 S 2) and apostolic investiture (Mk 1) the, vocation is seen in a strictly "timeless" fashion. Eveything is decided "from all eternity," even before the subject is born ("You are a priest forever"). It is as if God were disinterested in the psychology of the subject, in his cultural and social environment.

Following this, the Church has often viewed vocation as a state of life independent of contingency. In seminaries that are (in the etymological sense of the word) too premature it has set children apart, and given such candidates an obsession about the loss or rejection of vocation. Ignoring the influence of sexual or affective impulses, it has devalued everything that might threaten the sacred trust.

Choice from one's mother's womb, in the sense of today's reading, sets up too exclusive an idea of vocation. God's choice is primary of course, but it is only in the actual course of a human life that it can take actual shape. Every vocation reveals itself at the term of a journey that is constantly being made. It is common to every man. He detaches himself from an illusory self, and plunges to depths of his being that bring him closer and closer to God's plan. Vocation is never an affair of previous call only. On the contrary it is always concerned with openness to the future, the unknown. It is not so much a trust to be preserved as a constantly growing openness to the unpredictable. No man is shut in a particular frame of life in such fashion that its maintenance is guaranteed once for all. The priest is neither the proprietor nor the prisoner of his state. If this is the meaning of what Scripture has to say about God's absolute priority in vocation, it is very true indeed.

SIXTEENTH WEEK

I. Exodus 14:5-18
1st reading
1st cycle
Monday

In this account it is not easy to distinguish the contributions by the three classic traditions. We may give the lion's share to the Yahwist, with its emphasis on psychology, fondness for the highly colored and distaste for the historical. The priestly tradition can be detected in a theme dear to it, the hardening of Pharaoh's heart and personal intervention by Moses in dividing the waters (v. 16). The Elohist influence (v. 19a) introduces God's messenger where the Yahwist prefers intervention by the cloud (vv. 19b-20).

a) Having fled Egypt in great haste the Jews found themselves suddenly face to face with the sea, with the pharaoh's army at their heels. Immediately there were recriminations on all sides (cf. Ex 5:20-21). It was better to "serve" in Egypt than to "die" in the desert in the name of a God who was so unhelpful, even if they had quit Egypt preferring to "serve" Yahweh than to "die" in chains. It is the constant dilemma of people whose *faith* is subjected to severe trial. They must choose between the threatening power of Egypt's armies and the invisible power of God.

Moses' appeal is to pure faith, absolutely stripped, to something one cannot see, but trusts. Such is the Yahwist version (vv. 10-14).

b) The priestly tradition (vv. 15-18) recounts the same episode practically, but with much less vigor. We are not so conscious of the drama of personal faith. All attention is concentrated on the divine *power* which makes the event a single combat between Yahweh and Pharaoh.

c) The Elohist has the incidents depend not on God or Moses

but on a "messenger of God" (v. 19), with whom the Yahwist juxtaposes intervention by the cloud (vv. 19b-20).

All this shows that the biblical traditions did not have an accurate historical description of the events, and tended to give importance now to the cloud, now to God's angel or again to Moses' staff. What counts is the absolute belief of each author, despite the diversity of witness, that God was conducting events. The account is not historical but theological. It is a profession of faith that God is present in human *history*.

This moment in history when the Jews placed the sea and the desert between Egypt and themselves is a moment for considering the magnitude of their decision, and particularly the meaning of their passage from service of the pharaoh to service of God. They had actually placed themselves in a state that is now called civil disobedience. The Exodus event proved decisive for their history. From now on it would be impossible for them to encounter any political situation without being aware of the possibility of insubordination, because the political domain was secularized. They had dared to emancipate themselves from the sway of a sacralized monarch, one established by divine right and himself divinized. Thus they would never pass under the control of another sacralized monarch. For them God himself alone was sacral. Political authority was conceded to competence only at least during the period of Judges. Kings there would be, but kings bereft of priesthood. In the northern kingdom in any case, no dynasty was ever sure of the throne. In the southern, even the dynasty of David disappeared without great regrets.

It was at the Exodus then that politics were desacralized, and this has continued into our own day. It explains why the first Christians prayed for the emperor but never offered him incense. It kindled opposition to Nazism, that modern attempt to sacralize power. It lies behind the ideal of a classless society, deprived of any sacral character, or any claim by one group to dominate another.

II. Micah 6:1-8
1st reading
2nd cycle
Monday

This passage, which is apparently original, begins a series of Micah's oracles (6:1-7:7). It depicts a sort of indictment by God against his people.

The divine displeasure is directed against two faults of the people: their ingratitude (vv. 3-5) and the superstition of their sacrifices (vv. 6-8). The whole is very vividly presented: the judge's entry (vv. 1-2), the indictment (vv. 3-5), questioning of the accused about the value of his plea (vv. 6-7), and the prophet's conclusion to the debate (v. 8).

III. Matthew 12:38-42
Gospel
Monday

This particular passage of the gospel is highly complicated. The juxtaposition of episodes and teachings is so artificial that no single lesson emerges. We shall restrict our commentary to verses 38-42 (the sign of Jonah and the Ninevites' fast). The following verses (43-45, the return of the demon) are only understandable in the light of Matthew 12:24-30. The final detail (vv. 46-50, the beatitude of those who hear) must be taken in conjunction with the cure of the deaf man in Matthew 12:22-23. Thus the Hebrew procedure of inclusion has had full rein in the passage. We should really begin at verse 12 to appreciate this properly.

a) We have four references to the famous *sign of Jonah* (Mt 12:38-42; 16:1-4; Lk 11:29-32; Mk 8:11-12) in gospel tradition. The different versions are certainly traceable to words spoken by Jesus himself in some context where a thought, the meaning of which is now lost, was easily understood. In any case it is certain that the Matthean interpretation of the sign is late.

Doubtless Jesus wished to tell the Jews that, for conversion, they would experience no greater signs than the Ninevites did

(Jon 3:1-10). The mere presence of God's prophet and the content of his message ought to suffice for conversion (cf. Mk 8:11-12 and Mt 16:1-4). However, the more the primitive community pondered about Christ, his style of speaking was regarded as a clue to his personality. Thus he himself became the awaited sign. We find this already when Luke 11:29-32 likens Jonah to the "Son of Man."

Meditation about the meaning of Jesus' personality went on, and became more and more concentrated on his paschal mystery. A parallel was found between Jonah's three days in the sea and the three days of the Lord's Pasch. The primitive community made the "sign of Jonah" the very sign of Jesus' obedience and resurrection. This is the fairly allegorized version we have in Matthew.

Thus in Matthew we have actually two concepts of the sign. The prophet's word is its own confirmation and needs no extrinsic proof. Secondly, the true sign offered for men's faith is none other than the death and resurrection of the God-man.

b) Today's gospel then is an *exposé* of the *signs of faith*. The Jews took the most exterior view. For faith and conversion the miracle was needed. Jesus goes to the heart of the problem when he affirms that faith is based exclusively on confidence in the person of the envoy. The primitive community went further: apart from the death and resurrection of the envoy there is no faith.

Modern man is not likely to err on the side of the Jews. He has a distaste for material miracles, and will believe in spite of them rather than because of them. There is of course a certain attitude towards miracles which suggests that God is only to be found in what transcends man, whereas the truth is that he is present in all human activities.

The material miracle will only have meaning when it is an expression of the personality of the miracle-doer and a challenge to the witness. That is why most of Jesus' miracles are cures, signs of his messianic role and his goodness (Mt 8:17; 11:1-6), even of his relations with the Father (theme of "signs" in the fourth gospel). It is also the reason why most miracles are a summons to faith and interior conversion. They summon to faith, but do not give faith. The previous action of the Spirit in a man's heart is necessary, so that he will accept, as suppliant not as judge, the sign proposed by God.

Nevertheless we may indeed wonder why God, and Jesus, do not make things easy for Pharisees, or atheists today, by providing the signs they want. Why for instance is not the name of God written so visibly in the heavens that doubt becomes impossible? The greater humanity's progress towards secularization, the more it is "desacralized," and the manifestations of God seem to be withheld.

But were God to provide "signs from heaven," he would no longer be the God who chose to become man's servant so as to win his love and confidence. He would be some sort of public portent that no one could resist. He would break down all human resistance, true . . . but would he still bear witness to the free quest of a free and trusting love? There are really no signs other than that of Jesus. God decided not to put man under constraint, but to win his love by dying for him. It is precisely because he is the God of love that there is no other sign but Jesus.

The genuine believer, though he does not discount the ultimate role of miracle does not seek exterior signs, because in the person of the God-man Jesus Christ he discerns the intervention of God. The true miracle is of the moral order. It is Jesus' human state. It was assumed in fidelity, in obedience and in absolute love. It was totally irradiated by the divine presence to the point that, even in death God was with his Son to raise him up. All the gospel miracles culminate in this sign of Jonah. They are all a summons to conversion and openness to God's salvation. They are signs of the spiritual presence which is at work in the struggle against sin and death.

IV. Exodus 14:21-15:1 *1st reading 1st cycle Tuesday*

Here we have a description of the final episodes in the passage of the Red Sea. We must interpret this account according to its own particular style. It is normal for peoples to resort to epic style in recounting their beginnings (Pss 77/78; 104/105; 113/114; Wi 10:18; 11:14). The text is actually a resumé of distinct traditions in which either Moses (*priestly*) or God and the wind (*Yahwist*), or again God's angel (*Elohist*) is responsible for dividing the waters. All traditions however are at one in proclaiming the providential and striking character of God's intervention, as he leads his people to liberty by the destruction of the enemy cavalry and chariots.

Manifestly then the authors of the different traditions had no first hand knowledge of the facts. Their outlook is above all religious, an anxiety to demonstrate that the beginnings of the Jewish people are due to *divine initiative*. All the details mentioned: the angel of Yahweh, the staff of Moses, the column of fire and the patriarch's prayer have the single purpose of stressing the priority of God's action in salvation and the establishment of his people. There is no need to see God's initiative in terms of the extraordinary, however—a suspension of water in vertical masses, for instance. God rather tends to act in accordance with the laws of nature. There are places where an arid wind might render passable a fairly shallow body of water. In this context the emphatic tone of the priestly version, and this version only, does no great service either to God or readers.

Religious man tends to see God's presence in nature, above all in strange or mysterious phenomena. A nature that is stronger than man, a threat to his projects, a source of fear and insecurity, easily becomes a symbol of a god who is powerful, formidable and retributive. We have this note in the miraculous events of the Exodus account. But we have more as well.

It is remarkable that the religious authors of these traditions see God, not in nature untamed, but in nature that is controlled by man and blended into his history. Because of what man has done, from now on nature will speak of God. This is in its way a tremendous wager. Wherever God is present he is the initiator, and now he is to be found not only in nature as given to man, but in man's manipulation of nature. All generations of believers have made the same wager. Faith depends on our capacity to discern God's initiative even in human initiative and human decisions.

V. Micah 7:14-15, 18-20
1st reading
2nd cycle
Tuesday

The book of Micah ends with a series of pieces that date probably from the return after the exile (Mi 7:8-20). Our piece today is a prayer after the manner of a psalm addressed to God who pardons the faults of his people.

Yahwism, at its beginnings, put itself forward as a religion of fidelity to the Sinai covenant, human fidelity manifested by scrupulous observance of the law, and fidelity on God's part because he accorded the promised blessings to those who avoided all fault.

Very soon man failed. Different rites and ablutions proved vain: the human being seemed incapable of fidelity to the covenant. The most hardened and the most proud became convinced of this by the exile.

Then God showed his anger and expelled his unfaithful spouse. Despite the sin however, he remained no less faithful to the covenant, and did not cease to love his people. The most important discovery during the exile indeed was the divine fidelity and benevolence that went on manifesting itself in mercy, pardon and *grace* (v. 18). It is this tenacious love of God despite infidelity (cf. Ex 34:6-7; Jl 2:13; Pss 50/51:3 102/103:8-14; Lk 7:36-50; 15:1-

31) that forms the principal topic of today's reading. Words like grace and fidelity, pity and pardon, become interchangeable.

Modern man does not like to speak of God's mercy, not so much because of the sentimental and paternalist overtones of the word, but rather because of the suggestion of religious alienation. Is not this constant recourse to a merciful, pardoning God simply a way of salving the conscience?

The truth is that God's mercy summons to return and conversion. The one who experiences it is impelled to exercise mercy in turn (Lk 6:36). There is nothing alienating here. On the contrary there is exercise of responsibility.

VI. Matthew 12:46-50
Gospel
Tuesday

Each evangelist has interpreted in his own way Jesus' attitude to his family, and his affirmation of solidarity with the spiritual family of those who do the Father's will. In Mark 3:20-35 this comes immediately after the designation of the Twelve. In drawing the contrast, Mark doubtless reflects the differences between the apostles concerning succession to the Messiah. Was the Church to be governed in dynastic fashion by the "brethren of the Lord," or charismatically, by the Twelve.

Luke makes it the conclusion to Jesus' teaching in parables (Lk 8:4-18) concerning the coming of the Kingdom, the spread of the Word and the conditions for its reception, faith in particular. He shows that mere physical adherence to Jesus and his Kingdom signifies nothing unless it is given true meaning by hearing the Word and by faith.

In Matthew it is the conclusion, and illustration, of the combat between the two spirits, clarifying the healing of the mute (Mt 12:22-25). The exclusive condition for access to the Kingdom is openness to the Word and the Spirit.

The majority of world religions are based on the natural community of the family, somehow sublimated into a basic religious community. Jewish law and wisdom made much of the family, and other religions followed the same principle. Jesus however based his religion, not on familial ties, but on the selective type of community where people chose one another freely on the basis of faith.

The development of our technological world has tended to detach men from natural communities and involve them in others, more "artificial" or "selective." The family in our time has been experiencing a conflict of generations: it is not always suited to the demands of a community of worship. Parents may pray better in group meetings than *en famille* with their children; and children better in their own particular groups. This is a normal development which ought not to cause misgiving. We must remember that Christianity does not depend on natural community for faith and worship. The family spirit is not necessarily the Holy Spirit. Indeed the Holy Spirit may be much more manifest in groupings that arise from a need for liberty and brotherhood. A good criterion of the real religious character of such groupings, and the presence in them of the Holy Spirit, will be the adjustment of their members in the natural groupings to which they belong.

VII. Exodus 16:1-5, 9-15
1st reading
1st cycle
Wednesday

The redaction of the account of the manna "miracle" is rather late; it is agreed that it depends on the postexilic priestly tradition. It follows the literary genre of midrashic homily, embroidering upon traditional data. Consequently we cannot regard it as strictly historical. We could take it, for instance, that the manna was the result of exudation from a particular tree, that was one day so extraordinary as to suggest a divine intervention. The primitive traditions certainly described the prodigy as a single occurrence. The exaggeration of the event and its religious meaning, and its daily repetition, were the result of later traditions.

a) The religious dimension of the episode rests on the people's certainty of a particular intervention by God. They were going through a severe crisis of discouragement, and questioning the very reality of their liberation (vv. 2-3). At this point came an extraordinary phenomenon (v. 4) in which they discerned a sign of *divine presence* meant to reassure them.

This is the essential point of the Yahwist tradition (v. 4). The priestly tradition adds some particular details, placing Aaron at the side of Moses (vv. 2 and 6), recalling the Sabbath legislation (v. 5), and stressing the mediating function of the priesthood ("we, who are we . . ." vv. 7 and 8). It also emphasizes that the heavenly food is the essential basis of the people's nourishment (v. 4).

b) Throughout all the nuances of the different traditions one idea however is common. The desert experience is above all an experience of divine *providence*. Day after day, according to the needs of each, the people are led. They are not allowed to think of tomorrow or seek means of subsistence. The manna then is a trial: it teaches the Jew to become "poor."

Probably no one is converted any more by the divine interventions in the Sinai desert. Modern man does not readily believe in God's direct interference in the course of events. God uses secondary causes only, it will be said (in this instance, a possible exudation from a desert tree). However it requires the light of faith to see God even in these. There is nothing self-evident about it, and we Christians are always being challenged to revise our hermeneutic by atheists who see no religious significance in secondary causes. We may well ask: what *is* faith? At least it can be said that Christians and atheists are at one in no longer seeking God in the extraordinary. We must all look for him in the projects that make for human advancement.

VIII. Jeremiah 1:1, 4-10
1st reading
2nd cycle
Wednesday

In a poem of three strophes Jeremiah describes his vocation.

a) The first strophe concentrates on the prophet's *predestination* (vv. 4-5). There are three aspects of this: preexistence in the thought of God, consecration in his mother's womb, and official investiture as prophet of the nations. This is a way of stressing the total communion between God and his prophet by an image of temporal predetermination.

b) Human language is altogether incapable of conveying God's word. Jeremiah comes to realize this more fully because he has some difficulties in expressing himself (vv. 6-7). The theme is a common one in describing prophetic vocations. Moses stammered (Ex 4:10-12), Isaiah had to purify his lips (Is 6:1-6): the greatest proclaimers of salvation were often victims of *dumbness* or stammering (Mk 7:31-37). This stresses the communion between God and his prophet, and God's prior initiative in the ministry. It also shows that the messianic times, when speech (that is to say the means of communion) will be abundantly distributed to everyone (Lk 1:65, 2:17, 38; Jl 3:1-2; Ac 2:1-3) are about to be inaugurated.

c) The final strophe stresses the courage that will be necessary for the prophet (vv. 8-10). When Jeremiah was composing the poem he had already experience of the people's hostility to him. He compares himself to a soldier face to face with the enemy, or an upright judge who pronounces sentence without allowing himself to be influenced.

When everything is going well structures are sufficient to express God's presence in events. They make it precise, guarantee it, and disseminate it through the whole. Such were the priesthood and the legislation in Jeremiah's time. Such are certain doctrinal and administrative organs in the Church.

Comes the time of revolution however, events become precipitate. God continues to be present as he was in past events, but the person or institution of the moment may not be adequate for the circumstances. If they show themselves, for instance, too stubbornly opposed to changes of mentality and style they will become incapable of discerning God's presence. At such times every man, and every Christian as well, has to fall back on his own conscience.

A conscience that is sufficiently delicate to discern the divine presence clearly in the new developments becomes prophetic. Sometimes it clashes with structures, and is sometimes victimized. But as a result the institutions are renewed and brought to see God's presence in the new. At a time so turbulent as our own we need a great many Jeremiahs. In so far as our structures can avoid lulling consciences into torpor, we can look for them to arise.

IX. Matthew 13:1-9
Gospel
Wednesday

The parable of the sower poses three problems to the reader: the meaning of the parable as delivered by Jesus (vv. 1-9); the emphasis given by Matthew in inserting it at this point in his Gospel; finally the meaning given to it by the primitive Church (vv. 18-23).

a) In four successive scenes, prefaced by a description of the sowing (v. 3) and concluded by one of the harvest (v. 8) the chief interest of the parable proper is the fate of the seed in the four different terrains. The scenes culminate in the vision of an extraordinary yield from the *seed.*

The harvest theme, an image of the final times, is traditional in Israel (Jl 4:13). What is new is the emphasis on the laborious sowing which prepares it. Thus Jesus is modifying slightly the eschatological dimension of the coming of the Kingdom (the harvest) and concentrating rather on the arduous process of bringing it about. He does proclaim the coming, but stresses the slow growth and coming to maturity.

b) By placing it where he does Matthew gives the parable a christological interpretation. Jesus is contemplating the reasons for the resistance and stumbling blocks to his message: the Scribes' blindness, the superficial enthusiasm of the crowd, the distrust of his relatives, etc. He tries to give meaning to this lack of understanding, and finds it in the contrast between the relative futility of the sower's toil and the very abundant harvest when maturity comes. He thinks of his trying *mission*, and analyzes it in the light of the judgment to come. This will reward the understanding his disciples seem to show (vv. 10-17), which compensates for the indifference of the other classes of listener.

c) The primitive communities gave the parable an ecclesiological interpretation. It was no longer the mission of Christ which had to be explained, but the motives for their own conversion. They thought not so much of the harvest as of the daily difficulties presented by persecution (v. 21).

Then came an allegorizing turn. Each scene was taken to illustrate a type of conversion. It is not the seed that is important but the manner of its reception. Even the eschatological emphasis is obscured in favor of considerations that are principally psychological and paraenetic (v. 24). Where Jesus was optimistic concerning the meaning of his mission, the primitive Church gives evidence of more tension.

X. Exodus 19:1-11, 16-20
1st reading
1st cycle
Thursday

Chapters 19-24 are the heart of the book of Exodus. Here we have the account of the preparation of the covenant (Ex 19:1-25 and 20:18-21); the decalogue (20:1-17); the Code of the alliance (20:22-23, 19) and the account of its celebration (24:1-18).

In our passage today the three traditions are interwoven in fairly complex fashion: the priestly (vv. 1-2a), the Yahwist (vv. 9, 11) and the Elohist (vv. 2b-3a). Finally, we have additions by the deuteronomist redactor (vv. 3b-8).

a) The priestly tradition, by fixing *Pentecost* fifty days after the Exodus (third month, vv. 1-2a) made the feast the celebration of the covenant's promulgation. Gradually however, as the chosen people became aware that God was more the God of history—their history—than the God of nature, they made these traditional agricultural festivals memorials of one or other desert event. Pentecost became the feast of promulgation of the law and the establishment in the covenant of the chosen people. We have few enough evidences in Scripture of this reinterpretation, but in other Jewish documents they are frequent. They are sufficient to explain that it was while celebrating the Jewish Pentecost, the memorial of the people's establishment, that the apostles discovered the new reality, the Church (Ac 2:1-4).

b) Yahweh assisted Israel to cross the desert to Sinai in order to make a *covenant* with her (v. 4b; cf. Dt 32:11; Ho 11:3-4; Is 46:3-4; 63:9). This is not a bilateral contract, even if there are reciprocal obligations. The initiative is God's alone: he alone has prepared it (v. 4). Nor is it some sort of definitive regulation which determines forever a framework for the people. Everything indeed is in the future ("I shall have you as a people . . . you will be . . ."). The very best definition of the covenant would seem to be: the beginning of a relationship, with all the risks involved in this.

c) This relationship with God immediately establishes the people as a free entity, described (vv. 5-6) as a *kingdom* of *priests* and a *holy nation*. The first phrase doubtless recalls that the people had left Egypt to "serve God" (Ex 12:31) and ask him to bless the pharaoh (Ex 12:32). The people would exercise before God, in the name of all nations, the mediating role that the priestly caste played for all the people. They would be persons set apart to represent humanity before God, intercede for it, and convey the divine will (Is 61:6). The second description follows from the first, with emphasis on the fact of belonging to God. Israel as a nation would be involved in all the evolutions of history, as she developed. As a holy nation she would be somehow separated. She would always have to live the event in communion with God.

These phrases from Exodus are one of the best definitions of the Church, and New Testament writers refer to them on several occasions (1 P 2:5-9; Rev 1:5-6; 5:10; 20:6). From this definition springs the concept of the royal priesthood of the Christian people, which had been for long forgotten, but which present-day renewal stresses.

The priesthood of the faithful finds expression in the power of the whole Church to baptize those who are converted to the Lord, to pardon sins (Mt 18:18), and to share the body of Christ in a spiritual sacrifice. But such cultic expressions only have meaning because they indicate the vocation of all the faithful to bear witness to God in the world, and their duty to offer their own lives as a spiritual sacrifice for the world.

They share the unique and universal mediation of Christ, and thus have direct access to God (He 10:22; Ep 2:18). They rejoice in the certainty that their offering of themselves for the world (Ph 4:18; 2:17; He 13:15-16) is accepted by God in Jesus Christ.

XI. Jeremiah 2:1-3, 7-8, 12-13
1st reading
2nd cycle
Thursday

This oracle is one of Jeremiah's first interventions. Nabopolassar has just succeeded Assurbanipal (626). The threat of the Medes has begun to disturb the empire, while Egypt has regained her independence and is again a cause of unease in Palestine. Judah's future seems very gloomy, and Jeremiah draws up the indictment of faults that have brought her to this pass.

a) He first turns his attention to the desert covenant, which ancient sources presented sometimes as a vassal contract or military treaty, sometimes as a *betrothal.* The latter image is borrowed from Hosea (8th century) and several Canaanite traditions.

For Jeremiah, Israel is still but one of those young maidens

(v. 2) who were married in the East at the age of twelve. The image is highly idealized, but it enables Jeremiah to contrast the former fidelity of the people with their present infidelity, the youth of former days with the aged politicians and priests of his own day.

b) The essential burden of his complaint is the rejection of *knowledge* of Yahweh. Those responsible among the people, priests, lawyers, kings (-shepherds) and prophets have failed to recognize Yahweh in the gift of the promised land, anymore than in the law, worship or power (vv. 7-8). It is not surprising that their legal or liturgical systems, cut off from the source of living water, are cisterns incapable of holding water (v. 13). Every religious project that is set up without God's aid and knowledge of his presence is vain and futile.

Jeremiah's opposition to the doctors and commentators of the law is typical of the whole prophetic tradition, which is the least legalist of Jewish institutions. The law is not regarded as an ancient document that must be interpreted, but as the expression of God's actual will for his people, which determines present behavior and prepares the future. Regarded as the presence of God among his people the law is permanent. From the point of view of the conditions in which people live, it is variable.

That is why, as against commentators on the ancient text, he proclaims a "new law" written in the conscience of every man, concerned with the demands that arise from a dialogue between the believer and God (Jr 31:31-34). Here he goes further than even the contemporary authors of Deuteronomy, who put forward love in the context of the ancient law.

XII. Matthew 13:10-17
Gospel
Thursday

Between the parable of the sower (Mt 13:1-9) addressed to the crowd (Mt 13:3) and the explanation given to the disciples (v. 18) Matthew inserts this passage, which is manifestly adventitious and meant to serve as a transition. The synoptics are in agreement about the content of the parable and its meaning, but display great individuality in the redaction of this transition (Mk 4:10-13; Lk 8:9-11). The kernel of the passage is in verse 11. Verse 12, which is certainly a late addition by Matthew (cf. Mk 4:25), could be a restriction of the previous verse in regard to Judas (?). Verse 13 draws conclusions from verse 11 that the long citation from Isaiah 6:9-10 (vv. 14-15) is meant to confirm. Verses 16-17 are also drawn from another context (Lk 10:21-22).

a) In Jewish literature *those who are outside* generally indicates the Gentiles (cf. 1 Co 5:12-13; 2 Co 4:16; Col 4:5; 1 Th 4:2). Mark however gives them another sense (Mk 4:11). He is thinking of those who, when Jesus is speaking "in the house" (Mk 3:20) to his apostles and disciples, are outside (cf. Mk 3:31). His relatives that is to say and the Pharisees (Mk 3:22). The phrase then for him would mean the Jews themselves. They cannot be converted and enter the kingdom (Mk 4:12) until their unbelief is ended.

Matthew's interpretation is altogether otherwise. He does not have Mark's context, and applies the phrase in the ordinary sense of the time.

b) The whole text indeed has a manifest apocalyptic coloring like that of the book of Daniel. We have the same revelation in two stages of a "secret" or a "mystery" (Dn 2:47), first by visions, symbols or parables, then by explanation. Then there are the phrases which emphasize the privilege enjoyed by those who can hear and understand such things. The apocalyptic form (which is also found in Mt 11:25) is designed by Matthew to give Jesus' teaching in parables meaning as genuine *revelation* from on high.

c) His citation at length of Isaiah 6:9-10 (vv. 14-15) sets in relief another intention of Jesus. He realizes that he is a *prophet* and accepts the opposition and rejection inevitable to this ministry. He has just encountered it in his teaching in parables which has drawn the line of demarcation between faith and incredulity.

He is explaining his lack of success. It is in conformity with the Scriptures, particularly Isaiah. He himself is journeying towards his Passion.

The use of the Isaiah quotation differs in Mark. For him speaking in parables is an act of God whereby he proposes to judge and condemn unbelievers. The modifications introduced by Matthew ("because" instead of "so that" and "see not" instead of "see, but do not perceive" in vv. 12-13) show that the reason for speaking in parables should not be sought in God, but in the hostile dispositions of the listeners. It is the passion of the prophet rather than the judgment of God that is considered.

d) Matthew's use of the text unites the apocalyptic and prophetic dimensions. To the optimism of the first about the privilege of those who receive revelation, he joins the pessimism of the other concerning those who reject the prophet. This procedure gives the ensemble a new emphasis, opposition between believers and unbelievers. The *secret* of God and his mystery (apocalyptic dimension) is made to be this opposition, though this was not the thought of Jesus.

e) Matthew (like Mark 4:1-34) writes at a time when the infant Church is disturbed about the *unbelief of Israel.* Chapter 13 is his solution to this. Mark 4:11-12 emphasizes the fact that Jesus only reveals his secret to the disciples, leaving those without in ignorance. By his teaching in parables he is exercising a sort of judgment between believers and unbelievers. Matthew solves the problem by showing that lack of understanding of Christ's teaching if it is willed by God, is not the result of arbitrary decision, but of inadequate spiritual dispositions.

Jesus questions himself about the reason for failure in his prophetic ministry and his conclusion is clear. The Passion has already begun. Death looms at the end of his mission and will prove his fidelity.

The primitive community also questions itself about the failure, which for it is the reason for Israel's refusal to join it in the faith. It finds the answer to an anguishing problem in Jewish apocalypse. This division of men into believers and unbelievers is the "secret" of God. It is the preparation for the judgment of humanity.

The Church now too questions herself about her apparent failure and her dwindling influence in the world. She is careful to avoid having recourse to Jewish apocalypse and dividing the world into good and bad. The line of demarcation between good and bad passes through the heart of every man. The only view left for her is that of Christ. Because he has entered into glory, she is not dispensed from the law of failure and the paschal lesson of trial.

XIII. Exodus 20:1-17
1st reading
1st cycle
Friday

We have two versions of the decalogue: that of Deuteronomy 5:6-22 which is the echo of Josias' reform, and that of Exodus 20 which goes back to ancient Yahwist and Elohist sources. It was however reworked by the priestly tradition, not to speak of subsequent efforts at formulation such as those of Ezechiel 18:5-9 and Psalm 14/15.

The precepts are formulated according to a characteristic literary form. It is the apodictic genre, with precepts in the second person (you shall not kill) grouped in tens or twelves, with a particular phrase rhythm. The style is distinct from the normal juridical style in the East, a conditional form in the third person (if a man kills . . . he will be: the more usual style in Israel).

The apodictic formula presents itself absolutely, purporting to express a will that cannot be discussed (God or the legislator). So absolute is the form that there is no question of sanctions, particular cases, exceptions or consequences, unlike the normal juridical proclamation.

a) The apodictic nature of the decalogue, both in Deuteronomy 5 and Exodus 20, facilitates presentation as the word of

God (cf. Ex 20:2; Dt 5:6), though it seems that the association between the precepts and God's presentation of himself (I am Yahweh) is relatively late. We find proclamations in such form in certain treaties between suzerains and their vassals in the ancient East. The Hittites framed their oath of allegiance in a formula that the Hebrew decalogue had only to copy:

1) preamble and mention of the suzerain: cf. Exodus 20:2 and Deuteronomy 5:6.
2) preliminaries recalling the historical circumstances in which the suzerain imposes himself on the vassal: cf. Exodus 20:2 and Deuteronomy 5:2-4.
3) declaration of principle concerning the absolute loyalty of the vassal, and a prohibition of entering into relations with foreign powers: cf. Exodus 20:3-6 and Deuteronomy 5:7-9.
4) particular arrangements with regard to goods, boundaries, military assistance, tribute, etc., secondary obligations generally: cf. Exodus 20:8-17 and Deuteronomy 5:12-21.
5) arrangement for the text of the treaty to be placed in the temple and read regularly: cf. Deuteronomy 5:22b.
6) formula of malediction and blessing: cf. Joshua 24:35 and Deuteronomy 27.

Thus the Jewish people find themselves placed by the decalogue in a state of vassalhood to their suzerain, in a treaty of *alliance* which is above all the proclamation exclusively of the latter's will. It is more than a simple declaration of the natural law. The Israelite faith is not concerned with the elaboration of a universal ethic. It is a matter of discerning the personal will of God and living in communion with it.

b) It is also possible that the apodictic form is due to the exercise of authority in family and clan. In this social unit the precept was formulated absolutely by the elder or the father who ordered the child (as in the books of wisdom: Pr 22:17-24, 22). The great effect of the Sinai alliance was to substitute a higher authority for that of the clan chief, that of Yahweh himself, the father of all clans. From now on he himself declares his will, as the *father of the family* did previously. He adopts the apodictic formula of the father of the family, and has the power of life and death that the father had.

c) In the course of the people's history the text of the *decalogue* was certainly reworked. Precepts 6, 7 and 8 are so brief that it seems likely all the others were originally brief in a similar fashion. We may also take it that all the precepts were originally formulated negatively (the only exceptions now are 4 and 5, at least partially; but we still have their negative form in Ex 35:3; Lv 22:3b; Ex 21:15; Lv 20:9). In so far as this is possible we could reconstruct the primitive decalogue thus:

There shall be no other gods before you
You shall not make graven images
You shall not take the name of Yahweh in vain
The seventh day is Sabbath, you shall do no work
You shall not "dishonor" your father or your mother
You shall not kill
You shall not commit adultery
You shall not steal
You shall not give false witness against your neighbor
You shall not covet the house of your neighbor

The killing forbidden in the sixth precept is killing only outside the legal community framework. Adultery concerns every sexual act which violates the integrity of another's marriage. The use of God's name (3rd precept) has doubtless magic in mind in the Exodus 20 text, but false oaths in Deuteronomy 5.

The decalogue is interesting not only in content, but above all in form. It is not a reflection of natural law or any ethical structure: it is principally an expression of a will. Such too is the basis of Christian ethic. The Christian's behavior is dictated by a commandment of God. This can extend to ten precepts or to the single commandment of love. It can be mediated by the law or by conscience. The ultimate reasons for it can never be confined to general ethics or a philosophic concept of God.

This does not mean that there is a Christian ethic which is not a natural ethic. It simply means that the latter is embraced by the Christian at the very depths of his being. That portion of him which communes with the God who is revealed in Jesus Christ.

God's commandment as such is always addressed to a person, and is the word of a person. It can only be lived in a context of alliance and communion. As such it covers all one's life and all one's activities, not in analytic fashion, but as a central directive.

XIV. Jeremiah 3:14-17
1st reading
2nd cycle
Friday

Jeremiah doubtless is thinking of the events of 587. He has witnessed the fall of the northern kingdom, and now Jerusalem itself has been pillaged by the Chaldeans. In this debacle the ark, which was preserved in the temple, has disappeared.

The disappearance of the ark is not a catastrophe. It stood for an archaic religion, with nationalist emphasis. A new law has been promulgated by Josias: Deuteronomy. It is more up-to-date, more suited to current conditions. If people are converted to it with all their heart, the presence of God, previously symbolized by the ark, will be found in the community. Jerusalem as a whole will inherit the prerogatives of the ark (v. 17; cf. Ex 25:10). But the change to a more spiritual religion, where the community itself will be the ark of the covenant, can only take place through a conversion of heart (v. 14), an openness to universalism (v. 17).

We, who are undergoing such tension in the Church today, can understand the malaise that set in at Jerusalem after the disappearance of the ark. In their case as in ours the crisis could only be surmounted by a reevaluation of the supernatural. The

Jews may have thought that in losing the ark they were losing their faith. But in reality they were only losing the symbol of it that had been set up. They found themselves without a sacral point of reference, as many Christians do now as a result of the tide of secularization.

The reevaluation undertaken by Jeremiah is precisely what many Christians are trying to do now. He reminded his contemporaries that they ought to live in community with their compatriots, but also with foreigners, and give themselves totally to this relation. He goes no further; but we realize that in giving oneself to others we become identified with the gift of Jesus to the Father. If every man, Jew or Christian, lives the terrestrial condition for its own sake, if he liberates himself from archaic sacralizations, he will discover the one and only sacral value, the only definitive ark of the covenant, the gift to the Father of Jesus' life.

XV. Matthew 13:18-23
Gospel
Friday

This gospel was commented on with that of Matthew 13:1-9, above, p. 199.

XVI. Exodus 24:3-8
1st reading
1st cycle
Saturday

Here we have the two versions, Yahwist (vv. 1-2 and 9-11) and Elohist (vv. 3-8), of the celebration of the covenant between God and Israel. For the former it was sealed by a sacred meal, for the latter by sacrifice and blood.

a) For both versions the ritual of the *covenant* is identical (cf. further Dt 27:2-10; Jos 24:19-28): first a proclamation of the law and its ratification by the people (v. 7), then the offering of sacrifices which seal the covenant (vv. 5-6, 8), finally the creation of columns as witness for the future (v. 4; cf. further Gn 28:18; 31:44-54; Jos 4:4-7; 24:26-27).

b) The covenant however is more than a ritual ceremony: it is a sharing of the same life (later Hosea will speak of conjugal love). The initiative comes from God. What we have is "all that Yahweh has said" (v. 7a). The people freely give their answer. They will be Yahweh's people and he will be their God (v. 7b). The adhesion will be something much deeper than mere conformity to a law: it is the fusion of two lives. Life is in the blood (Lv 17:14): thus the best symbol of sharing of lives is *sharing blood* (v. 8). By spreading the blood of victims (cf. previously Gn 15:17-18) on the altar (which represents Yahweh) and on the people Moses unites the life of God (cf. Ex 20:24) and that of the people. Thus they are brought together effectively.

c) The *meal* ceremony suggests the proximity and intimacy to which the covenant gives a right. This was by no means for the general body. The people remain at the bottom of the mountain, outside the domain of God (vv. 1-2). Only Moses and the elders are admitted to the "vision" of God (v. 9), to some understanding that is of what God is undertaking (cf. Is 6:1-5 and above all Ez 1:26), and to a meal with God (v. 11) which consisted doubtless of the sacrifice victims.

From now on the Jews can boast that they have been at table with God, Yahweh's "sons of the table." It is well known that in the East he who could boast of being at table with the king commanded great respect.

During the course of Jewish and Christian history the covenant will be often renewed. In a common life fidelity must be always getting rebuilt and renewed. The rite of blood was not renewed in Israel. Once life is shared it cannot be separated again: a child does not lose the blood of his father. Christ himself renewed it, once for all (Mt 26:27; 1 Co 11:23-25). But the life he shares with men in the Eucharist is truly a new life, which makes men children of God, and opens for them the gates of eternal life (He 9:15-18; Jn 6:54-56).

XVII. Jeremiah 7:1-11
1st reading
2nd cycle
Saturday

Jeremiah is certainly one of the first to attack openly the formalist cult of the Jerusalem temple (in 608). He is destined indeed to be arrested for blasphemy (cf. Jr 26:1-19), as Jesus would be later, for a similar reason (Mt 26:39-61).

By casting doubt on the continued presence of God in the temple as long as the people surrenders itself to sin, and is content with a formalist cult he is laying the foundations for a theology of *spirtual cult.* He is not opposing the temple as such or the priestly function: he is simply criticizing usage. The prophet and the priest are not irremediably opposed. The former is more committed to the absolute indeed; but he has never wanted the abolition of the priesthood. Prophets have simply wished the abolition of deviations in the shape of formalist liturgy, devoid of any moral justice.

What Jeremiah is really reacting against is the false security which the temple cult fosters in the people (cf. Mi 3:11; 2 Ch 13:10-11). It seems to dispense them from any quest for Yahweh or knowledge of him, as if liturgy could be a substitute for personal living and genuine contact.

XVIII. Matthew 13:24-30
Gospel
Saturday

Like most of the parables, that of the tares must be subjected to strict rules of interpretation. We must distinguish the thought of Jesus from the several rereadings. We have the common synoptic tradition, and that of each individual evangelist, not to speak of parallel, noncanonical traditions such as the Gospel of Thomas. Generally the evangelists have tended to allegorize (give each detail a symbolic meaning) something that, for Jesus, was merely a parable (the ensemble providing a single lesson).

The thought of Jesus becomes clear if we compare the long version given by Matthew with the short one in the apocryphal Gospel of Thomas.

The patience of Jesus where his enemies, the Pharisees, were concerned, and his more hesitant disciples, scandalized the apostles. They were disturbed by the opposition of the former (Lk 9:51-56) and the defection of the latter (Jn 6:60-71). Urged by them to transform his community into a sect of the pure, Jesus reveals the *patience* of God. He postpones the judgment so that the sinner will have time to be converted. He forbids men to arrogate divine prerogatives by judging others. The last times have indeed been inaugurated, but they are not times of power and judgment as the Jews imagined. They are times of delay and tolerance (cf. 2 P 3:4-9; 1 P 3:20; Rm 11:25-27; 8:1-18), marked by collaboration between God and man's frail liberty.

To the primitive account some characteristic details are added by Matthew. The tares (v. 26) are more dense than usual. They are sown by the "enemy" (v. 28), gathered first and bound in bundles to be burned (v. 30). Further, he devotes considerable attention to the sifting of the tares and the wheat. His viewpoint is no longer exactly that of Christ. He is less concerned with explaining the delay of the Kingdom and God's patience than with the elaboration of a small eschatological treatise, which clearly describes the fate of the good and the wicked at the last *judgment*. He goes on to emphasize this viewpoint in an explanation which is not in our reading (Mt 13:36-43).

Intolerance and sectarianism has at all times been the strongest temptation for human beings, especially during periods of mutation. Had God been intolerant, Israel would never have survived her numerous infidelities. The Old Testament indeed is a chronicle of God's patience towards his people. They however, far from drawing the obvious conclusions, continued to have the concept of a violent God who would not hesitate to punish the Gentile nations.

Once Jesus proclaimed himself the Messiah, and the Son of man entrusted with judgment (cf. Dn 7), his listeners expected to see him judge and condemn. They were scandalized when they found him the universal pastor, anxious to encounter sinners, patient with their delays. The secret of Jesus' patience lies in his love, which invites to dialogue. He addresses himself to all men, with infinite respect for what they are, summoning them to respond freely as partners. This response takes time, and becomes a genuine spiritual pilgrimage where reverses are succeeded by advances. Jesus loves men even in their reverses. Even when human sin nails him to the cross, his love persists and deepens.

Because the Church is the Body of Christ, she is too, in the world the sign of tolerance and patience. She trains her members to have respect for the other (Rm 14), something that is slowly acquired. It takes a long time to recognize the other for what he is, someone God has called toward himself.

Missionary activity is also a sign of tolerance. Only little by little does the missionary learn to share the life of the people among whom he labors, and reach the proper degree of abnegation. Such a patience is not just a moral virtue. It is an expression of the love with which God loves men. That is why it is nourished by the eucharistic word and the eucharistic bread, the signs of Christ's patience on the cross.

SEVENTEENTH WEEK

I. Exodus 32:15-24, 30-34
1st reading
1st cycle
Monday

Moses comes down from Sinai with the tables of the law. Doubtless in Egypt he had acquired the art of writing: writing on stone was already known at the time. He may indeed have been one of the first to use that proto-alphabetic writing of which the earliest examples are precisely from Sinai. The finger of Moses engraving the decalogue on the rock becomes the very finger of God (v. 16).

a) Returning to the Israelite camp, he finds the *calf of gold* (vv. 17-18), and, confronted by such a divorce between the monotheistic spiritualism of the tables and this materialist, naturist cult, he is aghast. In his anger he destroys both the tables of the law and the statue (vv. 19-20), doubtless casting the debris into the stream where the people would drink, a ceaseless reminder, as it were, of what they had forfeited, which they would have to drink to the dregs.

b) Aaron defends himself so miserably for his part in the worship of the calf (vv. 23-24) that there could be no question of his priesthood reconciling Yahweh. Only Moses has sufficient integrity to exercise this *mediation* (vv. 31-32). It will be often thus in Israel. The clergy, grown too compromised, will have to be replaced by the prophet, one day by that unique prophet who is called Jesus Christ. The mediation of Moses is not successful. Punishment will fall upon the people, even though their pilgrimage toward salvation will not be compromised.

We encounter here two conceptions of religion. One sees God as hidden behind nature. A terrestrial symbol of strength and fecundity (the golden calf) has to be interposed between an all powerful God and a crushed humanity. The other sees God within man, whose undertakings he inspires (written on stone by Moses), and only a person can be interposed between God and man, someone who can represent both one and the other. Since Jesus Christ the second concept has prevailed: it is the only one which advances mankind.

II. Jeremiah 13:1-11
1st reading
2nd cycle
Monday

The episode of the spoiled loincloth is probably a parable rather than a gesture imposed on the prophet. We can hardly suppose that Jeremiah traversed four times the thousand kilometers that separated his country from the Euphrates.

Just as Jeremiah attires himself in a new *loin-cloth* and binds it about his loins, thus Yahweh has attired himself with Israel. She had been for him a true ornament, cleaving to his skin, so intimate were their relations.

However she had become detached from him just as easily as the loincloth becomes unknotted. And, just as the prophet's loincloth had spoilt at contact with the water of the Euphrates, so Israel had become good for nothing (v. 10).

It is a vivid image. Yahweh had made Israel his own and she lived in his intimacy. But no sooner did she become detached from her master than she lost all *raison d'etre,* decayed and became moldy.

III. Matthew 13:31-35
Gospel
Monday

Our passage today is taken from the Lord's discourse in parables concerning the growth of the Kingdom of God. We have two short, fairly similar parables, that of the mustard and that of the leaven, with an allusion to Scripture to confirm Jesus' manner of procedure. Previously in Matthew we have the parables of the sower (Mt 13:3-9) and the tares (Mt

13:24-30), of which Jesus furnishes an explanation himself (Mt 13:18-23 and 36-43). The whole discourse concludes with the parables of the treasure, the pearl and the net (Mt 13:44-50).

The parable of the mustard seed is given very differently in Mark (4:30-32) and Luke (13:18-19). Matthew's version is intermediate. That of the leaven we know only from Matthew and Luke, and the versions are practically identical.

a) Mark makes the mustard seed a similitude only, whereas it is a "parable" for Luke (probably accurate originally when we consider its similarity with the leaven). Matthew corresponds with Luke in the narrative style, and with Mark in the contrast between the seed and the majestic tree.

The tree certainly symbolizes God's kingdom on earth: it was a traditional image for the power of kingdoms (Ez 17:22-23; Dn 4:9-18).

In realizing the kingdom Jesus likens himself to the man who, in order to have a tree, buries a seed in the earth. Between the seed and the tree there is contrast, but yet continuity. Thus the kingdom is already present in *Jesus' ministry*, however meager its results. Understood thus, the parable is a justification for Jesus and his disciples of the insignificance of his preaching and its fruits. There was no question in the original of light on the future: it was a justification of present failure.

Matthew however attempts to read into it the conditions of the Church in his time. The seed is still in its minuscule state, but he thinks of the efflorescence of the Church when it will be spread over the earth.

b) The three measures of meal mixed to make the bread recall Sara's mixing for her guests (Gn 18:6), Gideon's offering to the angel of Yahweh (an *epha* = 3 measures: Jg 6:19) or Anna's offering with her son Samuel (1 S 1:24). It seems likely that Jesus wants to suggest that this is not a normal repast, but a biblical one, in accordance with God's plan.

The leaven image very clearly suggests the insignificance of

Jesus' mission, though it bears the most overwhelming eschatological import. But Matthew doubtless discerns in the enormous quantity of bread the *growth* of a Church that was astonished by the success of her first missions.

IV. Exodus 33:7-11; 34:5-9, 28
1st reading
1st cycle
Tuesday

After the golden calf incident, a rupture developed between God and his people. Moses indicates this by carrying his own tent (not the sacred tent which is only found in subsequent priestly traditions: Ex 24:8-9) outside the camp (v. 7). From now on God will not speak any more to the people, but only to Moses, and through him to those who leave the accursed camp and join him (v. 7).

a) This rupture makes us think of the mystical life of the patriarch. All contact between God and man is not cut off. Moses remains a *friend of God* (v. 11), provided he separates himself from the crowd. All that the people can do is follow the goings and comings of the holy man, and imagine the nature of his conversations with God.

b) Emboldened by these privileged contacts Moses demands to see God (Ex 33:18-20). Against all expectations his prayer is heard. Yahweh passes before him revealing all his principal attributes (vv. 6-7). The proclamation with which God manifests himself is made up of a series of ancient liturgical invocations (v. 6: cf. Jl 2:13; Jon 4:2; Ne 9:17; Pss 85/86:5; 102/103:8; v. 7: cf. Nb 14:18; Na 1:3), an archaic formula (v. 6: cf. Ex 20:5; Jr 2:18) and two phrases of deuteronomic origin (Dt 5:9; 7:9). Man cannot *see God* beyond the sensible world. What he can know of him is his goodness to man, to whom he never ceases to "do grace." This is what God himself seems to say in giving the exegesis of his name (vv. 6-7) in formulae and phrases that suggest his love for the sinner. Chastisement and punishment do indeed exist and fall on man up to the fourth generation, but the love of God has repercussions up to the thousandth generation.

Moses approaches God in terms of religion, but is made to fall back on faith. He looks for what is "beyond existence" but finds a "preexistence." He thinks of some divine domain which is beyond the terrestrial. He is made to discern a God who is precisely the unexpected, the Totally-Other, insofar as he is for the world, about to suffer in Jesus Christ for it. In all Moses discovers that God is free for man, and in that degree free of man.

V. Jeremiah 14:17-22
1st reading
2nd cycle
Tuesday

In the time of Jeremiah, Judah went through a period of catastrophic drought. The prophet delivered several oracles at this time, being anxious to discern God's presence and his will in the calamity (Jr 15:1-4; 5:20-24; 8:18-23). It seems likely that chapter 14 has assembled elements of a liturgy of supplication celebrated during the course of the drought, and largely composed by the prophet himself.

Our passage today would be the second public confession of the people's faults. Doubtless it echoed, at the end of the celebration, another confession (vv. 7-9) which began the ceremony.

The collective *confession* of sins follows the traditional schema of such innovations, very frequent in the psalms. First we have a sort of challenge to God's mercy—can he really forget his covenant and his promise (v. 19)? So absolute is the tone that we ask ourselves whether this is not deliberate extortion of God's love, or evidence of boundless faith in a God who is greater than any human sin.

In the second part of the confession we have the avowal proper (v. 20). It is for the most part brief and recalls somewhat the sins of ancestors, a not unusual procedure of the sinner who looks for extenuating circumstances.

Nor is the third part (vv. 21-22) any more spiritual. The prophet does begin by recalling the glory of God: can it be in his interest to let his faithful languish under punishment? Yet the argumentation is poor. There is perhaps a profession of monotheism (v. 22); but we have also the concept of Yahweh as a God of nature, the only one capable of giving rain.

VI. Matthew 13:36-43
Gospel
Tuesday

This gospel was commented on with that of Saturday in the previous week (Mt 13:24-30), p. 212.

VII. Exodus 34:29-35
1st reading
1st cycle
Wednesday

Those verses belong to the priestly tradition. Probably they allude to some detail of the high-priest's vesture in the temple: he had perhaps to wear a mask when proclaiming the divine oracles, or a coiffure which symbolized his belonging to the divine domain. Greek tradition interpreted the original badly, imagining the face of Moses ringed with horns, or rays resembling horns.

Whatever it may have been, tradition emphasizes above all the radiance in Moses when he spoke of God. He seemed a man of God, able to approach Yahweh and his mystery. What is being thrown into relief is his role as *mediator*. One day another will display more marvelously still in his lineaments the very presence of God (2 Co 4:6; He 1:3; Col 1:15).

VIII. Jeremiah 15:10, 16-21
1st reading
2nd cycle
Wednesday

By this particular arrangement of Jeremiah's first "confession," the lectionary is following exegetical evidence. Exegetes consider verses 11-12 as a dittography, and verses 13-14 as a doublet of Jeremiah 7:3-4. We may add that verse 21 too seems to be a late gloss.

The prophet is the first one in Israel to challenge God and call him to account. He has given his life to the service of the Word so that people may be converted, but all he finds around him is a pack of contemptuous accusers (v. 11). Fidelity such as this has cost him dearly (v. 17). Why does not God give better recompense to one who has given himself altogether, and who finds himself alone in loving God's word (v. 16)?

Doubt invades his soul: could God be a deceiving water (v. 18)? The only solution is conversion to God and blind confidence in his mystery (vv. 19-20). To resolve his doubt by denying God or withdrawing from his engagements is unworthy of the mystery of God. The only way open to a man is to live with doubt, and ceaselessly try to probe the mystery. God would not be God unless it were open to man to doubt him.

IX. Matthew 13:44-46
Gospel
Wednesday

In this gospel we have conjoined two parables of fairly different tenor, that of the hidden treasure and that of the pearl. The lesson they propose is somewhat identical, and they are presented together even though they were delivered on different occasions with a different viewpoint, as the Gospel of Thomas suggests (nos. 76 and 106).

a) Accounts of treasure discovered are frequent in Eastern tales and Jewish traditions. The Gospel of Thomas, at least where this parable is concerned, yields to the marvels of this genre. The discoverer finds riches and happiness and marries the daughter of a landed proprietor from whom he buys a palace and slaves, to the great discomfiture of the despoiled heir (another example in a *midrash* on the Canticle of Canticles 4:12).

We have nothing like this in Matthew. The *treasure* discovered is the kingdom of God. The man who finds it, by chance as it were, is so aware of his good fortune that, instead of thinking like the heroes of the Eastern tales of all that he can buy, he considers how unpardonable it would be to lose it. What is emphasized in the parable is not the man's sacrifice but his motive. The discovery of the Kingdom is regarded as something which governs all one's subsequent life.

b) The parable of the pearl seems different. The Kingdom of God is no longer likened to a thing (a net or treasure) but to a person, as we have elsewhere in the New Testament in the case of the good Samaritan, the good shepherd or the sower. Wherever there is question of a person, he stands for God himself or Christ. There are more textual differences between the two parables than average versions would lead us to think, so that an original parallelism between them is doubtful.

The pearl parable seems to have been allegorized to the point that it represents God himself establishing his reign over humanity (represented by the pearl according to a current contemporary symbolism). He sells all that he possesses (his divinity "humiliated" in the incarnation of his Son). So that we would have, at least in the secondary stage, an allegory of the *divine kenosis* in search of humanity.

Such an interpretation disappeared fairly quickly, and the parable was reduced to a simple sapiental proverb, fairly like Proverbs 3:13-18. The association of it with the treasure parable culminates in a common meaning. So imminent is the Kingdom that one should abandon everything to obtain it (cf. Mk 1:18-20).

X. Exodus 40:16-21, 34-38
1st reading
1st cycle
Thursday

The liturgical law is presented twice in Exodus, first (Ex 25-31) as orders given by Yahweh ("you shall do") and second in a very similar formula ("you shall do" is replaced by "this is done") in a more descriptive section (Ex 35-40). Chapter 40 then is simply a replica of chapters 25-27. The only originality is the form, and the conclusion (vv. 34-38).

This group of chapters comes from priestly sources: they are not only late, but actually anachronistic. The desert tent has the dimensions of the Jerusalem temple. It resembles the temple in many unlikely ways, and is made from materials not available in the desert, with an artisan skill certainly unknown to nomads.

Our reading gives only the portions about the consecration of the tent and the furniture, and the description of the apparition of Yahweh which sanctioned the ceremony (vv. 32-36).

a) It is very difficult to say what the *tent of meeting* was like in the desert period. The sources which describe it were too thoroughly remanipulated by priestly redactors. We may be sure that it was a product of desert style, that it was the shelter for the ark, and the scene of Moses' encounters with Yahweh, precisely because it contained the ark, the place of Yahweh among his people.

b) The presence of God in the tent soon required *consecrated ministers* (v. 15; cf Ex 28:1-5; 29:1, 44). One did not undertake this office of one's own accord: one was summoned. Such is the import of the anointing of Aaron and his sons (vv. 9-15), and their solemn vesture. The double investiture with anointing and clothing comes probably from a later ritual, already influenced by diverse elements. Anointing we may take it was a royal ceremony that was only used for the high priest after the disappearance of the royal dynasty. Its meaning changed too. To the king it gave strength and wisdom, to the priests holiness rather. But in any case it indicated that the recipient belonged to the divine domain.

c) Tent, ark and priesthood all assured the people of the mysterious *presence of God* (vv. 34-36). It was not however an automatic presence. At the time of compilation of the text the priests realized that Yahweh was only present where fidelity and conversion prevailed, above all where he could encounter the "poor" (Is 56:4-8; 57:15; 58:13-14; 60:1-18; 63:15-19; 66:1-4).

XI. Jeremiah 18:1-6
1st reading
2nd cycle
Thursday

The episode of Jeremiah's visit to a potter (probably from Anatot his native village) is doubtless contemporaneous with those which determined his vocation. The account displays a vivid imagination which makes a symbol of the smallest detail. He compares the potter's freedom in casting aside a spoiled vessel to rebegin another, with God's freedom in his covenant with Israel.

The theme of *God as potter* is common in Scripture. The Yahwist account of creation is largely inspired by it (Gn 2:7), and Isaiah uses it to describe the absolute dependence of the creature on God (Is 29:16). The difference about Jeremiah's use is that the image is transposed into the theology of the covenant. Should the chosen people revolt, they will weigh no more in Yahweh's hands than a spoiled vessel in the potter's. God will have no difficulty in fashioning another people, more faithful to his mold.

The use of the image both in creation and covenant theology stresses God's absolute initiative in the relationship with man. The image however, if it were exclusive, would be erroneous. It would suggest that God does just as he pleases, and would equate man's liberty with that of a pot in the potter's hands (cf. Jr 19:10; Ps 2:9; Si 23:7-13).

As Old Testament revelation draws to a close however, we have Third-Isaiah giving a more benign interpretation (Is 6:7). The potter-God is no longer the formidable, autocratic judge. He is faithful to the relationship with his own, sinners though they be. There is nothing here of the capricious God. The image is demythologized. Soon the time will come when the potter-God will let himself be broken on the cross, in order to maintain his relationship of love with free men.

How should we now interpret the image? Creation is not an action, but a relation, not an action from above, but a relation to God that grows within a man. We should avoid presenting the image in terms of external "fabrication." Rather should we see it in terms of inner relation, where liberty, on hearing the Word of God, is fully expressed.

XII. Matthew 13:47-53
Gospel
Thursday

This is the last of Matthew's parables concerning the Kingdom.

The parable of the net, like that of the tares, shows how the kingdom which Jesus inaugurates necessarily needs time for conversion and increase before reaching plenitude (theme of the "full" net). The phraseology largely resembles that of the tares parable (Mt 13:40-43), which suggests late redaction.

We should distinguish the teaching of the parable itself, with its insistence on a period of transition between the establishment of the kingdom and its fulfillment, from the more restricted, allegorical interpretation. The latter confines it to the last judgment.

The encounter between God and man, which is proclaimed in the parables of the treasure and the pearl, will only reach accomplishment in the final phase of the world's history. Meanwhile patience is *de rigueur:* any procedure of condemnation could block men's conversion and its growth.

XIII. Leviticus 23:1, 4-11, 15-16, 27, 34-37
1st reading
1st cycle
Friday

This passage is one of the latest versions of the Jewish liturgical calendar, but not necessarily the most elaborate. It is indeed surprising enough that what we find in it is the most "naturist" concept of the festivals. Everything seems to suggest that the natural rhythm of harvests and vintage was still imposing itself on religion.

The Pasch is presented as simply the occasion of eating unleavened bread (v. 6), a survival of an agricultural rite, and of offering God the first of the new harvest (vv. 10-11). The Feast of Pentecost is scrupulously calculated to allow the people to offer their last sheaves (v. 15). That of Tabernacles appears less clearly as the vintage festival (during which people dwelt in huts or tents).

These agricultural festivals had been detached by the prophetic current from their naturist context, and make memorials of various stages of salvation history. The Pasch became the feast of the passage of Exodus, Pentecost that of the Sinai covenant, Tabernacles that of the desert sojourn. But we find no echo of this in Leviticus 23, unless it is the importance given to the Pasch which now begins the year, formerly a function of Tabernacles.

The inadequate notion of the liturgical year conveyed by this passage at least enables us to measure the distance between these primitive festivals and Christian feasts. We see the ever present danger of degradation to the inferior level. In Leviticus 23 the feast is that of the peasant who clings to the law of nature, and thinks to find God behind nature. This is the reaction of pre-technological man, subject, to the point of alienation, to nature.

The Jews kept the calendar, but gave its feasts another meaning. It is not a matter now of man's submission to nature, but of his communion with God in the fulfillment of salvation history. Festivals celebrated the principal stages (in the past, or eschatological) of the collaboration between God's liberty and man's. They both work for the building of the world and the direction of its history.

It was only in the person of Jesus Christ that the collaboration was perfectly successful. He is our Pasch, our unleavened bread, our new covenant, our promise of happiness. A Christian feast is essentially the very person of the man-God and the union with him and his love experienced by all who celebrate it. Were this dimension not present the feast could become a simple anniversary, not to say a simple naturist or magic rite.

XIV. Jeremiah 26:1-9
1st reading
2nd cycle
Friday

Jeremiah's invectives (Jr 7:1-11) against the temple and Jerusalem's formalist cult (in 608) were the occasion of his arrest. Jesus would be arrested for similar reasons later (Mt 26:59-61).

By casting doubt on the continued presence of God in the temple as long as the people surrenders itself to sin, and is content with a formalist cult, he is laying the foundations for a theology of *spiritual cult.* He is not opposing the temple as such or the priestly function: he is simply criticizing usage. The prophet and the priest are not irremediably opposed. The former is more committed to the absolute indeed; but he has never wanted the abolition of the priesthood. Prophets have simply wished the abolition of deviations in the shape of formalist liturgy, devoid of any moral justice.

What Jeremiah is really reacting against is the false security which the temple cult fosters in the people (cf. Mi 3:11; 2 Ch 13:10-11). It seems to dispense them from any quest for Yahweh or knowledge of him, as if liturgy could be a substitute for personal living and genuine contact.

These invectives are the core of the "desecurization" process undertaken by Jeremiah where all Jewish institutions were concerned. He foretold the end of the temple, queried the current messianism (cf. Jr 30:18-22), mocked the legalism (cf. Jr 2:1-13), and questioned current ideas about the retribution of the just and the wicked (Jr 25:7-11). Not a single institution of ancient Israel escaped his criticism. In his own day he brought about what secularization is doing now in the Church: a devaluation of the security that depends on institutions. We must return to the religion of a mysterious and invisible God, to be sought out by faith in disquiet and torment, with no other assurance than the love inscribed in our hearts.

XV. Matthew 13:54-58
Gospel
Friday

Having finished his Galilean ministry, Jesus returns to Nazareth. Here, during the course of a Sabbath meeting in the synagogue he speaks (Mk 6:1-6; cf. Lk 4:16-28). Matthew enlarges the scope of this account. He suppresses mention of the Sabbath, and in speaking of "their" synagogue (v. 54) as in Matthew 4:23; 9:35; 10:17; 12:9; 23:34, he indicates Judaism as a whole rather than a particular synagogue. The phrase describes at once the ideal platform for Jesus' preaching, and the place where unbelief and opposition were manifested.

It is Matthew's purpose above all to present Jesus as Master and rabbi, and so the Nazareth episode naturally becomes with him a sort of general "summary" of Christ's preaching. The following verses describe the attitude of a crowd which is no longer just that of Nazareth, but the Jewish audience in general. In spite of his wisdom and his miracles (v. 54) they only see in Jesus an ignorant man of humble origin (v. 55).

In order to understand verse 57 it is necessary to remember the general tone of the passage. "House," unlike Mark 6:4, probably does not indicate Jesus' family, but is a synonym for "country."

The Pharisees (cf. Mt 15:10-20), a social and intellectual elite, exercised their influence on the doctors of the law and their teaching, not on the people. Though he chose to become a rabbi, Jesus refused to join the doctors of the law, Pharisees for the most part, in order to remain near the *poor* and the little ones (Mt 11:25-30). He based his doctrine on the messianic hope of the people, elevating popular values like poverty, solidarity and the hope of a better world.

Nevertheless this very attitude led to a lack of understanding not only on the part of the Pharisees but also of the people. The former were scandalized by his ideology, the latter by his miracles and messianic pretensions. They expected a more mysterious Messiah.

Ties of the flesh and contiguity could prove an obstacle to recognition of Jesus' personality. His parents' poverty was a stumbling block to the faith for those who expected a marvelous Messiah (Jn 7:2-5). Jesus wanted, on the contrary, to reveal the salvific meaning of this poverty. Happiness would no longer be based on extraordinary events, signs of divine power, but would come from a God who assumed humanity totally, including its poverty.

This is the only way that does not alienate man. It is alienating to leave him in his poverty, or relieve him of it in paternalist and miraculous fashion. With Jesus poverty itself is elevated into a means of salvation and acquires its full dignity.

XVI. Leviticus 25:1, 8-17
1st reading
1st cycle
Saturday

Every seven years Jewish law prescribed a sabbatical year. This was originally based on the need to leave somewhat poor land fallow (Ex 23:10-12). Very soon it became the occasion of liberating slaves (Ex 21:2-6). Such an arrangement must have come to seem utopian, because the priestly legislation replaced it by the creation of a jubilee year, every fifty years.

The idea of the *jubilee* probably originated with the necessity, after fifty years, of adjusting the solar year to the lunar. But at the time when priestly legislation was at its height, this origin was probably forgotten. The sole idea was to reproduce the dispositions of the old sabbatical year.

Accordingly the purpose of the precept was the restoration, at the fiftieth year, of all the lands that had been bought during preceding years. Basically this transformed all purchase contracts into rentals. It was hoped thus that proprietors would never definitively lose their patrimony, and the family heritage, to which priestly legislation attached great importance, could be maintained. In the background of these socio-economic considerations however, some religious considerations begin to emerge which are of interest in the future development of the jubilee year. First, the idea that the land belongs to God. This is the basic reason why it cannot be definitively alienated. Next, the idea of "repurchase" which underlies the prescriptions of the jubilee, and which requires that family property be "repurchased" by priority by a relative (the "goel"), so as not to escheat. Finally, the idea of remission, not only of debts, but even of sins. This we find, but only faintly as yet, in the fact that the jubilee year opened on the tenth day of the seventh month, the day of Expiations. A sort of connection is established between the remission of debts and the remission of sins.

They are three very important ideas, however sketchily they appear in the text of Leviticus. Because of them the prophets will be able to save this institution from the decadence into which it would inevitably fall. They will reestablish it in the eschatological future, where such ideas can acquire their proper spiritual level. This we owe to Third-Isaiah (Is 61:1-3). No longer is the sound of the trumpet necessary to proclaim the year: the prophet's word suffices. It was in this context that the word "gospel" had its origin, as if the essential thing in the gospel was the "good news" of the Lord's "year of grace." Indeed the very first discourse delivered by Jesus will be a commentary on the text of Isaiah which proclaims the spiritual year of jubilee (Lk 4:21).

He saw his ministry as a veritable jubilee year. Time and again he demonstrates this by references to the text of Isaiah (Mt 11:2-6; Lk 1:77; Ep 1:7). He demonstrates it especially by the use of his power "to forgive sins," which scandalizes the Pharisees (Mt 9:6).

His whole ministry indeed was an uninterrupted succession of liberations, healings, remissions of debts and sins. When he returned to the Father he attached this jubilee power of remission of sins to the dominical liturgy, bequeathing it to the apostles at his first appearance by the gift of the messianic Spirit (Jn 20:22-23).

So that, apart from the Sunday, we do not have to seek in Christianity for any survival of the sabbatical and jubilee years. This is where the remission of sins takes place: this is where we live in anticipation the messianic era when freedom and ransom become realities.

XVII. Jeremiah 26:11-16, 24
1st reading
2nd cycle
Saturday

In Jeremiah 26 we have a second version, from the hand of Baruch, of the violent invective against the Jerusalem temple (Jr 7). It is more circumstantial than the first. The discourse itself is somewhat abbreviated, but the events following are given in detail. The prophet is arrested and appears before the royal council. At the very moment when he undertakes the defense summarized in today's reading, a sentence of death hangs over him.

a) The discourse in the temple is concentrated on two points. A cult which is celebrated in the midst of moral decadence is rejected (Jr 7:3-11; 26:1-5). The approaching chastisement of the holy city and its temple (Jr 7:12; 26:6) is proclaimed. His accusers fasten on the curse of the city, which they regard as a sacrilege. How can a prophet who purports to carry the Word of God contradict so unequivocally the previous oracles of Yahweh on Jerusalem, the promises of happiness and the blessings? Consequently Jeremiah's own prophetic mission is queried, and the accusers feel no obligation to consider his message.

b) Jeremiah replies with three arguments. He himself is a

prophet of God (v. 12) and his words are an expression of the divine will. Even if he is put to death, the Word he carries will endure. Yet everything can still be saved if Israel is converted (v. 13). God will *repent* of his proposed punishment. But, if he is put to death, innocent blood will be spread over the city, crying out, like that of Abel, for vengeance to heaven (vv. 14-15).

Every time their ministry is contested, the prophets, Jesus and the apostles reproduce these three arguments. They reaffirm their vocation and their fidelity to it (Jesus: Jn 18:37; Paul: Ga 1:11-23). They proclaim the destruction of the temple unless the people are converted (Jesus: Mt 26:61; Stephen Ac 7:48-51). They protest an innocence which calls to heaven for vengeance, if it is not a source of expiation (Jesus: Mt 27:25) and conversion (Stephen for Saul: Ac 8:1 and 9:5; Jesus for the centurion: Lk 23:47).

Would Jeremiah, Jesus or Stephen abandon such arguments if they returned today? Would they have the same fear as we have of displeasing authority? Would they have less confidence in the Word?

XVIII. Matthew 14:1-12
Gospel
Saturday

Matthew recounts the execution of John the Baptist in order to put an end to rumors current about the resurrection of John in the person of Jesus (v. 2; cf. Mk 6:14; 8:28). Herod himself, in his remorse, is not insensitive to them (v. 3). There is no question of resurrection: John is dead and there are witnesses who know the place of his burial (v. 12).

a) While his main intention is to dispel any confusion between John and Jesus, the evangelist gives numerous details concerning the circumstances of the Baptist's martyrdom. In lessening the responsibility of the weak Herod (v. 5) to fasten guilt on the odious Herodias (vv. 3 and 8), he strengthens the parallel between *Elias* and the Baptist (cf. Mt 17:10-12). Both confront wicked kings (Achab, Herod) and still more wicked queens (Jezebel, Herodias; cf. 1 K 21). In the Bible, disaster often falls on a dynasty where an idolatrous woman exercises too much influence. Athalia, Jezebel, Herodias and others brought many kings to disaster.

b) In his account Matthew has some details borrowed from the book of Esther. It was an oriental custom that the queen should present herself at the king's banquet in full natural beauty. Vasthi paid with her crown for her refusal to appear thus before the court (Esther 1:7-12). The young Esther had less scruples at the festival organized in her honor (Esther 2:18), in the course of which the king offered her "half his kingdom" (Esther 5:6; 7:12; 9:12). Matthew is probably thinking of such scenes when he describes Herod's banquet. Herod he represents as a king, though he was only a simple tetrarch, in order to stress the resemblance to Assuerus (v. 9). His step-daughter dances before the guests (v. 6) like Vasthi and Esther, and he makes the same promise that Assuerus did to his wife (v. 7; cf. Mk 6:23). All of this contrasts the *luxury and license* of the royal palace with the poverty and purity of the prophet (cf. Lk 7:25).

This time the new Elias is really dead and has brought with him the end of the old economy. He does not return, or even mount to heaven like his predecessor. He dies a victim to the dominance of politics over the spiritual, of blind impulse over spirit. In this he is a true precursor of Jesus, because he shares with him the role and mission of "suffering Servant." He did not cease to live in his disciples who were among the first founders of the Church; in Jesus his principal disciple, head of the Church; and in all Christians who gather in eucharistic assembly to give witness in face of the powerful of this world.

XIX. Exodus 31:12-17 *alternative reading Liturgy of the Word*

This extract from the Jewish legislation on the Sabbath is a relatively ancient text, but it was not inserted in the code until after the exile. It concerns the furniture and personnel of the sanctuary (Ex 25-31), and the purpose doubtless was to feature more strongly the liturgical aspect of Sabbath observance.

The *Sabbath repose* in its pagan beginnings was already an expression of man's anxiety to be associated with the gods' time and share its advantages. It was his way of putting himself under the shelter of the gods' intervention in nature. He would avoid any disappointment and conform as much as possible to the rhythm of the gods' life. Semitic, Summarian and Babylonian cultures all obliged their workers to observe repose certain days of the month, under penalty of divine vengeance.

At this stage the day of communion with the gods was distinguished by prohibitions of work. It was as if some of man's time had to be taken in order to be associated with divine time and its laws (cf. Ex 16:21-30, one of the most ancient traditions). Probably we owe to the Jews the institution of the weekly day that was common to everyone. But in order to make the Sabbath an official institution, or indeed a national one (cf. the theme of "sign" in verse 13), Jewish law gave it an original interpretation. It is no longer so much the day when one becomes associated with God by taking from human time, as the day when God brings to human time a little of his divine freedom. Already apparent in Exodus 23:12, this concept is above all the work of the deuteronomic school (Dt 5:12-15). The Sabbath is the day on which one communes with God's life, by a sharing of the liberty God himself granted his people by bringing them from Egypt. Observance of repose on this day is not so much a way of "doing nothing." It indicates a man's liberty *vis-a-vis* the cyclic round of nature and toil (1 Mt 2:32-41; 2 M 6:11; 15:1-3).

In the midst of a pagan world where man is crushed by nature and his toil, the Jewish day of repose began rapidly to assume the allure of a sign, the sign of Israel's privileged covenant with Yahweh (v. 13; cf. Ez 20:11-13). As allies of a holy God, ought not the people be sanctified, separate themselves, that is, from the usages of the world? This notion of being set apart, communing with God's life, will be sanctioned by the death penalty for transgression of the Sabbath (v. 14). Judaism went on to define the manner of "sanctifying" this day by an extraordinary multitude of prescriptions. Sometimes the latter destroyed the spirit, and Jesus often had to say this and act accordingly (Mk 2:23-3:5).

EIGHTEENTH WEEK

I. Numbers 11:4-15
1st reading
1st cycle
Monday

We have here an extremely old tradition about the manna (vv. 7-9) and the unexpected arrival of a flight of quail (vv. 31-32), prepared by the prayer of Moses (vv. 10-15). And in the background: a vivid impression of constant murmuring by the people (vv. 4-6).

a) Some time or other during the desert sojourn the people doubtless had benefited from unexpected nourishment. Normally they could live apparently on the produce of herds, but there may have been periods of drought or epidemic in the course of which they came on unhoped for food. In the Sinai desert great swarms of birds, exhausted by struggling against the wind, will fall to the earth. There are also trees, which in June-July, exude a gum that is perfectly edible and fairly plentiful in the morning. Thus did manna become the daily food in the desert (cf. Ex 16:1-30). It was providential, and tradition went on to stylize the episodes, insisting on the miraculous character of such food. It was genuine supernatural *nourishment,* the result of Moses' prayer, a sign of providence and of choice by God.

b) Subsequent reflection contrasted this food that came from God with earthly food (Dt 8:3-18; Ps 77/78:24-25; Wi 16:20). It stressed the *murmuring* of the crowd, who were so seized with longing for the nourishment of Egypt that they were incapable of depending on God for subsistence.

The Jewish contrast between terrestrial and supernatural nourishment was made as if both were of like nature. In fact there is no such contrast: the contrast is in the use made. Indeed it is only in the search for just distribution of terrestrial nourishment that one can come to partake of the nourishment given by God. It was in the very act of distributing bread to the hungry (Jn 6) that Jesus revealed himself as the "bread come down from heaven." If a selfish use is made of terrestrial nourishment, through the deviations of profit or interest, all reference to divine nourishment is lost. Murmuring is the opposite of faith.

II. Jeremiah 28:1-17
1st reading
2nd cycle
Monday

Here we have an episode that is frequent in the lives of Yahweh's prophets. They would often have a confrontation with hireling divines, where the genuine prophet would have the courage to predict misfortune for the people, whereas the false prophet would prophesy in terms calculated to ensure his own success.

Jeremiah gives us the criteria of the true and false prophet, but his confusion and hesitation can be discerned in the account. Is he sure he has the truth? If it is true that truth is the end of a quest that all men make, believers or not, at what point and by what criterion can the believer draw apart from his unbelieving brethren, and elicit the truth from his contact with God and God's Word?

The diatribes of the prophets, of Jesus and Paul against false prophets receive new clarification in our modern world and Church. The false prophet is he who condones the gap that separates his own word from that of God. He realizes it is there; but because of circumstances, to compromise, or for advantage, he glosses over it.

In our environment the gap can manifest itself between the truth of establishment or law, and the truth of conscience. Often conscience is suborned to the other considerations through lack of sincerity. Many a politician or ecclesiastic can persuade himself he is right in maintaining the truth of the institution. But he may be avoiding the truth of conscience, his own, or that of others.

The thing of basic importance is sincerity, that virtue, which, tardily enough, has come to assume "cardinal" status for modern man. It is not enough to be faithful and upright (these virtues regulate human conduct in the exterior domain). One must be true to oneself, with the fullest degree of lucidity.

Many men indeed have by tradition inherited the virtues of fidelity and uprightness, but often they are little concerned about sincerity. For reasons of state or Church they are ready to compromise in this domain. It is a compromise that is distasteful to the modern mind: it lays too much emphasis on society in the relation between individual and society. It is not conscious enough of the necessity for individual integrity, and thus represents an adequate view. We cannot have an ethic where the individual does not find himself, and yet society brands as disobedient those who simply seek to be true to themselves.

The individual on the other hand who wants to find his true self regards this attitude of society as comparable to that of the false prophets. One truth is suppressed for the benefit of another. The attitude is often trumpeted with such publicity and vigor that the individual has to accept it in order to be noticed, or in order to avoid trouble. A society that deals in such terms cannot pride itself on its ethical standards.

However, false prophets are not always on the side of the establishment. We find them advocating sincerity as well. We find fanatics in the cause of lucid sincerity, who think they possess the only possible truth. There are people who insist on isolation, whereas truth must be sought and found in company with others. There are those who want only to be heard, not to listen.

III. Matthew 14:13-21
Gospel
Monday

This passage is taken from the portion known as "section of breads" (Mt 14:13-16; 12; Mk 6:31—8:26; Lk 9:10-17), so-called because it is built around the two multiplication narratives. Mark and Luke introduce the section in anecdotal fashion: Matthew connects it with the death of the Baptist. But in each of the three gospels the initial verses are designed exclusively to explain why Jesus is in the desert (v. 13) confronted by a crowd who are without food (v. 15), and to set up a parallel between him and Moses. Mark develops the parallel from the theme of the flock without a shepherd, John from that of the mountain, Matthew from the flight and the "crossing" of the water. Behind all the variants, the same lesson manifests itself. Jesus puts himself forward as the *successor of Moses,* capable of nourishing the people with food and bringing them to definitive pastures. Throughout all the section of breads we have this new Moses providing a manna that is far superior to the old (Mt 14:13-21; 15:32-39), triumphing over the waters of the sea (Mt 14:22-33), liberating the people from the legalism into which the law of Moses had fallen (Mt 15:1-9), and providing access to the promised land, not only for members of the chosen people, but even for the Gentiles (Mt 15:21-31).

Moses' role as legislator is set in the context of the economy that had been founded with Abraham, and is based on faith and the promises. His law indeed is meaningless except as a realization of the spiritual pilgrimage undertaken by Abraham with the discovery of the totally-other God. It can never be reduced simply to a moral code, unrelated to the salvation events which provide its context. Essentially it is a platform for the exercise of faith. Isolated from this, it becomes inevitably involved in a process of degradation, and legalism is substituted for faith.

Jesus can claim the title of new Moses because in his personal life he restored the ideal of obedience to the law, under the regime of faith and attachment to the Father. Having demonstrated in his own flesh the fidelity required by the true covenant, he could impose his pattern on all humanity. The demands of such a fidelity did indeed, it is true, expose some limitations in the previous covenant. It was a fidelity based on a deeper, more all-embracing obedience, the sign of which was death itself.

Christ is not manifested to the world by the moral "good example" of Christians. Atheists as well as Christians can lay claim to ethical standards. The presence of the new Moses is indicated by the Christian's faith in his loyalty to the "Totally-Other." This he will demonstrate by his confrontation of the trials of daily life, of death and sin, of the great problems of war, hunger and social injustice.

For renewal in these attitudes the Eucharist is our great source. It unites us in a real fashion with the major event whereby the new Moses showed his fidelity to the mysterious design of his Father.

IV. Numbers 12:1-13
1st reading
1st cycle
Tuesday

Though of Elohist origin, this account has been reworked by a priestly hand.

There is no question of confusing Moses' extraordinary personal charism with the simple charism of prophecy. He is more than a *prophet* subject to the criticism of others. He transcends criticism.

It will be thus where Jesus, the Scribes and Pharisees are concerned. They will not speak the same language. The prophet's authority does not depend on external criteria only: it depends on the mystery of his person and his communion with God.

V. Jeremiah 30:1-2, 12-15, 18-22
1st reading
2nd cycle
Tuesday

Here we have an authentic oracle (vv. 18-21) delivered doubtless by the prophet shortly after the fall of Jerusalem (587). It was subsequently glossed (21b-22) by another redactor, who was inspired by another important passage of Jeremiah (Jr 31:33).

Jeremiah is formulating his *messianic* ideal. The "city" that will be rebuilt is no longer Jerusalem necessarily. It is not named by the prophet. Nor is the king who will lead the people necessarily a davidic figure. Jeremiah had experienced too much suffering at the hands of Jerusalem and the royal dynasty. He is too convinced of their responsibility in the catastrophes of the moment to contemplate in this context a new Sion and a new son of David. His ideal indeed seems to look back to the period prior to the kings. The leader he foretells resembles somewhat the judges raised up from among the ancient people to save them from their enemies.

Thus in Jeremiah's time we find that the royalist messianism of Isaiah is in crisis. We no longer hear of a shoot of Jesse, of a child born of a queen, of a king filled with the Spirit. The prophecy of Nathan about the perpetuity of the davidic dynasty means nothing to Jeremiah.

That is not to say that he will not contradict himself and proclaim a davidic renewal (Jr 22:4; 23:4-6, and on the contrary Jr 22:30). His present oracle troubled the subsequent redactors and they interpolated promises of restoration for Jerusalem and the davidic line. This falsifies the prophet's thought. His real concern is not with a future king, but with the future community which will no longer be limited to Jerusalem (Jeremiah is no friend of the nascent Judaism) but will include the northern tribes too (vv. 20-21). The basic covenant will no longer be that of David, but the half-forgotten one of all the desert tribes, at the time when God made them his people and became their God (v. 22).

But messianism of course is not dead. It will be revived in the apocalypses of the exile. The king will be altogether different. He will be shorn of arrogance and absolutism, and display the more authentic trait of "service" to the flock (Jr 3:15, 18; 23:4-6). Jeremiah as prophet marks the end of a particular concept of authority and the maturation of particular concepts of the people and the community.

The point of all this is not confined to ancient history. The recent crisis of authority in the Church has a good deal in common with that of the king of Judah. The old concept of the papacy as the focus of devotion for the people, the exclusive vehicle of truth, is yielding to a more modest one of something which serves the people of God. They must be assisted, enabled to express themselves, to coordinate varying mentalities and cultures, to bring all usages into authentic harmony with love and truth. For the concept of *dominium* that of *servitium* is being substituted. It is becoming more and more clear today that in this process certain attitudes sometimes have to be discarded. Just as in the case of the royal house in Judah, some actual styles to which authority had grown accustomed may be about to undergo purification in a totally unexpected fashion.

VI. Matthew 14:22-36
Gospel
Tuesday

In both Mark and Matthew this episode follows immediately the account of the multiplication of loaves. The initial two verses here (22-23) are still influenced by the content of the miracle. Realizing that the crowds continue to regard him as a conquering and vengeful Messiah, Jesus abandons them to devote himself to the training of the disciples. We might regard the storm episode as the initial lesson in this. We should note Jesus' particular solicitude where Peter is concerned (cf. Mt 16:16-21; 17:24-27).

a) God's *victory over the waters* is a highly important theme in Jewish cosmogony. Following ancient Semitic traditions the Bible presents creation as God's victory over the sea and the evil monsters it contains (Pss 103/104:5-9; 105/106:9; 73/74:13-14; 88/89:9-11; Ha 3:8-15; Is 51:9-10). The victory over the Red Sea (Ps 105/106:9) and the eschatological victory over the lake (Rev 20:9-13) are also regarded as decisive stages in salvation history.

Thus the first Christians saw in the stilling of the storm and the walking on the waters (Mt 8:23-27) a manifestation of the one who brings to fulfillment the work of creation, and a sign of the advent of the day of Yahweh (Ha 3:8-15; Is 51:9-10; cf. v. 33). The walk on water is as it were a sort of epiphany of the divine power which resides in Jesus.

b) The victory comes at a decisive moment in Jesus' life. His role as itinerant rabbi, the idol of the crowds, corresponds no longer with the salvific will of the Father (cf. the prayer of v. 23). He decides to give himself wholly to the intensive training of the apostles, and of Peter in particular. He will reveal his messianic power to them and win their confidence. His walking on the waters has this double intent. He convinces Peter that he really has in him the power to conquer evil (symbolized by the water on which Peter walks, 28-29). And he makes him realize that this is not a magic faculty but one that is based on his fidelity (vv. 30-31). Thus power over the forces of evil is offered to the apostolic group in proportion to their attachment and loyalty to the person of Christ.

When we make the affirmation that Christ has conquered the domain of evil, we are recognizing the cosmic dimensions of his work. Prior to him all creation was involved in the solidarity of sin; but he burst this yoke.

The Christian's victory is not only a victory over himself: it too has a cosmic dimension. He really does conquer the world and control its elements, as Christ and Peter dominated the sea. His mission is to come to grips with evil wherever it still manifests itself, especially in death, its greatest minion. For this he is strengthened by the Eucharist, because it enables him to share Christ's victory over Satan and death.

VII. Numbers 13:1-2, 25-14:1, 26-29, 34-35
1st reading
1st cycle
Wednesday

At the time of the definitive redaction of the book of Numbers (after the exile), the ancient Yahwist and Elohist traditions about the desert sojourn had already been assembled in the book of Exodus. Some of them however had been discarded or forgotten. It is to the credit of the Numbers author that he included some of these latter (Nb 10:29—12:15; 13:7-14; 25, etc.) in his book.

Their collection however, in his case, is inspired by one purpose only, to allay disquiet among his contemporaries who were discouraged by Israel's state of dispersal among the nations, and by the continued evidence of sin among the people. He wants to discern God's omnipotence at work in history in spite of the obstacles placed by man, and disseminates the hope of a new Moses.

The *rebellion* of the "bad heads" where manna is concerned is somewhat similar to that in the case of the quails (Nb 11:31-34). Two theological arguments are sufficient to deal with this revolt (and also the murmurings of the author's contemporaries). First, history never goes back upon itself. Wishing to return to Egypt and dreaming of a revival of the past is an attitude contrary to the true spirit of revolution (Nb 14:4-5). Second, fear of a hypothetical enemy or of future obstacles shows a lack of confidence in God (vv. 8-9; cf. Jg 16:20; Is 30:2).

The account in Numbers of the desert revolt gives us the priestly author's interpretation of the events many centuries after their occurrence. In the clerical, theocratic society to which he belonged, no other view would be possible. It would be very wrong however to apply the same principles to all human revolutions. Christians indeed have often been mistaken because they had no other criteria to apply. They have often taken revolutions as mere material revolts after the pattern of that in the desert, where folk grew weary of austerity. Their reaction was the restoration of established power in the name of God (cf. Nb 14:4).

In fact, of course, revolution is often the occasion on which new values are brought forward. The value of community is emphasized, whereby people are liberated from the control of a single individual or slavery to the machine. The masses are led toward some standard of human dignity. These great objectives must not be lost sight of because of the abuses and extremes that characterize most revolutions. Wherever the cause of humanity is advanced we have the presence of Christ: the sign of salvation for which the Christian stands has a place.

Christians, distressed by revolutions which they cannot always properly evaluate, tend to stand apart from them, if they do not actually oppose them. The result is that no "sign" of salvation is manifested, and human progress seems divorced from a Christian dimension.

VIII. Jeremiah 31:1-7
1st reading
2nd cycle
Wednesday

The two chapters, 30 and 31, of Jeremiah are set in dramatic form. In today's brief extract we can clearly discern the genre, particularly by omitting verse 1, which is probably late. The people speak first (vv. 2-3), recalling the desert covenant and the love then shown by Yahweh. Yahweh replies (vv. 4-6) by proclaiming that the former love will be renewed. To prove his generosity he will restore Israel. Finally the choir hymns the new *alliance* to come (v. 7).

IX. Matthew 15:21-28
Gospel
Wednesday

The "section of breads" continues. Though Jesus has given bread to all who wished it (Mt 14:13-21), twelve baskets of crumbs and fragments are collected. The remainder of the section is devoted to an explanation of why so much remains. Two reasons are given. First, the Pharisees, by their rules about ablutions, place too many obstacles in the way of those who wish to eat bread (Mt 15:1-20). Second, the Gentiles seem to be denied access to the fragments (v. 24). Today's passage is concerned with the second topic.

The account of the miracle at Tyre is proper to Matthew (15: 21-28) and Mark (7:24-30). The differences between the two versions indicate the different approaches. Matthew has the Syro-Phoenician woman come into Jewish territory to be heard (Mt 15:22, as Naaman the Syrian). According to Mark Jesus, the itinerant rabbi, goes as far as Gentile territory to proclaim salvation (Mk 8:24; cf. Mk 5:1 and 6:53). He avoids reproducing the extremely harsh phrase which Matthew places on Jesus' lips (v. 24). Nor does he, like Matthew (v. 22), have this Gentile woman confess the Messiahship of the Son of David. Both evangelists however have the exchange about the crumbs of bread, because they see here a possible allusion to the fragments after the multiplication.

Their common purpose is evident. The Gentiles too will share the bread of salvation, because they in their turn will experience the Lord's pity (cf. Mt 14:20; 15:32). One day the table of the disciples will be open to them.

By being no accepter of persons, whether Jews or Gentiles, men or women, children or adults, poor or rich, Jesus is following a most explicit tendency of the Jewish law itself, and establishing the very nature of Christian worship. In so far as all men eat at the same eucharistic table, they bear witness to Christ's sacrifice "for the many," and they hasten the moment when human beings will be gathered together in the glorious Body of Christ.

X. Numbers 20:1-13
1st reading
1st cycle
Thursday

In this passage we have an ancient tradition, the primitive content however of which is not well preserved. The final redaction is priestly and thus postexilic. But there were other traditions, sometimes Elohist sometimes Yahwist, which recounted an identical incident in somewhat obscure language. They place it at a different site in the desert (Ex 17).

Moses doubtless displayed some powers as a sorcerer at a time when the people were in particular need of water. The incident was not preserved for its own sake, all traditions being concerned to draw the doctrinal moral.

a) The people are thirsty and *murmur*, calling in question the presence of God at their side and displaying disbelief in their interpretation of events. True, they do not directly address their recriminations to God: Moses (and Aaron, according to the priestly version) have to meet the challenge. In the New Testament this murmuring is made characteristic of the attitude of those who rejected Christ (1 Co 10:1-10; Jn 6:41, 61). They cling to their own judgment when everything suggests they should take a new stand.

b) There is little point in trying to determine the exact nature of their experience, but as a result of it the Israelites constructed a whole mystique about the *rock of living water*. They had frequently the experience during the desert sojourn (Ex 17; Nb 20), and indeed in Jerusalem itself which was watered by a single fountain (2 K 20:20; Is 7:3), of what a blessing the discovery of a spring could be. The theme of living water is one of the most powerful in suggesting God's presence with his people. When God dwells with his own a stream of water refreshes Sion (Ps 45/46:5), all the rocks are changed into springs (Is 30:25; 35:4-7; 41:15-18), and innumerable waters gush from the temple (Ez 47; Ze 13:1). There was even a festival of water in the liturgical calendar during the feast of Tabernacles, and it is even possible that verse 8 alludes to one or other detail of this ceremony.

According to the tradition a rock of living water accompanied the people throughout its long history (1 Co 10:4). In fact Christ distributes this living water, the gift of his own life (1 Co 10:1-11; Jn 7:37-38). He is able to provide water charged with the vitality of the Spirit (Jn 1:31-34; 4), and describes eternal life as a diffusion of living water throughout the universe (Rev 22:17; Jn 7:37-39; Rev 22:1-2, 17; 7:15-17).

Water symbolism had a prominent place in the life of the chosen people, as it had for Jesus himself. People today are not so sympathetic towards such symbolism. The association of God's presence with water seems indeed to belong to another age, or to be an overly poetic concept.

At a time when man believed himself inferior to nature, it was normal that he should see Yahweh on the side of the more powerful element. Nature was a main source for religious symbolism: water because of its purity and necessity for fruitfulness proved an obvious choice.

Now however men do not see the universe as an image of God. Creation as such does not immediately evoke the idea of God as architect. Rather do we tend to see the world built by human toil as the image of God, a suggestion of the transcendent.

We could indeed retain water as a divine symbol, but in a radically different context. There are the projects for converting water power into energy for desalting sea water, for irrigating arid deserts, for controlling rainfall. All these attempts to build a better world, more humane, more spiritual, can turn the mind to God.

XI. Jeremiah 31:31-34
1st reading
2nd cycle
Thursday

If this passage is from the hand of Jeremiah, it is the crowning point of his reflection. Nowhere else in the Old Testament do we have so rich a text. It is extensively used by Jesus, Paul and the author of the letter to the Hebrews, either to clarify the essence of the Eucharist, or the position of Christianity *vis-a-vis* traditional Israel.

Under the old covenant, ratified on Sinai (v. 32), the law was something essentially exterior to man. The deuteronomic reform had already discerned the need for an *interior law* (Dt 6:6, 11, 18; 30:14), but such interiorization was the fruit of human effort, a gradual assimilation of the external law. The Jeremiah text goes much further, indicating that the internal law is a gift of God. There is nothing to suggest that he wants to abolish all external law: his close association with the deuteronomic reform suggests indeed the contrary. But he does stress the need for a moral attitude that is not exclusively based on an external law or on human effort. Its source should be the communion of the deepest self with God.

How did Jeremiah arrive at such a concept of God's law written in the heart? For him God is an examiner of the heart and the loins in the sense that he is present in our very thoughts (heart) and our instincts (loins) (Jr 11:20; 12:3; 17:10; 20:12). In any case it is only after examination of the heart and the loins that he admits men to his presence.

The reward of this presence of God in men's hearts will be a softening of their hardness of heart (Jr 3:17; 7:24; 9:13; 11:8; 12:12, 23, 17) and a close union between Yahweh and his people (v. 33). The latter is depicted by Jeremiah in the conjugal image "They shall be my people and I will be their God" (Jr 7:23; 11:4; 24:7, 30:22; 31:1; 32:28).

The covenant was the last area in which the Old Testament could bring itself to be contemplate renewal. A new Jerusalem, a new temple, a new king . . . were readily enough envisaged, but the covenant seemed so definitive that there was no thought of change. The new Testament will often refer to a new convenant. This was what Jesus had brought (1 Co 11:25) when he celebrated the Supper (cf. also 2 Co 3:1-2; Gal 4:21; He 8:6-10). However it does not seem that the term was used in condemnation of the old covenant. It was one and the same act of divine mercy that was envisaged. The new covenant bestowed what the old one had promised.

XII. Matthew 16:13-23
Gospel
Thursday

The account which exegetes agree in describing as the "confession of Caesarea" is a fairly homogeneous passage in all the symoptics. It comprises Peter's confession of messianic faith, the first announcement of the passion, a moral application (the apostles too must carry their cross) and, finally the account of the transfiguration. It seems reasonably probable that the whole belongs to the primitive catechesis (Mt 16:13-17:9; Mk 8:27-9:10; Lk 9:18-36), even though it seems clear that the different episodes brought together took place independently of one another. There are many indications that Matthew's version is the best, but the redaction appears to be the work of the primitive community which places a post-paschal mission before the resurrection.

We have a structure somewhat as follows:

v. 13 Christ's address	v. 21 Christ's address
v. 16 intervention of Peter	v. 22 intervention of Peter
v. 17 thoughts of God not of men	v. 23 thoughts of men not of God
v. 18 you are the rock of the Church	v. 23 you are a rock of scandal

a) Thus the whole account is built around the double *exchange of titles* between Jesus and Peter. Peter gives Jesus the title of Messiah and Jesus responds by giving him the name Peter, and conferring on him the messianic power of the keys. Peter refuses to give Jesus the title of suffering Servant, and Jesus replies by calling him the rock of scandal.

b) The title given to Jesus is essentially *messianic:* "you are the Christ." But Peter strengthens it by adding "The Son of the living God." The phrase does not seem to be an affirmation of divinity strictly speaking. It is often employed in the Old Testament to designate the angels (Gn 6:1-4; Jb 1:6), judges (Ps 81/82:6-7) and the king (2 S 7:14; Ps 88/89:27-28). It is then merely a doublet of the title Christ, an affirmation of the divine origin of his Messiahship. Messiahship indicates such a man as will never be again, one capable of giving meaning to life and bringing it to fulfillment.

c) Scarcely has his Messiahship been recognized when Jesus, at least in Matthew's version, hastens to share it with Simon. First of all he gives him the title *Peter* (v. 18) which will henceforward be his personal name. He is transmitting the prerogatives of invulnerability and firmness associated with David, Sion and the Messiah (theme of the gates of hell: v. 10; cf. Is 28:16).

Then he gives the power of the keys (v. 19). Here there is a whole hinterland of biblical imagery. The Messiah has the keys to David's dwelling (Is 22:22): he is the major-domo of the Father's house (Mt 16:19), and entrusts this function to Peter.

Finally Peter receives the power of binding and loosing, to be exercised in collegiality with the others (Mt 16:18; cf. Jn 20:22-23). The force of the expression, which combines two contraries, is to indicate fullness of power. The apostle is a veritable plenipotentiary.

By a single act Christ confided his Church to the college of apostles and to one among them, Peter. The basic reason for the apostolic college was the necessity for fraternal accord in setting up the Church as the Body of Christ; and the basic reason for Peter's office was in order that the college should incorporate within itself its living norm. Saint Irenaeus described Peter as the one "presiding over charity."

Papal primacy is necessary for the exercise of collegiality because it is the norm of apostolic brotherhood for the building in charity of the Church. It is a service rather than a power.

XIII. Deuteronomy 4:32-34, 38-40
1st reading
1st cycle
Friday

The verses here, with some others not included in the reading, constitute the conclusion to a series of exhortations addressed to believers. Between the introduction (v. 32) and the conclusion (v. 40) we have two strophes which culminate in the same refrain (vv. 33-35 and 36-39).

a) The piece is really a commentary on the first commandment of the decalogue. Israel is to be *monotheist.* How could it be otherwise in view of all the indications Yahweh has given of his choice of her.

b) Thus it is through reflection on *salvation history* that the author's faith in the one God is established. This history culminates in three decisive events, which throughout Deuteronomy are the promise to the patriarchs (v. 32; cf. Dt 1:10; 26:5), the flight from Egypt (vv. 32-37; cf. Dt 4:20; 5:6; 7:8; 9:26) and finally the entry to Canaan and the promulgation of the law (v. 31 [covenant]; cf. Dt 4:21; 12:9). Two important texts (6:21-23; and 26:5-10) put forward these three stages as the most decisive ones; and from this point of view the book is one of the most important for the elaboration of the doctrine of salvation history. The concept however has its limitations. The author does not envisage any fulfillment of the promises other than peaceful establishment in Canaan. His horizon is limited, deliberately so, in that he recounts only the promises concerning Canaan, and is silent about those which give a universalist dimension to the progeny of Abraham ("all the nations will bless you").

Deuteronomy is the first book to feature salavation-history by emphasis on three events of history. God came near to Israel by engaging himself in a promise to the patriarchs, by seeking out the people exiled in Egypt and leading them to the Promised Land. Why should not the same unique God who caused these three events be the author of events that trouble us now? He is the one God and his love is everlasting. His word is not conjugated in the past tense. It is for today and tomorrow as well. And the human response it requires is required now as well as then.

XIV. Nahum 2:1, 3; 3:1-3, 6-7
1st reading 2nd cycle Friday

The emperor Assurbanipal died in 625, leaving an empire too vast to be governed and too complex for the preservation of unity. The Medish king took advantage of the accession to the throne of the colorless Nabopalasar to invade the empire and threaten Nineveh directly. Numerous small nations which had been previously crushed by her secretly hoped for her downfall. The collection of texts grouped under the name of Nahum date from this period, and convey the hopes of the weak.

In today's reading we have an oracle of blessing addressed to Judah (2:1-3) and one of malediction on Nineveh (3:1-7). The prophet is proposing a reading of events which stresses the unicity of God. Because he is unique, an event which is accomplished at Nineveh has repercussions at Jerusalem, and a people which just now was plunged in misfortune recovers the happiness promised to their ancestors. Truly Yahweh is the master of all *history*.

God directs history, but with regard for human liberty. Men are not puppets manipulated by a despot. In the midst of their engagements, their failures and their dreams of grandeur, their projects and their oppositions, a sometimes tortuous road is being traveled. They are enabled to live these events in communion with God, if they are open, and welcome all things as the gift of his love.

XV. Matthew 16:24-28 *Gospel Friday*

This passage follows the announcement of the Passion, and gives the necessary conditions for following Jesus on the new road he has taken. It is an important turning in Jesus' teaching and the training of his disciples. This is evident in Matthew's suggestion of a new beginning: "he began to show" (v. 21). The teaching is new. Doubtless it is in order to bring about the necesary attention and understanding that Jesus has just reproached them for their lack of faith (Mt 16:5-12).

a) He is not content with pointing out the eschatological necessity of his own sufferings. He prepares his disciples too to accept a life of trial in the same spirit. To inculcate this lesson, Matthew has assembled a rather artificial anthology of Jesus' sayings.

The phrases "renounce," "take up the cross" and "follow Christ" are really synonymous. Each in its fashion describes the essential note of *Christian life*. If Jesus must himself expect the punishment of the cross for his nonconformist ideas, he is warning his disciples that they can expect no better fate if they remain faithful to his teaching. All personal security must be renounced. The counsels of the master (the rabbinic sense of the phrase "follow") must be accepted not alone in theory but in practice ("carrying the cross" v. 24).

Saving one's life in this context means abandoning the group around Christ, which has become dangerously revolutionary, to seek security. Losing one's life means risking it by remaining with the group (v. 25). It is only in complete solidarity with the person of Christ ("for my sake") that this risk can be encountered.

This solidarity, manifested throughout terrestrial life, entails active participation in his resurrection and eschatological kingdom (theme of "life" contrasted with that of the "world" in v. 26). So is accomplished for every Christian the paschal mystery. Christ's death and resurrection become the lot in turn of all disciples who carry their cross in order to live with him in glory.

b) By introducing the theme of the *Son of Man* Matthew describes this glory for which Christ and the disciples (vv. 27-28) are destined. In the prediction strictly speaking of the passion he had not alluded to this theme, unlike the other synoptics and Matthew 17:22; 20:18. Now, at the end of the passage, he takes it up very appositely. It is not only the theme of the suffering Servant that inspires the prediction of the passion: it is rooted also in the profound eschatology of the Son of Man.

The Son of Man of Daniel 7 had often been interpreted as a

symbol for the Remnant of the elect, the seed of the new humanity, The title was subsequently individualized until it came finally to designate Christ (Mt 17:22; 20:18, etc.). One wonders whether Matthew's particular placing of the allusion, not in the context of Jesus' personal sufferings, but at the end of his description of the common sufferings of Jesus and the disciples, does not still argue a collective concept of the Son of Man. He would be a symbol of the new humanity who had escaped death and judgment to constitute the eschatological kingdom. Whatever about the possibility of such an interpretation, it is essential to insist that, for Matthew, the Son of Man is also personalized and individual. It is only through association with Christ that man can be eventually included in the phrase, or share in the kingdom.

XVI. Deuteronomy 6:4-13
1st reading
1st cycle
Saturday

It is somewhat surprising to find the most explicit passages about God's love in a body of legislative texts. They are nevertheless relatively numerous. We find them incorporated in the very text of the code (Dt 13:4; 19:9), in the introductory discourse (Dt 5:10; 6:5; 7:9; 10:12; 11:1, 13, 22), or again in the final exhortation (Dt 30:16, 20). Verses 4-5 here may belong to the most primitive redaction of Deuteronomy; verses 6-9 belong to a second stage.

a) The concept of the *love of God* inculcated in Deuteronomy is above all one of cultic fidelity. It consists first of all in not rendering any worship to other divinities (v. 5: cf. 6:14-15; 11:13 and 16-17; 13:2-3; 30:16-18). Quite often the relations between the people and their God are described in terms of love (cf. Ho 1-4). So too the deuteronomic law concerning love of God is a precept of cultic fidelity to Yahweh.

But love of God is seen too in obedience to divine precepts. We should notice that today's passage is a code of moral precepts, the most basic code in all Hebrew ethics. Furthermore, by requiring that love of God be more than an external attitude (with all the heart, all the soul . . . v. 5; cf. Dt 10:12; 11:13; 13:3), Deuteronomy is contemplating a total, personal love unknown to previous legislation. Finally, the personal intensity is strengthened by the use of the second person singular (v. 5; cf. Dt 10:12; 30:6). Thus the love of God under consideration would be the "love" contemplated in the contracts of alliance between suzerain and vassal that were common at the time in the Near East. It implied fidelity, loyalty and obedience. The love of God does not yet seem to have been seen as a love of affection. It is still too close to juridical and cultic sources to convey what will be conveyed in the New Testament, or for that matter even in Hosea and Jeremiah.

b) The main interest of our passage is that it constitutes the *Schema Israel* (Hear, Oh Israel) recited three times a day by the faithful, particularly in the morning. The prayer expresses the essential attitudes of Jewish faith: affirmation of one God (v. 4), the summation of all the law in love (v. 5), and finally the commemoration of the covenant (vv. 10-12). It could very well serve as a common formula for Christians and Jews just as the *Our Father* does for Catholics, Protestants and Orthodox.

We might wonder how something so spontaneous as love could become the object of a legal precept. The answer that the content of the love in question consisted of cultic and moral regulations that fitted a legalist context is perhaps too facile. We must remember that the Hebrew notion of divine transcendence precluded an affectionate love for God. It would require a precept to force the pious Jew to take a step in this direction. The Law in any case was so much the normal context of relations between Jewish man and God, that the notion of love was easily absorbed into it.

XVII. Habakkuk 1:12-2:4
1st reading
2nd cycle
Saturday

The book of Habakkuk constitutes the formulary for one of the last great liturgical ceremonies in the old temple before the fall of Jerusalem (586). Habakkuk exercises the function of official prophet. The Chaldeans were threatening the city even as the King Jehoaquim was tyrannizing over Judah (the "wicked one" of Ha 2:6). Thus the people gather in the temple and request the prophet to address their complaint to Yahweh (Ha 1:2-4). God answers with an oracle (Ha 1:5-10) which seems too general to the people. They direct the prophet to address a second complaint (vv. 1, 12-17) which is answered by a second oracle, inscribed on a tablet by the prophet. It was a tradition, in temples of the period, to inscribe divine oracles thus (vv. 2, 1-5).

The text continues with five prophetic imprecations (Ha 2:6-20), then the chanting of a psalm where the people express their hope for an early intervention by God to free them from the tyrant.

a) The second complaint is constructed according to a classic formula. We have the initial invocation (in this instance charged with epithets) and the questioning about the meaning of the misfortunes that have come. Next comes the contrast between the just (the people?) and the impious (the king?) that is characteristic of the literary genre of complaint (v. 12; cf. Pss 21/22:15-16; 30/31:10-11; 37/38:11-12; Jr 20:10-11, etc.).

We notice the anxiety in the complaint to adhere to ready-made formulas. There is no originality or inspiration. He is a professional, cult prophet, and his thought is confined to the established style of his ministry. He does show considerable daring however in assembling the community in the temple to indict the reigning monarch before God himself. He even gives the title of "just" to the oppressed people (v. 13), and, like his contemporary Jeremiah, raises the problem of the suffering just one, a prelude to the *suffering Servant* theme.

b) The liturgy, which has been inaugurated by the two complaints of the people (Ha 1:1-17) reaches its culminating point in the oracle given by God in response (vv. 2:1-4). The prophet doubtless remained all night on the watch (v. 1) awaiting this reply. When God does manifest himself, Habakkuk understands that the oracle will only be fulfilled after a certain delay. Thus he arranges to have it conserved until its fulfillment (vv. 2-3). God's willingness to have his word engraved and made permanent is a sign of his fidelity. The oracle will surely be fulfilled.

It is extremely brief. The impious one (the king) will fall and the just (the people) remaining *faithful* to God, will be saved (v. 4). The text, with its atmosphere of mystery, the anonymity of the persons and its brevity, follows the established style of oracles.

Thus the whole liturgy, which begins with the complaints, is concluded with the certainty of God's proximate advent. The Chaldeans are not far from Jerusalem and will put an end to the despot's reign. As for the people, they must bend their back a little longer under the royal tyranny, the denial of justice the acts of violence, and the disastrous diplomacy. They must remain unswervingly faithful to God (cf. Rm 1:17; Ga 3:11; He 10:38). It is this fidelity which will save them in the approaching chaos.

XVIII. Matthew 17:14-20
Gospel
Saturday

The episode of the lunatic boy is in two parts: the account of the cure (vv. 14-18), and the exchange concerning the power of expelling demons (vv. 19-20). Verse 20b seems to belong to a different context (cf. Mt 21:21); and deliberately generalizes for all the disciples what has been said to the apostles alone.

The dialogue in the episode is quite artificial and the vocabulary inconsistent. In one portion we have mention of a sick person, in the other of a possessed man. The disciples play no real role except in the dialogue and the demon is spoken of only at his departure. Luke ignores the dialogue.

a) It seems possible that the account was originally confined to the narration, with the apostrophe of verses 17-18 designed to throw Jesus (and him only) into prominence as *thaumaturge.* As such it would have the effect of a liturgical proclamation.

b) Doubtless Matthew added to this a discussion concerning the faith necessary for the apostles to expel Satan, which took place on another occasion. Here he displays his catechetical bias. The faith in question is not the faith whereby a man adheres to the mission of Christ (Mt 18:6), nor yet the faith required by Jesus from those who benefit from his miracles (Mt 8:10; 9:2, 22, 28; 15:28; 21:21-22), but precisely that faith in a mission that has been given to his apostles by Jesus. These doubt their own power, and refuse to depend on the one who gave them their mission (cf. Mt 14:31). Where Mark will emphasize in the account Christ's victory over Satan, and Luke the idea of mercy, Matthew makes it rather a stage in the doctrinal preparation which Jesus imposes on his disciples.

It seems likely that Matthew gave this interpretation to the episode at a time when the primitive Christians were somewhat taken aback to find that the apostles did not have thaumaturgic powers comparable to those of Christ. He does not hesitate to reproach the apostles for lack of confidence in the powers entrusted to them. His message continues to have point. The Christian doubts the efficacy of the gospel message and waters it down. He loses faith in a humanity spiritualized by Christ. The hierarchy loses faith in the Spirit who animates all things. They are afraid of adventure and reject renewal and progress. They seek security in apparently powerful institutions, stopping short of loss of faith in the power of the Lord himself. It is undeniable that the world and the Church are confronting a crisis which shakes the foundations. But has not the Spirit been given to both so that they can witness the collapse of false gods and useless institutions? They must build something new, where the Lord's presence will be more evident than it was in outmoded structures which they try in vain to preserve. The faith that is capable of expelling demons and moving mountains is faith in a new Church in a new world arisen from the ruins that surround us now.

NINETEENTH WEEK

I. Deuteronomy 10:12-22
1st reading
1st cycle
Monday

This discourse comes at the very point where God is authorizing the conquest of the Promised Land (Dt 10-11). It is in four paragraphs centered on verse 16. Verses 12-13 and 20-22 are parallel and correspond to one another, as do verses 14-15 and 17-19.

a) The greater portion of the discourse is devoted to recalling the benefactions of Yahweh and the concrete signs of his *choice.* The election has been a gesture of love towards ancestors, that has been renewed for the new generation (v. 15; cf. Dt 7:8). Not only did God love the patriarchs: the love is ongoing, and the actual situation of the people is his concern. His love is not destroyed by pettiness (v. 22) or sin.

b) But Yahweh's election of the people, the revelation of his love, requires that the people reciprocate with *love* (v. 12) and attachment (v. 20) to him. This exchange, which constitutes the covenant, spurs the people to love the poor and strangers with the very love God is showing them (vv. 18-19). Such a concept is all the more extraordinary when we remember that the people are always engaged in conquest of a territory held by "strangers." Deuteronomy indeed contemplates many exceptions to this love for the other. Amalee can be completely exterminated (Dt 25:17-19). The tribes of Canaan will likewise perish or at least be ignored (Dt 20:17-18; 7:1-5). The nations living outside Canaan will however be respected (Dt 20:12-14).

c) The people's love for God is manifested above all in *circumcision of the heart* (v. 16). This phrase, of prophetic origin, is a reminder that membership of the chosen people is not merely an exterior mark. It depends on the personal knowledge that a man acquires of God's will and the love wherewith it is accomplished.

II. Ezechiel 1:2-5, 24-28
1st reading
2nd cycle
Monday

Probably compiled after the prophet's death, the first chapters of Ezechiel stress his prophetic vocation, and conjoin two different collections containing his major oracles. Verses 1:4-28 belong to the second collection (theme of the chariot), verses 1:1-3 and 2:1 to the first (theme of the book).

Thus the chariot theophany was not originally associated with the account of Ezechiel's vocation. It should be interpreted apart as a symbol of Yahweh's *mobility*. He is not bound to the temple or the Promised Land and can remove himself to Babylon if he sees fit (cf. Ez 10 and 43) where the departure and return of Yahweh are contemplated. Here we have a lesson of encouragement: for love of his people God will renounce his attributes of immutability.

The God of revelation is not the changeless God of the philosophers. The God that Israel experienced is a God of mobility. The God of power and glory as defined by their forebears was discerned by the apostles in the poor and humble figure of Jesus Christ. The God who was seen in terms of eternity is manifested even in death. He who associated with absolute freedom lives in his son at the very limits of alienation.

III. Matthew 17:22-27
Gospel
Monday

The first portion of this passage gives us Jesus' second prophecy concerning his paschal mystery. It was discussed in treating of Matthew 16:24-28, p. 253. Here we shall confine ourselves to the second portion, where Jesus takes a position in regard to taxes.

This rather strange tradition is preserved by Matthew only. It seems to be quite primitive—notice the curious miracle which follows (v. 27). However it could have been reworked by the primitive communities. They were doubtless tried by the obligation of paying the imperial tax (cf. Mt 22:15-22; Rm 13:6-7) or by the obligation, still accepted in the Judaeo-Christian communities, of the temple tax.

a) The *temple tax* was obligatory, and was at the time of the Roman occupation a sign of religious fidelity (cf. Ex 30:11; Ne 10:32). It was collected by the Levites, as distinct from the imperial tax, which was gathered by publicans (v. 25). It amounted to a didrachma only, whereas the imperial tax was extremely heavy.

Probably the Judaeo-Christian communities remained subject to the temple tax, as their devotion to the temple continued to be considerable. However, as they began to be detached from Jewish institutional cult, the question of the tax presented itself. It caused a division between the partisans of fidelity and those of emancipation. The personal attitude of Jesus was invoked. He was above all anxious not to give scandal (v. 27), and this pointed towards a compromise between Jewish and Gentile Christians. The former were reminded that Jesus had dealt with the problem somewhat humorously: the latter, that there were emancipations more important than that from taxes: ransom from satanic alienation (symbolized by the fish taken from the "inferior waters," hell that is).

b) Possibly there are evidences of another interpretation too, designed to clarify the relations between Christians and the civil *State* in this regard. The tax was a sign of alienation because it was paid by strangers only (v. 25). Christians however were free, and "sons" (v. 26), because they had been ransomed by Christ. They must nevertheless make good use of that liberty, being careful not to scandalize others by challenging frontally the society by which they profited. The fundamental liberty they had acquired in Jesus Christ they must use to forward the good functioning of the State.

IV. Deuteronomy 31:1-8
1st reading
1st cycle
Tuesday

In this passage we have combined a very old tradition (vv. 1-3a), and a text that was added at the time of the definitive redaction of Deuteronomy (vv. 3b-8).

One leader goes and is replaced by another. God lets Moses know that it is time to transmit the investiture to Joshua. This intervention by God for the dismissal and investiture of *leaders of the people* is noteworthy. God, who is invisible, does not directly associate himself with such decisions. The author, by representing the intervention as explicit, simply indicates his keen sense of God's will and presence in the exercise of human authority.

Joshua's authority will be of the profane order. He will conquer a territory, provide encouragement and successful leadership for the people. The author tells us that God is with him, though no specifically religious mission is entrusted to him.

In order that his authority have a divine dimension, the political leader has no need of religious responsibility, still less of liturgical sacralization. He organizes the community in such fashion that they can achieve their destiny and spiritual ideals, something that is very much the province of God. Nor is it even necessary that he provide and maintain the right of each to follow the religion of his choice. We journey towards God not only by the exercise of religion but also by life in society. When the leader provides the optimum conditions for this life in society, his function has divine meaning.

V. Ezechiel 2:8, 3:4
1st reading
2nd cycle
Tuesday

The vision of the book belongs to the first collection of Ezechiel's prophecies, and recounts the choice of the prophet.

a) Like that of the other great prophets, the *call* of Ezechiel takes place by symbolic action. The point is invariably to show how God's word is found on the lips of a man.

An angel purifies the lips of Isaiah by fire (Is 6:5-7). God himself puts his speech in the mouth of Jeremiah (Jr 1:9). Ezechiel however lives at a time when writing has become part of civilization. What he receives from God is no longer a word but a book. He is in this respect the forebear of the Scribes and rabbis.

b) Where Jeremiah and Isaiah receive the Word of God passively, he eats, digests and assimilates the divine will. This will only be manifested in his own particular vision of reality. The word of God is only found in association with the word of man. It is an excellent introduction to the doctrine of *inspiration*.

There is a great risk run by God in deciding to associate his word inevitably with that of man. In Jesus Christ he had absolute success. So much in communion was he with the plan of the Father that his word, and his whole being, could only be the word and manifestation of God. In this respect Christ forms the center of Scripture, and he is that center in his capacity as total man, totally saturated with the thought of God. Just like the prophets, only in greater measure, he had to exercise all his human faculties, develop them to the fullest according to their nature.

When we study Scripture, it is important that we understand how these faculties function, the literary genre that is chosen for expression, the environment and traditions by which they are influenced. God's word is shorn of omnipotence. In humility human language is chosen for the revelation of what is to be revealed.

God does not choose some super-language: he becomes part and parcel of human language and communication.

VI. Matthew 18:1-5, 10, 12-14
Gospel
Tuesday

This is the introduction to what is called the "community discourse" (Mt 18:2-35). The original format is not preserved in any of the three synoptics. Nevertheless the primitive discourse can be reconstructed with fair certainty, like the primitive sources generally of the synoptics, by means of the key-words.

Preamble:
(a) circumstances of the discourse;
(b) insertion of the first key-word, *raba* (the greatest).

First article:
(a) development on "the greatest" (*raba*);
(b) mention of the second key-word: the *raba* should be *talya* (servant).

Second article:
(a) development on the *talya*;
(b) mention of the third key-word: the *talya* should be received "in the name of Christ" (*bashma*).

Third article:
(a) development on the *bashma*;
(b) mention of the fourth key-word: the little one (*qatina*) must be received in the name of Christ.

Fourth article:
(a) development on *qatina* (little one);
(b) mention of the fifth key-word: one must not scandalize (*macsheka*) any *qatina*.

Fifth article:
(a) development on scandal (*macsheka*);
(b) it is better to cut off a member which is the cause of scandal than to be thrown in the fire (*noura*).

Sixth article:
(a) development on fire (*noura*);
(b) mention of the seventh key-word: everyone must be treated by fire and salt (*melba*).
Seventh article:
(a) development on salt (*melba*);
(b) conclusion.
There follows the parable of "mercy" (vv. 11-14) which sets the tone for all Jesus' prescriptions for the leaders of the different communities.

a) In the hands of Matthew the discourse takes on a new emphasis.

1) The question of the "greatest in the kingdom" is often taken up in the gospels and we find it in Matthew too (Mt 11:11; 19:13-15; 20:26-27; 23:11-12; Lk 22:24-27).

2) However he omits three connecting phrases of the primitive discourse (Mk 9:35a; Lk 9:48d), because later on he is to return to the topic of the child.

3) Mention of the second key-word (*talya*) does not occur again in Matthew 18 (though we have it in Mt 23:11). This is to be expected because he gives us the example of the child in answer to the question about "the greatest." The passage to the theme of the *child* is easy in view of the double meaning of *talya* in primitive aramaic: *child* that is and *servant.*

4) The article with the child theme is found in the three synoptics (Mt 18:2-39); but Matthew adds elements from another context.

Verse 2 is taken from the episode of the blessing of the children (Mk 10:15). To enter the kingdom one must be despised as a child is despised.

Verse 4 gives us Christ's answer to the question "who is the greatest in the Kingdom?" Matthew had omitted it earlier but he now returns to it with specific emphasis on the child theme, using for this purpose a logion common in the gospel (Lk 14:11; 18:14; Mt 23:12).

5) The *talya* must be received "in the name of Christ" (Mt 18:5). Here Matthew gives us the first portion only of the complete text (see Mk 9:37 or Lk 9:48), and places it in a context where the sense is modified. Because the disciples are compared to children, the phrase "a single child such as this" indicates the same disciples. This is made all the more certain by the inclusion of the second portion of the phrase in the mission discourse (Mt 10:40b). The identification of the disciples with the children is proper to Matthew.

6) In the primitive discourse there was a further development on the theme "in the name of Christ" (Mk 9:38-40), which Matthew gives elsewhere (Mt 10:42). He modifies or totally suppresses the texts where John and James speak like Zealots (Mk 3:17; 20:20-23; Lk 9:53-56).

7) He also reproduces elsewhere (mission-discourse 10:42) the text with the fourth key-word (*qatina*). But, while suppressing the text, he retains the development on *qatina* (Mt 18:10, 14). Now comes the development concerning angels. It is divided by Matthew into two portions, one after the passage about scandal (v. 10), the other forming a conclusion to the parable of the lost sheep (v. 14). Doubtless he wished to contrast with verse 10, the punishment of him who scandalizes the little one, the promise made to him who receives him in the name of the Lord (v. 14).

8) In verse 6 of Matthew we have mention of the fifth key-word, scandal.

9) There follows the development on scandal. Matthew preserves it, with certain slight modifications, that associate it with a text already given in Matthew 5:30.

10) While omitting the verse which mentions the sixth key-word (Mk 9:45), he retains the development concerning fire (v. 9).

11) He omits the reference to salt, which he will return to later.

b) By their severe laws concerning purity and their insistence on ablutions before meals, the Pharisees had excluded from sacred meals the classes of sinners and publicans. To such ostracism Christ opposes the *solicitude* of God who ceaselessly tries to save sinners. Jesus himself is faithful to the Father's wish (v. 14) when he pursues to the limit the search for the lost sheep (Mk 10:6; 15:24; 9:36). Matthew is of course more restrained than Luke. He does not emphasize in the same way the theme of joy, nor the search by the shepherd. For him it is the lost sheep alone that counts. He is more precious to the shepherd than the ninety-nine others. What one has just lost acquires more value.

The Scribes and Pharisees see in the sinner only the enemy of God. This is the attitude of those who are judgmental; but God's manner of action is altogether different. He does not wait for repentance in order to love the sinner: he abandons everything to go in search of him. It is then the duty of the head of the community to let the sinner know that God loves him first (1 Jn 4:10, 19; 2 Co 5:20), and is concerned for the salvation of all.

Are the ministers of the Church always aware of this responsibility? Are they not perhaps too preoccupied with controlling the faithful flock to be concerned wih the "little ones"? Does not the Church herself often give the impression of being too institutional to encounter sinners and the poor, with full respect for their dignity?

VII. Deuteronomy 34:1-12
1st reading
1st cycle
Wednesday

Here we have a seventh century tradition providing details about the final moments in Moses' life, something that predates it by six centuries. The account then is more doctrinal than factual.

a) When Deuteronomy was being complied all trace of Moses' tomb at Nebo had been lost. For the author this does not matter:

God himself has buried Moses in a very secret place, like Elias and Enoch. He is being reserved for the *messianic times* (v. 6).

Moses then is not really dead. His return, like that of Elias, is contemplated in order to bring to men the revelation of God's mysteries.

b) The author of Deuteronomy was writing during the greatest Jewish prophetic period (Isaiah, Jeremiah, etc.). He makes Moses the greatest of the *prophets* in order to remind his contemporaries of the original character of the forgotten patriarch's mission (v. 10), and the determining role he played in reading the events that shaped the beginnings of the people.

VIII. Ezechiel 9:1-7, 10:18-22
1st reading
2nd cycle
Wednesday

Jerusalem's chastisement is beginning. Seven mysterious beings (vv. 1-2) will traverse the city to exterminate all sinners, beginning with the old men of the temple (cf. Dn 13; Jn 8:1-11). Those who remain faithful will be *marked* with a "T" and preserved from calamity (v. 4; cf. Gn 4:15).

So complete is the extermination that the corpses sully even the interior of the temple (v. 7), forcing the glory of God to withdraw from so unclean a place (10:18-22).

As in Ezechiel 2-3, we discern here the religion of the book. It is Yahweh's secretary, he who keeps the book of life to date, who will save the just (v. 2). The book of the law is the mirror of those who are faithful to it and who are marked with the first letter of the word "torah" (law).

The concept of a mark or seal suggests an exterior sign that liberates or sets apart people who are more or less acquiescent. Examples would be Jews during time of war, slaves in certain areas, or the doctrine of the "ineradicable" seal of baptism or ordination. It is a valuable concept for understanding the priority of God's initiative in salvation or in vocation. It would be wrong however to see this action by God independently of human freedom and collaboration. There is nothing automatic in the "mark" of the Christian seal. The mark has value in proportion to the quality of the engagement. The inspired author is aware of this. The mark for him is to be the first letter of the word "law," the symbol of conscious adhesion to the thought of God.

IX. Matthew 18:15-20
Gospel
Wednesday

Our reading gives us a portion of Jesus' discourse concerning the attitude to be adopted first of all with regard to sin and scandal (Mt 18:5-11), secondly with regard to the sinner. The second point indicates the Church's concern for mercy by recounting the parable of the lost sheep (Mt 18:12-14), and by full detail concerning the attitude of pardon. The sinner is to be confronted alone (note: the phrase "against you" is not found in the original text which speaks of the sinner in general, v. 15). He must then be brought before two or three witnesses (v. 16), and then challenged in full assembly (v. 17). For this, Jesus confers power on his apostles (v. 18).

The third portion of the discourse determines the attitude that ought to be adopted by the injured party towards the one who has wronged him. Here, the only rule is limitless pardon (vv. 21-22). Matthew continues the teaching with the parable of the unforgiving debtor (Mt 18:23-35).

Between the second and third portions (vv. 19-20) he inserts the Lord's logion about "two or three" being joined in prayer. He has just been dealing with the question of the value of the witness of "two or three" (v. 16). By inserting the prayer logion in this context of victory over sin, he may too wish to indicate that prayer is a weapon that triumphs over sin (Jm 5:15-16; Mt 6:12).

Undoubtedly the central theme of the passage is *pardon.* Jesus reminds people of the duty (vv. 21-23) and simultaneously gives the power (vv. 15-18). The new age is one in which the Lord offers man the opportunity not only to emerge from sin in his personal life, but further to triumph over it in the lives of others by means of pardon.

It is perhaps worthwhile to review the principal stages in Jewish law which brought about this law of pardon. Primitive society had reacted violently to wrongdoing by the individual. It had no provision for pardon, and could only avenge the wrong by a condign punishment, seventy times more severe than the fault itself (Gn 4:24). The *lex talionis* was a considerable step forward.

Leviticus (Lv 19:13-17) goes a step further. It does not of course introduce the notion of pardon strictly speaking (the only instance of pardon in the Old Testament: 1 S 24 and 26). It does however insist on the solidarity which unites brothers among themselves, and forbids them to have recourse to judicial procedure to settle their differences.

Christ's doctrine on pardon is a decisive advance. The New Testament instances are frequent. He pardons his executioners (Lk 23:24) and Stephen (Ac 7:59-60) and Paul (1 Co 4:12-13) and many others follow his example.

Generally the duty of pardon is associated with the imminence of the last judgment. If we are to be pardoned at this crucial moment, we must as of now pardon our brothers (partial sense of v. 35). Our measure for pardon must be precisely that which was the measure of primitive vengeance (v. 22; cf. Gn 4:24).

The latter notion which is based on the doctrine of retribution is still very Jewish. Gradually however the doctrine of pardon becomes specifically Christian: the concept is based on the fact that one is oneself pardoned by God (Mt 18:23-35; Col 3:13). The pardon we extend to others is no longer just a moral obligation: it becomes the visible evidence of God's reconciliation at work in everybody (2 Co 5:18-20).

The idea of pardon could never have been developed in an atmosphere where retribution is the dominant idea, and God's justice is regarded as distributive. Its proper atmosphere is one permeated by the mercy of God and justification for the sinner.

For all that Matthew 18:15-22 echoes this concept, it is still expressed after the Jewish manner. The evangelist however is at least aware that the Church is a community of the saved where the salvation of the sinner can be the only objective. If it is not achieved that is because the sinner hardens and refuses the pardon offered (v. 17). There is a distinction between the Christian community and the Jewish. It is only in pardoning the sinner that it judges him. Nor is the sinner condemned except in so far as he refuses to live in the bosom of the welcoming community.

The sinner will only encounter God's pardon when he rediscovers the mercy of God at work in the Church and the eucharistic assembly. What we have in the Church is no longer just a national solidarity requiring that brothers only be pardoned. The faithful are involved in a salvation history which leads all men towards God's judgment. And God's judgment is really his pardon, offered throughout time until the final consummation.

X. Joshua 3:7-17
1st reading
1st cycle
Thursday

Chapter 3 of Joshua, epic in style, depicts the passage of the Jordan as a marvelous proof of Yahweh's leadership of his people. The redactor has numerous sources and can thus properly formulate the religious lesson of the crossing.

a) The passage is seen as a replica of the passage of the Red Sea. The waters of the Jordan are "cut" (v. 13) as were those of the Red Sea (Ex 14:21). They form a "heap" (v. 16) as in Exodus 15:8 and make place for the "dry land" (v. 17) as in Exodus 14:21-22. The chroniclers clearly saw the crossing as a guarantee that the *paschal liberation* would be renewed each time the people needed it (cf. Jos 5:10-12). At the very moment of completion of the pilgrimage towards the Promised Land this new pasch is a reminder that the journey has been a long liberating trial, a liberation from all alienations and slaveries, not only those of Egypt, but those caused by sin throughout the desert sojourn.

b) The crossing is presented as a liturgical *procession* in the course of which the ark of the Lord is solemnly carried from one bank to the other. All attention is concentrated on it (it is mentioned 17 times in chapter 3 alone). It is carried by the priests (vv. 14, 15 and 17): the people receive precise instructions to file in front of it as a sign of respect. For the redactor the passage of the Jordan is Yahweh's solemn entry into the land he has chosen as a dwelling.

Doubtless the stoppage of the waters (v. 16) is due to a natural phenomenon. The hills of marl which border the river often slip into the water, on the last occasion in 1927, sometimes blocking the current for an entire day. The chronicler however sees this as a sign of God's presence by his people's side. Such indeed is the role of the prophet, to discern the meaning of the event, and see how it is the vehicle of God's word.

XI. Ezechiel 12:1-12
1st reading
2nd cycle
Thursday

Ezechiel has recourse to a symbolic action to proclaim the deportation of the people (vv. 1-3, 6-11). At a later stage a disciple of the prophet will understand this mime of the *emigrant* as a prophecy of King Sedecias' flight and will add vv. 4-8 and v. 12.

The lot that is described here as a chastisement is in fact the lot of a considerable number of our generation. Populations everywhere are in search of richer territories. Rural folk are being absorbed by the tentacles of the city. Manual workers from poor areas are being exploited by rich countries. Specialists leave their own countries to be swallowed by the industrial nations. In a less dramatic way holidaying tourists are bringing about the greatest deplacement of people that history has seen. Can we, like the prophets, see all this as a sign of chastisement? Though it would be ridiculous to affirm that God is punishing the world by displacing populations, we can scarcely isolate the phenomenon from human limitations, perhaps indeed human sin.

All displacement of populations means in fact a deracination of persons. It is an implicit acknowledgment of the failure of an environment to provide the necessary conditions for interpersonal relations and expansion of personality. It is an indictment of an economy which manipulates men for profit, and fails in equitable distribution of wealth and privilege.

The Christian carries the yoke of exile side by side with his brothers and realizes that he is bearing the weight of a humanity that continues to be selfish. When he welcomes the emigrant, and looks for solutions to the great problem of displacement, he knows that he is making humanity more conformed to the image of God, and alleviating the burden of punishment of which the prophet spoke.

XII. Matthew 18:21-19:1
Gospel
Thursday

The parable of the unforgiving debtor belongs to the fourth discourse of Jesus, which is concerned with the rules governing Christians' relations with one another. Jesus had already spoken of the attitude to be adopted towards the sinner (Mt 18:15-22), and of common prayer (Mt 18:19-20). Now in response to a question from Peter (Mt 18:21-22) he turns to the matter of mutual pardon.

a) Judaism was already familiar with *pardon for offenses;* but this was a fairly recent development, where precise tariffs had to be observed. Rabbinic schools required their disciples to pardon wife, children, brothers, etc., so many times, and the number varied as between school and school. Accordingly we can see why Peter asks Jesus for his tariff in this matter. He is anxious to know whether he is as severe as the school which required pardon seven times for a brother (Mt 18:21).

Jesus' reply is a parable which disassociates pardon from any tariff, and makes it the sign of pardon received from God. The primitive parable appears to have been fairly simple. The servant of a sheik has his debt remitted by the latter, but is incapable of remitting in turn a comrade's debt. The sheik reproaches him for failing to remit a debt *as* his own has been remitted.

Such is the nature of Christian pardon. One forgives as one is forgiven. One pities a comrade because one has been pitied oneself (vv. 17 and 33; cf. Ho 6:6; Mt 9:13; 12:7).

Pardon is no longer, as in Judaism, an obligation measured by tariff, but the symbol of the pardon one has received. It becomes a sort of theological virtue, extending the pardon of God that one has received to others (Col 3:13; Mt 6:14-15; 2 Co 5:18-20).

b) Matthew makes an allegory of the primitive parable. He substitutes awkwardly "king" for the "man" (v. 23), so that the reader immediately thinks of the king of heaven (same procedure in Mt 22:2). He fixes the servant's debt at ten thousand talents to emphasize the sinner's complete inadequacy *vis-a-vis* God (v. 24). He heightens the religious atmosphere of the tribunal scene (falling at the feet of the king, prostration, begging for pity . . . , v. 26) to suggest the last judgment. He stresses the disproportion between the ten thousand talents and the hundred pence (similar to the disproportion between the mote and the beam: Mt 7:1-5), to show the immense difference between human and divine concepts of debt and justice. Finally, he determines exactly the servant's punishment, torture to last until he repays the altogether improbable sum (v. 34), suggesting eternal punishment (Mt 25:41, 46).

Such a procedure places the duty of pardon in an *eschatological* context. The final times have come. They take the form of a sabbatical year (Dt 15:1-15) in the course of which God remits for humanity its unmeasurable debt and offers justification. Some however refuse to become the beneficiaries of divine justice and thus condemn themselves to endless unhappiness.

c) God could have exacted immediate vengeance for man's

sin, broken his covenant and precipitated the eschatological judgment. The parable shows how he substitutes pardon for judgment, postponing judgment to a later date. The servant's lifetime in fact is lifed between two sessions of divine judgment (vv. 25-26 and 31-35). The first issues in an acquittal: the second will come after the delay allowed by God. Man will be definitively justified if he uses this respite for pardoning and justifying too. Christian life is a sort of provisional acquittal that will only become definitive at the final judgment. What we have is a theology of the *time of the Church,* a time given to man for conversion (cf. Mt 13:24-30). The history of pardon runs throughout the whole life of the Church, not only through the sacramental ministry of the apostles and their successors, but also through the capacity of each member to manifest God's pardon in his love for others.

Our Sunday Eucharist has a clearly penitential dimension. God's pardon is proclaimed there, and is exercised by the Church because the Church is none other than the assembly of sinners awaiting God's initiative of mercy. This brotherhood in the Eucharist and in pardon will only become evident for the world to the extent that Christians collaborate effectively in human enterprises of pardon, particularly in work for peace.

XIII. Joshua 24:1-15
1st reading
1st cycle
Friday

Chapter 24 of Joshua is a sort of appendix, that was added a century or two after the Deuteronomic reform of the book. The account notwithstanding is based on a very old tradition of the Sichem alliance, anterior even to those of Joshua 8:30-35 and Deuteronomy 27:1-26. According to that the alliance was presented in terms of the treaties of alliance common at the time between suzerain and vassal. We have a preamble (v. 1), a discourse which recalls the previous relations between the contracting parties

(vv. 1-15), proclamation of the stipulations of the contract (vv. 16-18), enumeration of the maledictions and punishments which will visit failure to observe them (vv. 19-24; cf. especially Dt 27), finally, mention of the ceremony of alliance and the engraving of the contract on a stele (vv. 25-28). It was doubtless this primitive tradition which inspired the account of the Sinai alliance in Exodus. The promulgation of the code which Exodus fixes at Sinai must have really taken place at Sichem.

Indeed, for a time, Sichem was the place associated with the memory of the alliance with Yahweh, and the final redactor of Joshua 24 interfered considerably with the account, in order to transfer to Sinai the interest originally concentrated on Sichem.

a) The tribes assembled at Sichem comprised the clans who had dwelt in Palestine since the patriarchs, those who had returned from a foreign sojourn to Palestine before Joshua, and finally the "house of Joseph," the latest to regain the ancestral territory under the successive leadership of Moses and Joshua. Very soon the latter were to show themselves the more important, in any case the better organized and more cultivated. This was doubtless due to their Egyptian experience. They were capable of rallying the other tribes round about them and making their own history, that of the exodus and covenant, the possession of all the people. So it was at Sichem that the God of the house of Joseph became the God of all the tribes, and the traditions of all the tribes were fused to form the law of the *covenant*.

b) The dialogue between the people and God still retains some elements of the primitive tradition (vv. 14, 15, 18); the rest was added after the exile. The sign of true acceptance by the tribes of the conditions of the alliance will be the forsaking of false idols. Every alliance implies a *conversion,* in this case desertion of the Mesopotamian gods adored by Abraham's ancestors, and the Canaanite gods worshiped by those who remained in Palestine.

c) The purpose of the alliance between the tribes is not primarily political but religious: the *service of* God (vv. 14-15).

Probably the cult of Yahweh was organized on an amphyctionic basis. Twelve clans or tribes guaranteed, each for a month, the "service" of a common temple (perhaps the high-place of Sichem). However at the time when the final redactor was handling the tradition, the "service" of God had become more spiritual. Experience of infidelity in the previous centuries had taught him that serving God above all means fidelity to the stipulations of the law, as a vassal fulfills his suzerain's will.

The account of the Sichem assembly throws new light on the content of the alliance. It is not primarily the gesture of a God who recognizes a people, or an established people who acknowledge their God. It is the constitution of a people around a common faith and common worship. Culturally and politically, Israel is born in the moment when she recognizes her God. Nationality and religion cannot be separated. It is because they are a people that the Hebrews are "chosen": the religious alliance requires action in solidarity.

Whether we belong to the old covenant or the new, this dimension is a dominant one. The covenant is not confirmed to the relationships between God and the individual: it is principally a solidarity between people who serve the same God, a solidarity that can be divested of the nationalism that characterized Sichem. It is a service of God which since Jesus Christ has taken on unparalleled dimensions. Yet it always remains a solidarity in living because God lives with us.

XIV. Ezechiel 16:1-15, 60-63
1st reading
2nd cycle
Friday

Chapter 26 of Ezechiel is an excellent example of the midrash genre. It is a meditation by the prophet on the history of Jerusalem and her mission in the establishment of God's reign over the world.

a) *Jerusalem* is a Canaanite city, and from its very beginnings had a precarious existence. She was deserted by her founders, excluded from the Canaanite confederation (Melchizedek no longer had father or mother: He 7:3; and long before the Hebrew period King Ponti-Hefer wrote to the pharaoh complaining of his isolation), but nevertheless survived unscathed the Canaanite period (vv. 3-5). At the moment, the Hebrews were occupying the province and did not concern themselves with Jerusalem. They respected her and let her live her life (vv. 6-7; cf. Wi 19:11-12). It is not until the time of David that Yahweh enters into association with the city, making her his spouse (vv. 8-14) and bestowing on her the unforgettable glories of the reign of Solomon. His love for her seems a personal choice, a gift of the heart, a grace. It is conceived as a physical love in the sense that he loves her institutions, her political choices, etc. There is total communion: nothing in the city's life is without divine love and grace.

b) That is why her infidelity is particularly grave. The other Eastern cities condemned by Yahweh had not known his life and his love to the same degree. They had not been adulterous, and thus are less culpable than she (v. 15). We expect then that Yahweh will punish her as an adulteress (vv. 35-43, not in the reading). Her judgment must be even more severe than that of Sodom, Samaria and other pagan cities (vv. 44-52).

c) However at the very moment of her judgment she receives an unexpected mission, the *expiation* of the faults of her sisters Sodom and Samaria (vv. 53-58). It is rather a pity that these verses are not included in the reading because they are important. Her fall is so terrible, so much lower than that of the other cities; her fault is so great that the chastisement of God is exhausted in her case (cf. Mt 11:20-24). We are encountering already the doctrine of the suffering Servant, a victim suffering for the faults of others that she carries (Is 53).

d) If, even in her condemnation, Jerusalem justifies humanity and contributes to the building of a better world, she cannot be definitively abandoned by God. She enables him to fulfill his plan. The final verses in the chapter (vv. 60-63) proclaim that a new *alliance* will be sealed with her because of the justice her fate has procured for the world. If God declares that the sin of Jerusalem is expiated, with how much more reason will not the less grave offenses of Sodom and Samaria be expiated too (cf. Rm 5:20)?

A city that has not known sin and pardon cannot presume to the salvation of other cities. One cannot be the bearer and messenger of pardon and of God's justification except when one has benefitted from it oneself. Thus a Church which is altogether preoccupied with her own justice is by that very fact incapable of proclaiming pardon. When she realizes on the other hand that her own sin is the gravest of all, when she is ready to bear the consequences, her words of justice and pardon will reverberate throughout all the cities of the world.

XV. Matthew 19:3-12
Gospel
Friday

This passage concerning the indissolubility of marriage and continence is fairly identical with the parallel passages of Luke and Mark, apart from the phrase "except it be for fornication," proper to Matthew (5:32 and 19:9), and verses 10-11.

a) Jewish law allowed a man to repudiate his wife (Dt 24:1) if he found in her "some impropriety," doubtless some hidden, repugnant flaw. The rabbinic schools could never determine the interpretation which should be given this. Laxists maintained that a man who encountered a woman more beautiful than his wife could become so disgusted with the latter that he could validly repudiate her. Rigorists on the other hand interpreted the flaw as adultery, or at least very bad behavior.

The Pharisees' question for Jesus then is a trap. They want to force him to take sides between the two schools, and thus become alienated from at least one group of teachers and believers.

He escapes the trap by declaring himself opposed to *divorce* for whatever motive. He bases his view, according to usual rabbinic procedure, on two texts of Scripture, Genesis 1:27 and 2:24. He clearly gives more weight to Genesis 2:24 which he quotes in full (it is abbreviated in Mark) and comments on almost literally (v. 6). Matthew reinforces this impression by making Genesis 2:24 a "word of God" whereas it is simply a reflection of Adam.

God then wishes man and woman to be united as one flesh. Such a clear proclamation admits no revision. That which God has joined together, no man, not even Moses (vv. 10-12) may undo. Not only is marriage a contract between two persons: the will of God, written into the complementarity of the sexes, is involved. Thus, because marriage is not confined to the will of the spouses, divorce interferes with the design of a partner in marriage, God himself that is.

b) That the doctrine of Jesus will not be understood by all is demonstrated by verses 11 and 12. He does not say "not all will be able to fulfill this Word" but "not all can understand this word," as in verse 12 "Let anyone accept this who can." Verse 11 makes it clear that those only can understand "to whom it is given." What is contemplated is the interior inspiration given to the apostles and those who believe (Mt 11:25 and 16:17). But the inspiration does not cancel the necessary personal effort, as is clear from the final injunction in verse 12: "Let anyone accept this who can" (Mt 24:15; Mk 13:14; Mt 13:9; Lk 8:8).

What is to be accepted? The Lord makes the following pronouncement:

There are eunuchs who are so from their mother's womb
There are eunuchs made so by men
There are those who have made themselves eunuchs for the kingdom of God

The final affirmation being the most important. It is set in relief by the two previous ones (cf. with Pr 30:18 and following, or Mt 8:20). The first two are known categories. The third would be repugnant if it were understood materially. The phrase "for the kingdom of God" is the important one and the term eunuch is used analogically.

"For the Kingdom of God" should be understood, according to the immediate context (Mt 18:3; 19:14, 16), and Matthews' general use, as "in order to obtain (or enter) the Kingdom of God."

What is the relation between the apostles' response and the Master's saying? Or between the two logia, that on divorce and that concerning eunuchs. We know that the first Gospel tends to group sayings in order to stress a precise teaching. Compare Matthew 5:27-28, 29-32 and 19:3-12:

Matthew 5	Matthew 19
Condemnation of lust	Condemnation of remarriage after divorce
If your eye scandalize you pluck it out	Those who make themselves eunuchs for the kingdom

The final verses in chapter 19 then indicate that a man who repudiates an unfaithful spouse cannot remarry, and should "for the kingdom" accept a continence that makes him like a eunuch. Because it is couched in general terms, the logion refers not only to separated spouses, but to all those who for one reason or another have renounced conjugal life for the Kingdom.

XVI. Joshua 24:14-29
1st reading
1st cycle
Saturday

This passage was commented on with the preceding one (Joshua 24:1-15), p. 277.

XVII. Ezechiel 18:1-10, 26-32
1st reading
2nd cycle
Saturday

Chapter 18 is one of the most important passages in the whole book of Ezechiel (cf. Ez 14:12; 33:10-20; 34:16). The prophet is summoning the Jews to conversion, but encounters a fatalist attitude. What is the point in conversion when they are expiating the sins of their fathers? This popular notion was based on texts such as Deuteronomy 5:9; 29:18-21; and Exodus 20:5, and on proverbs such as that refuted by Ezechiel in verses

1-4. Here he alludes to a sort of decalogue that was familiar to his contemporaries (Ez 18:5-9; 11-13; 15-17) in order to show that the duty is one of personal responsibility.

Later (Ez 18:21-32) he shows that on the personal level there is no fatalism. God will only judge the individual on his personal justice or injustice. If the sinner is converted he can combat the threat of punishment; but his weakness can cancel his right to reward. This forms the conclusion to today's passage.

Ezechiel understood the people's solidarity in fault and the collective punishment that was the result (Ez 16; 20; 23). But he realized also that collective punishment is never inevitable, and that a massive conversion on the part of the people can retard its onset (cf. Am 6:1-6). His essentially original idea however is that God is preparing a *new covenant*, which will give each man a new heart and a new spirit (v. 31; cf. Ez 11:19). Access will be opened wide for just and unjust.

God does not will death or punishment (vv. 23 and 32) but the life of the greatest possible number. The new covenant is designed to bring this about: man's portion in the project is to be his conversion. In conversion of course everyone is personally involved. Yet we cannot really say that the prophet is putting forward a particularly individualist view of personal responsibility. Even though the cases described in verses 26-28 are individual, he is nevertheless addressing the whole "house of Israel" (vv. 24, 29-31). He is envisaging the conversion of the people as a whole and their restoration in a new life by a new covenant.

XVIII. Matthew 19:13-15 *Gospel Saturday*

The ascent of Jesus to Jerusalem is marked by numerous episodes where he deliberately encounters the humble and despised, to the great scandal of those with him. It is as if in realizing his own role of despised and suffering one he draws near to those in like condition (cf. further Mt 20:29-34).

a) Jesus' reception of children has to be seen in the context of Jewish thinking where the child was regarded as an insignificant being, even though an addition to the family was welcomed as a divine blessing. By welcoming children (v. 14; cf. Mt 21:15), he indicates his intention of admitting to his kingdom and his liturgy those who had been excluded by Judaism.

He wants then to be associated with those who have the same lot that he will endure in his passion, and to affirm his desire for a reassembly and liturgical gathering that will bear witness to the *universality* of salvation. A liturgy which excludes any class of human beings would not meet the universal demands of salvation.

b) Without doubt this is the proper interpretation of Jesus' gesture. However the first Christians interpreted it in support of *infant baptism.* They gave the imposition of hands (v. 15) a liturgical value which it did not originally have, and repeated the phrase "do not prevent them" in their pre-baptismal interrogations (cf. Ac 8:36; 10:47; 11:17; Mt 3:14).

Now, at a time when the importance of faith in the action of a sacrament is being once more realized, the question of infant baptism is posed afresh. Many parents would be inclined to have their child baptized at an age when he could make a personal decision.

In fact we may very well expect that infant baptism will be less prominent in future Church discipline. In greater and greater numbers parents will come to realize that they do not have the faith necessary to raise their child in the Church and will request that baptism be delayed. Priests moreover, without claiming the right to refuse the sacrament, will tend to interpret the obligation *quam primum* more broadly to meet circumstances. However infant baptism can never be altogether suppressed. Such a decision would be a denial by the Church of her essential function, which must be a witness that salvation is accessible for all classes of men. It would also run counter to the principles of psychology. According to these an infant is not unconscious but preconscious. After his fashion he is already in contact with the world and profoundly influenced by environment.

TWENTIETH WEEK

I. Judges 2:11-19
1st reading
1st cycle
Monday

This passage is taken from the deuteronomist author's introduction to the book (Jg 1:6-3:6) where he expounds his philosophy of history.

The people's *history* is a constant passage from fidelity (v. 7) to infidelity (vv. 10-12). Every time infidelity takes possession of their hearts, they are immediately decimated by invasion (vv. 14-15), and thus restored to fidelity and the service of God by the intervention of a liberating "judge." When he dies, they fall into error once again (v. 19). So very important does the author consider this view of history that he reproduces the passage at the end of each judge's biography (Jg 3:7, 11-15; 4:1-2, 6; 10:8, 33; 10:6-17).

The Church does not escape the vicissitudes of history. Our age carries all the symptoms of infidelity, just as the preceding one gave every evidence of fidelity. We shall be wise to abstain from judging and confine ourselves rigidly to the symptoms. African Christians, the urban ones at least, have abandoned religious practice in large numbers once their countries have gained independence. "Dechristianization" has still a long way to go in the West. Priests leave their ministry without bothering to regularize their situation with the institution they abandon. Christians seem to want to live their faith not only in a secularized world, but in a secularized manner too.

In brief our infidelity seems to be concentrated chiefly in rejection of all ecclesial institution. Traditional formulations of faith, liturgical styles, the hierarchy, do not control our lives as they used to. The actual confines of the Church seem to have become blurred. Concerned Catholics find themselves considerably closer to Protestants, or even involved atheists, than to integrist or conformist fellow Catholics. Is not this state of affairs comparable to the situation described by the author of Judges when the enemy was encroaching on Hebrew territory?

The moral of Judges remains valid for the ecclesial situation now. Neither in Israel or the Church is the solution to be found in the institution itself: it must be charismatic. The Church however has one advantage over Israel: it knows its liberating judge already, Jesus Christ. He is already at work in it, and his action takes place through the instrumentality of the whole people, lay and cleric. The people are both prophetic and charismatic. It will be their business, in spite of confusions and delays, to discover how the faith can be lived in a secularized world where the Church wears a new visage.

II. Ezechiel 24:15-24
1st reading
2nd cycle
Monday

Ezechiel's wife died on the very day of Jerusalem's fall; and he makes this the occasion of another, particularly painful, symbolic action. Verses 19-22 were probably interpolated after the exile. They are in any case superfluous, and divert attention from the primary sense of the passage.

Ezechiel has lost his *spouse, the "joy of his life,"* and in the fall of Jerusalem, he sees Yahweh also losing a spouse. Between the faithful spouse of Ezechiel and the adulterous one of Yahweh there is of course a great difference. Yet Ezechiel transcends his personal situation, and makes himself mime before the body of his spouse Yahweh's apparent insensibility to the fall of Jerusalem. Where custom calls for strident cries at the obsequies, he remains mute. His silence will inspire the Judaeans to forego their lamentations over Jerusalem's fate.

III. Matthew 19:16-22
Gospel
Monday

In chapter 19 Matthew considers the effect of the Christian concept of the final times on moral behavior. For this purpose he assembles fragments of Christ's discourses on marriage and celibacy above all (Mt 19:1-12), on being despised and rejected (Mt 17:13-15), on the use of riches and poverty (Mt 19:16-29).

He stresses the imminence of the final times which force the disciple to adopt intransigent attitudes, and the upheaval this means in human affairs. He shows how novel and austere Christ's teaching can seem (v. 25; cf. v. 10). Finally he so disposes the account of Christ's remarks to those who wish to follow him in his messianic ministry (the "eunuchs" of v. 12; the rich young man of vv. 16-22) that they seem valid for every Christian.

a) Matthew made *perfection* the *leitmotiv* of the sermon on the mount (Mt 5:48). Not the formalist, scrupulous perfection of the Scribes and Pharisees, but a perfection that transcends the law (Mt 5:20-48), simply because the time has come to bring everything to fulfillment. This implies not only the wish to set up an ethic more elevated than the law, but above all the intention of giving this an eschatological meaning.

It is for this reason that he gives us the episode of the rich young man. Doubtless this individual asked Jesus' permission to "follow" him as disciple, and thus share his messianic adventure (cf. "if you will" in vv. 17 and 21). Matthew however hardens the position of Christ. It is not sufficient to obey the law, even the two most important commandments (vv. 18-19). One's attitude must be an eschatological sign of radical breach with the world (v. 21).

Perfection then consists in accomplishing the divine will as Jesus did, transcending the ancient commandments by the gift to God of all that one is and all that one has. It is not a matter of "doing" (what must one do? v. 16), but of relationship (come, follow me, v. 21). This is to say that Matthew is rejecting in advance the distinction between commandments and counsels. For him the Christian is called to perfection as a sign of the final times.

b) The rich young man (v. 22) failed to reach perfection because his attachment to *riches* interfered with his relationship to the person of Christ. Jesus' audience is astonished to see a rich man lose the Kingdom, because it regards riches as a blessing from God (Jb 42:7-16). Jesus does not, according to Matthew, say that one must be poor to share the Kingdom. For Luke however (cf. Lk 6:20 and Mt 5:3) Jesus' point is that God is no longer associated with the blessings of riches and abundance. These have lost their religious meaning: salvation is due exclusively to the divine initiative (v. 26). In so far as riches give social status, become a right that must be maintained, they imperial one's sense of God's gratuity, and fail to manifest the salvation that is at hand. Likewise the legalist justice of the Scribes and Pharisees stifled good conscience and openness through self-sufficiency.

IV. Judges 6:11-24
1st reading
1st cycle
Tuesday

Gideon is a typical "judge" of the preroyalist era. He has a charismatic power which he places at the service of the tribe (at this stage there was no question yet of a people) to combat the invasion of the Madianites.

The marvelous consumption of his sacrifice will be the sign from heaven that will enable him to be accepted by his peers in the coming struggle.

The account of Gideon's vocation (vv. 11b-18) was much affected by successive traditions. He was himself probably a Madianite, and his legend was connected with the foundation of the high place of Ophra (vv. 11a, 19-24) even before the Hebrew arrival in Palestine. Subsequently the account of the foundation of another high-place (Jg 6:25-31) was added to it, because perhaps of certain similarities. A final tradition (Jg 6:32) transformed the name Gideon into Yerubbaal, doubtless to give the paternity of Abimelek (Jg 9:1) more verisimilitude, and to incorporate the legend in the people's history.

V. Ezechiel 28:1-10
1st reading
2nd cycle
Tuesday

The prophet does not believe that his ministry is bounded by the confines of Israel and Judaea. One God governs the destiny of the world. His prophet then can address all people, the king of Tyre in this instance whose power over the sea, regarded as divine, was so great that he could look on himself as god.

The oracle against the king of Tyre echoes many traditions of Ras Shambra and Phoenicia, above all the account of the terrestrial paradise. The man who wants to make himself god will be punished for his *pride* and will perish.

VI. Matthew 19:23-30
Gospel
Tuesday

Here we have an extract from Christ's discourse on the use of riches (Mt 19:16-30). The discourse follows the usual structure: a brief narrative first (vv. 16-22), then statements by Jesus on the topic (vv. 23-24), finally questions by the disciples (vv. 25-29). Verse 30 belongs probably to another context.

a) Because the primitive communities were very troubled concerning the attitude to be adopted to *riches*, such discourses must have been frequent among them. The matter was especially important in the Jerusalem community, which was composed of the poor exclusively (Ac 4:34-5:11). From verse 23 onwards a challenge is laid down. The rich will have great difficulty in adjusting to the Christian community (and hence to the Kingdom which cannot be longer delayed and coincides with the community). The "eye of a needle" probably designates a known spot near Jerusalem, so narrow that it could not be negotiated by caravans of camels (v. 24).

The disciples are all the more astonished by the difficulty for the rich in sharing the Kingdom, because the Old Testament had often made wealth a sign of blessing and of membership in the Kingdom (Si 31:8-11).

b) Yet it is not necessarily because the rich have difficulty in entering the Christian community that entry to the Kingdom will be forbidden them. What is impossible here below may with God be possible. To some extent the terrestrial Church is relativized *vis-a-vis* the *eschatological Kingdom* by verse 26. It is so to speak already the Kingdom, and yet it is not. True, some primitive communities were over-particularist, over-linked sociologically with the poor (cf. Lk 6:20-24) to be able to absorb the rich (otherwise in Mt 5:3; Co 13:11). However the fact that the Church shows herself, at this or that point in her history, incapable of absorbing a particular mentality or culture does not mean that these cannot be integrated into the eschatological Kingdom. This depends, not necessarily on visible membership of the Church, but on the grace of God. Of course the Church is the sign of salvation in the sense that all men are saved by her mediation and her mission. Visible membership however is not necessary for salvation. Salvation is something that transcends the institution, something that is a gift of God. Discord between a particular class (rich or poor) and the Church at any particular time does not mean this class is precluded from salvation.

c) Peter's intervention (vv. 27-30) makes a discreet allusion to the incident of the rich young man (vv. 16-22). Jesus had required from him a *renouncement* in order to enter eternal life. Where the young man had refused, Jesus' own companions had accepted. What would be their reward?

There are two parts in Jesus' answer. The first which is addressed to the apostles only (v. 28) is peculiar to Matthew. The second on the other hand is common to all the synoptics and concerns anyone who practices renunciation ("whoever": v. 29). Whoever abandons all to follow Jesus ("follow" in this context suggests Jesus' final journey towards death) obtains life eternal. Matthew suppresses mention of God's blessing "in this world" (cf. Mk 10:30) and associates the "hundredfold" with eternal life. Corresponding to the death and resurrection of Christ are the ideas of Christian life and life eternal.

d) The renunciation of the apostles will however be rewarded in a particular way. They will sit on twelve *thrones* at the entrance to the Kingdom, and will exercise with the Messiah judgment concerning entry or exclusion (cf. Is 3:14). Such an archaic view of the apostolic function is a far cry from the more missionary view of the twelve we now have. Nevertheless the apostles themselves retained it for a considerable time. After the death of Judas they wanted to re-form their group (Ac 1), and they wished to remain at Jerusalem and await the coming of the Judge rather than go out to encounter the world.

VII. Judges 9:6-15
1st reading
1st cycle
Wednesday

This, with 2 Kings 14:9, is the only instance in the old Testament of a fable. In course of transmission however it received several different interpretations, and it is not easy to be precise concerning the details.

a) Originally perhaps the fable had to do with the people of Sichem who were proud and stubborn. No one would agree to rule over them because they were ungovernable. Their *ambition* however would not ultimately benefit them, and sooner or later fire would put an end to their projects (cf. Wi 9:57).

It is possible that later the fable was used in the *anti-monarchist* struggle that began in the time of Samuel. The purpose may have been to cast ridicule on people who had chosen their king not from among the competent (the friut trees) but from among useless and parasitic elements. Or it may have been the discrediting of the monarchy itself, as a parasitic and pretentious institution.

VIII. Ezechiel 34:1-11
1st reading
2nd cycle
Wednesday

When the elite were deported the ordinary folk remained in Palestine. Thus there was a collapse of authority. Armed bands set up a reign of terror, placing improvised chieftains at the head of local administrations. This was the situation depicted in Jeremiah 41. Verses 2b, 3, 6 and 8b seem to belong to another discourse on the same topic.

a) Ezechiel invieghs against those bandits who practice extortion on the "fat" sheep, or take the "puny" ones as hostage (v. 4). The only remedy for such a situation is the return of a king who will take the country in hand, a *shepherd* who will be representative of Israel's only true shepherd, Yahweh himself.

b) The shepherd image is not new. Saul and David had been shepherds before becoming kings. Jeremiah compares the kings to shepherds (Jr 23:1): in the East kings often received that title. What is however absolutely new in Ezechiel 34 is the attention given by the shepherd to each of his sheep, from the puny to the thriving. It is here that the prophet displays his concept of *personal religion.* He is logical. Having vigorously defended individual responsibility (Ez 18), it is to be expected that correspondingly he will stress God's personal attitude towards each one. Previously he had discerned in the watchman (Ez 3:16-21) not just the anonymous figure responsible for the city, but the pastor of each citizen.

The parables of Jesus on the lost sheep and the good shepherd vindicate the personalism of Ezechiel.

IX. Matthew 20:1-16
Gospel
Wednesday

This passage has been re-read in so many different ways, each time with a different interpretation and conclusion, that the original meaning is obscured. To recover that we must first of all omit the final phrase (v. 16b), which is probably an addition by the Church in the second century, absent in a number of manuscripts. It appears in its proper context in Matthew 22:14, from which doubtless it was taken. According to this late tradition the parable would concern the call of "many" to the vineyard of the Lord. It would affirm that not only was it necessary to be "called" but to be "chosen" also. This latter was the privilege of a few only. The sentence is probably due to a reaction by the second century Church against the *simpliste* mentality of some Christians. It is not sufficient to belong to the Church in order to be saved. However valid in itself, this interpretation strains the original meaning of the text.

a) The conclusion provided by verse 16a (the first shall be last and the last first) is from Matthew's hand. This does not necessarily mean that it was pronounced by Jesus at this point, or that its connection with the parable was already established. Furthermore the point of the sentence is not so much that the last will go *before* the first (v. 8), but that both will receive the same treatment. The sentiment that "the last will be first" is frequent in the synoptics. Mark 10:31 and Matthew 20:16 have it in another, more natural context. And Luke is more moderate than Matthew: "some" first will be last and "some" last first. What we have apparently is an isolated saying of the Lord, which the evangelists, with greater or less success, tried to place in a different context. Matthew, whose gospel emphasizes the importance of Gentiles as against Jews, places it after the vineyard parable, so that Christians will understand the *reversal of situation* that has come about between Israel and the nations, now that the latter have accepted the faith. Though perfectly valid in the first century, and throughout Church history, this interpretation nevertheless strains the original meaning of the parable, where there is no question of priority of the last over the first.

b) We have Jesus' own conclusion to the parable in verse 15. The basic complaint against the master of the vineyard (God) is his lack of "justice." This had already been the complaint of the elder brother of the prodigal to his father (Lk 15:29-30), that of the "good" Jews when they heard the doctrine of retribution (Ez 18:25-29), and that of Jonah when God pardoned pagan Nineveh (Jon 4:2). In all these cases the texts contrast the justice of God as seen by men with his mercy, unanticipated by men (Lk 15:1-2). Jesus answers this by an argument *ad hominem.* The master of the vineyard is "just" (after the human fashion) with the first, because he gives them what has been agreed. He is "just" in the divine manner with the last, because he is not tied by any contract in their regard. The argument however is weak, because the complaint lies not in any of the attitudes taken singly, but in the contrast between the two. Accordingly Jesus passes to another consideration, and affirms the primacy of God's goodness. His manner of action is not opposed to human justice, but transcends it altogether in love. The pact entered between the master of the vineyard and the workers is an image of the covenant between God and his people. This has nothing in common with the "*do ut des*" contract the Jews wished to discern in it: it is a gratuitous act of God (Dt 7:7-10; 4:7). The gift of the Father's *gratuitous love,* it is based on his total freedom and implies ours (Ga 3:16-22; 4:21-31). By the different treatments meted out to both groups, God wishes above all to show his love for both, accordingly to the situation of each.

The purpose then of the passage is to give Jesus' listeners an understanding of God's mercy. They must transcend the narrow limits of human justice and bilateral contracts which govern too exclusively human relations.

X. Judges 11:29-38
1st reading
1st cycle
Thursday

The sacrifice of the daughter of Jephthah must not have shocked the author's contemporaries in the same way as it did fervent Yahwists at a later stage. Jephthah is a loyal devotee of Yahweh, but he expresses his devotion in unconsidered fashion by vowing to sacrifice the the first person he met.

The account is actually less concerned with human sacrifice (cf. Gn 22:1-19; 2 K 3:27; Mi 6-7), which was certainly practiced at the time, than with the obligation of fulfilling vows. That is the understanding of Jephthah (v. 35) and his daughter (v. 36). Nothing, not even the hope of motherhood, can interfere with a sacral pledge (Nb 30:3). If there is a moral in the passage, it is that an oath should not be taken without sufficient motive, and that the person should always be preferred to sacral procedures.

XI. Ezechiel 36:23-28
1st reading
2nd cycle
Thursday

We have to understand this passage according to the vocabulary and liturgical outlook of the prophet. The whole oracle (vv. 16-32), pronounced at Babylon about 585, is full of allusions to ritual ablution. Terms like pollution (v. 25) and dung (modified by the Jerusalem Bible to "idols"), like holiness profanation and ablution, suggest preoccupation with ritual purity.

a) Ezechiel however transcends this sort of ritualism. In the future there will be no more baths of ablution: they will be received from God. There will be a change of minister. Priest or believer will no longer wash themselves, but will receive *purifying water* from God. It would be premature perhaps to discern a prophecy of Christian baptism in this text, but we can discern the economy of the final times when God will deal directly with his own by means of sacraments that will clarify his action, and liberate men from magical and ineffective rites.

b) This action by God is presented as a *new creation*. God will send his spirit into man as he did formerly into Adam (Gn 2:7). What is contemplated is a principle of life or new vital force, that will enable a man to do what was formerly impossible, obey the law spontaneously. It had been hitherto something external; from now on it would be associated with an interior dynamism.

Ablution with clear water also indicates God's action. It would give man real purity and cleanse him of pollution. Above all it would give him a new being, capable of preserving his recovered purity.

XII. Matthew 22:1-14
Gospel
Thursday

This passage of Matthew is noticeably different from the parallel text of Luke (Lk 14:16-24). The principal addition is the reference to the wedding garment (vv. 11-14), by means of which the banquet is made a wedding feast (v. 2), shared by the "bad and good" (v. 10).

A comparison of both versions enables us to reconstruct the words of Jesus as he proclaims the messianic times by using the image of a messianic feast (cf. Pr 9:1-5).

Luke has reinterpreted the message in the light of the problems of the Christian assemblies in admitting the poor and sinners. Still influenced by Judaism, he has throughout his gospel associated the theme of poverty with that of eschatology (Lk 6:20). Matthew, who has greater experience of the life of the first communities, goes further. He realizes that mere material poverty has nothing to do with the justice of the Kingdom. That is why he stresses moral behavior and justice: to remind Christians that mere external membership of the Church does not guarantee their salvation.

a) Aware too as he is of the atmosphere of increasing *hostility* to Jesus which is the context of this parable of the feast (Mt 21-22), he differs from Luke by associating with it the parable of the murderous vineyard workers (Mt 21:35-45), and that of the two sons (Mt 21:28-32). His account has a purpose altogether more polemic than Luke's.

We notice this principally in the royal character of the principal person (v. 2) and in the elaborate preparations for the wedding. Verse 7, with its mention of anger, army and punishment, can fit a royal context only. The parable of the murderous vineyard workers is constructed in the same way (Mt 21:33-41): we find the same personages and the same punishments.

b) Accordingly where Matthew describes a *wedding* feast (v. 2, above all vv. 11-13), Luke speaks of a feast simply. Matthew is solely responsible for the addition. We can clearly see his procedure in verse 4 where he retains the term "banquet." This in fact designated a midday meal, whereas wedding feasts were in the evening. He introduces the wedding theme in order to associate the parable with that of the wedding garment (vv. 11-13). Christ had often presented himself as the Spouse (Mk 2:19; Jn 3:29; Mt 25:1-13; 9:15; Ep 5:25; 2 Co 19:7-9; 21:2, 9; 22:17) joined to his own like the royal spouse of the Canticle or of Ps 44/45. The wedding feast of the Messiah was to take place in messianic times, and Matthew's parable indicates the welcome reserved for the King in the final days.

c) We notice that the words "invite" or "call" (*kalein*) recur regularly in the account (vv. 3, 4, 8, 9, 14). The *call* takes on a special character because of the fact that the servants are sent twice. Their message and the response of those invited are only described at the second call. And the sending twice is introduced only to strengthen the association with the parable of the murderous vineyard workers, where we have messengers twice also, but with more reason (Mt 21:34-36). The mission however in both cases is not similar. In the vineyard parable it precedes the sending of the Son, but in our parable the Son is already present. The first envoys, for Matthew, are the prophets of the Old Testament: the second, the apostles of the New. Matthew in fact likes to emphasize that the same fate is reserved for both one and the other (Mt 5:12; 10:17-18, 41; 13:17; 23, 29, 35, 1 Th 2:15). If the second call is more pressing than the first, that is because the apostles are commissioned to proclaim the imminence of the Kingdom (Mt 4:17).

d) The behavior of those first invited, in Matthew (vv. 5-6), is fairly curious. Where Luke tries to excuse them, he is content to list the occupations they leave in order to slay the servants. This strange behavior finds its explanation in the association with the parable of the murderous vineyard workers (Mt 21:36). These murderous guests stand for official Judaism, as in Matthew 21:36. Their punishment will be swift (v. 7). The "army of God" (a very biblical idea: Is 5:26-29; 7:18; Jr 5:15-17; 6:22-27; 4:13-17) stands for the foreign invaders God will use to punish the city of Jerusalem, as in the vineyard parable (Mt 21:43). The *fall of Jerusalem* at the hands of the Roman army is contemplated. Here we encounter one of Matthew's great preoccupations. He is addressing Christians who are tempted to revert to Judaism, and uses anything that will enable them to grasp the passing nature of the Jewish economy.

Once Jerusalem is destroyed the wedding feast can begin. The Church can go to the world (same idea in Mt 24:15-36). Primitive tradition did indeed associate the birth of the Church with the fall of the Jewish city. The beneficiaries of the feast are no longer just the poor as for Luke 14:21, but the "greatest possible number" (Mt 22:9-10), including good and bad, as the chaff is mixed with the good grain, and bad fish with good (Mt 13:24-30, 36-43, 47-50). We have the same viewpoint in chapter 24, where Matthew describes the assembly of all humanity after the fall of Jerusalem (Mt 24:30-31).

The parable could have stopped there. It could clearly manifest

God's plan. Christ comes to bring a message of Israel that is not heard. But God's plan cannot fail. If necessary his messengers will bring his message again.

e) At the time of redaction of this parable, Christians were despised and persecuted by the Jews. They had to be assisted towards perservance in the faith, shown that their temporary misery was God's will and presaged early punishment for the persecuting Jews. Matthew also adds to the parable the detail of the *nuptial garment* (vv. 11-13). Conceivably the juxtaposition of the two parables may have been suggested by Zephaniah 1, verse 7 of which could have inspired the first and verses 8-9 the second. The episode of the garment is a description of the last judgment. The verb "enter" (v. 11) has an eschatological overtone (Mt 25:10, 21, 23; 7:13), and the place of darkness and grinding of teeth traditionally designates hell (Mt 8:12; 13:42, 50; 24:51; 25:30).

Side by side the two parables emphasize the time of the Church in the design of God. With the rejection of the Jews and the call of the Gentiles a first stage has been reached. But a long time of testing of the conduct of each one must elapse. External membership of the Church is not sufficient, unless it includes the moral preparation that is here presented in the image of the wedding garment.

The garment image reminds us of the theme of clothing and its symbolic meaning in the order of salvation. Clothing humanizes the person, helps him take his place among his peers, takes away anonymity. It becomes a natural sign of the covenant between Yahweh and Israel. Like a bridegroom God stretches a fold of his garment over his bride (Ez 16). She however is unfaithful and exhibits herself to every comer. Her garment decays if it is not withdrawn by Yahweh, who relinquishes his spouse to nakedness and anonymity.

Jesus before the cross is stripped of his garment, for greater solidarity as it were with sinful humanity, in face of a death which strips away all false securities and appearances. But soon he will be reclothed at the resurrection in divine glory.

"Putting on Christ" then or "putting on the new man" (Ga 3:27-28; Ep 4:24; Co 3:10-12) means sharing the order of salvation that follows the road of Christ's despoliation and resurrection. The fullness of sharing must be postponed to the eschtological moment when all humanity will put on incorruptibility, and be clad for the eternal Spouse (Rev 21:2).

The wedding garment however must be donned before sharing the eucharistic banquet. Such sharing in other words has moral requirements that the sharer must honor, by accepting the despoliations that come his way.

XIII. Ruth 1:1-6, 14-16, 22
1st reading
1st cycle
Friday

The book of Ruth was written about 400, at the time when Esdras forbade mixed marriages (Es 10:15, 44).

a) The primary purpose of the book then is the permission of *mixed marriages.* What was a contemporary of Esdras to do? Choose between the police law and love for a foreign spouse? The author is concerned to resolve this dilemma, and draws from ancient history, especially the line of David, instances of good marriages contracted with strangers. In particular he describes the virtues of love, fidelity (cf. vv. 14-16) and discretion in the foreign spouse, anxious that the clergy of his time should show somewhat more respect for feminine qualities.

b) Behind this open, avowed purpose however is hidden another. The author makes his book a secret midrash on the history of Israel. He wants to reassure his compatriots who are disappointed with the conditions after return, but in such fashion that the occupants will not understand.

All the protagonists are in fact symbolic and designate a stage in the people's history. Israel rejoices in divine "favor" (Naomi). God has chosen a dynasty to which he promises perpetuity (Elimelech); but the kingdom is divided (Mahlon, the "puny" and Chilion) and the two kings are dead. Their descendants in exile are mingled with strangers (Orpah and Ruth). But the tribe of Judah, where Boaz figures, will be the seed of restoration. In it will be found that messianic seed which is God's gift, even through the medium of mixed marriages. Ruth accordingly becomes the mother of the Messiah (Is 9:5). She receives the divine seed from Boaz. The daughter of Sion, returned from exile, can be certain that her hope of bearing the *Messiah* will not be in vain.

XIV. Ezechiel 37:1-14
1st reading
2nd cycle
Friday

In exile on the banks of Kebar, the prophet meditates on the future of his people. Probably the beginning of this account is actually to be found in Ezechiel 3:16a, 22-24a. Verses 12-13 were added after the exile by a disciple of the prophet.

a) As he surveys the plain stretched out before him, Ezechiel thinks of the numerous ossuaries where the corpses of his compatriots dry in the sun, having given their flesh to the rapacious birds of the air. For the Bible the *bones* are the radical, resistant part of the being. Thus what is represented here is the better element of the people, the very essentials of its life (v. 11; cf. Jr 8:1-3).

The prophet tells the people that all is not lost. There will be, by God's will, a national restoration comparable to a new creation. God will not bring this about directly himself, but will entrust it to the prophetic ministry. The new man henceforward will be inspired by the breath of prophetic inspiration: the breath of Yahweh as in Genesis 2:7, now become a prophetic word and a new spirit (vv. 5-10).

What is foreseen then is a national restoration after the manner of a re-creation. The prophet will breathe into the heart of the new people the spirit of a new covenant, and will give them the strength to adhere to it (cf. Ez 11:14-20).

b) A disciple of Ezechiel, under the influence of Isaiah 26:19 and Daniel 12:2-3, has added two verses which make the passage a prophecy of the *resurrection of the body* (vv. 12-13). He wished to show by this that the national restoration would be postponed perhaps to the final times. In any case those Jews who had died before the final times would arise to be associated with the happiness of their descendants. This gloss colored not only the later interpretation of Ezechiel 37, but also the redaction of several New Testament passages, notably Revelation 11:11; Matthew 27:51-54; John 5:28.

XV. Matthew 22:34-40
Gospel
Friday

Jesus has just dealt with the Pharisees' trap concerning the tax (22:15-22), and replied to the Jewish question concerning the resurrection of the dead (22:23-33). Now he is asked about the greatest commandment (22:34-40).

The Bible gives us three different versions of the first part: the commandments of *love*.

1) In Luke (10:25-28) the lawyer himself states the commandment. There is no question of the "greatest commandment." Such a typically rabbinical problem would be of no interest to the readers.

2) In Matthew (our text) the question is not put to Jesus in good faith. His answer is so clear that there is no further rejoinder.

3) In Mark (12:28-34) the Scribe approaches Jesus in good faith with an honest desire for enlightenment.

In verse 34, in the very terms of Psalm 2:2, the evangelist notes that the Pharisees are meeting together: *principes convenerunt in unum.* A polemic atmosphere of conspiracy is thus set up at once.

Then immediately Jesus affirms two commandments (vv. 37-39), not one. Mark simply gives the gist of the commandments and Luke combines the two in one. In giving the two, Matthew says that the second is like the first.

In the case of the first, Jesus' answer reproduces Deuteronomy 6:4-5, but in the version given by the Jewish morning and evening prayer. The formulation of the second is from Leviticus 19:18.

Matthew concludes with a phrase which is peculiar to him: "in these two commandments is resumed all the law and the prophets" (v. 40: cf. Mt 7:12; 5:17). He is affirming that these are the pivots as it were on which all the rest depends: abolish them and the edifice crumbles. There is perhaps a reference to the attitude of the Pharisees, who prefer "all the rest" to charity and duties towards God. Love is the key to the law, which cannot really be fulfilled without it.

XVI. Ruth 2:1-3, 8-11, 4:13-17
1st reading
1st cycle
Saturday

This passage was commented on with Ruth 1:1-6, 14-16, 22 on Friday of this week, p. 301.

XVII. Ezechiel 43:1-7
1st reading
2nd cycle
Saturday

The new temple described by Ezechiel from chapter 40 onwards is a creation of fantasy which will never be realized. However the prophet was thinking less of the construction of a new edifice than of basic reform of cult and the priesthood. His abstract architecture is a way of affirming the demands of monotheism in the liturgy.

He concludes the description of his *temple* with a ceremony of reintegration within its walls for Yahweh. He had written at length of the departure of the glory of Yahweh from the old temple, where the worship discouraged him (Ez 10:2-5, 18-19; 11:22-23). He is happy to proclaim the reentry of Yahweh, a divine seal set on the liturgical reform, which he had labored so hard to program.

It is rather surprising that he, who had proclaimed the building of a spiritual temple which might be anywhere on earth, returns now to the construction of a material, localized temple. At the time of Deuteronomy, the temple, previously a simple chapel in the royal palace, became the visible symbol of the unity of the people, assembled around the unique God. A prophecy of its reconstruction then becomes a proclamation that the people will return to its fidelity to Yahwist monotheism.

In the temple-vision we have an example of prophetism abdicating in favor of priesthood. The religion to come would be perhaps more pure and holy than previously, but it would be essentially ritualist. In such fashion does the institution always devour its prophets.

XVIII. Matthew 23:1-12
Gospel
Saturday

This passage is the preamble to the maledictions on the Scribes and Pharisees (Mt 23:12-32). At the second verse Jesus indicates his adversaries. They are usurping the chair of Moses. According to the law the teaching and interpretation of God's Word was to be reserved to the priests exclusively (Dt 17:8-12; 31:9-10; Mi 3:11; Ml 2:7-10). By usurping the function, the Scribes had introduced a profound change in religion. They had substituted a sort of intellectualism for faith in the Word, legalism and casuistry for obedience to God's plan. By cursing the Scribes, Jesus is rejecting this human concept of religion.

The words in verses 8-10 are peculiar to Matthew. Joined with the preceding text by the key-word *rabbi,* this passage is constructed in a sort of ternary rhythm, with mention successively of "Master," "Father" and "Teacher" (or better, "Director"). It is not so much these titles that Jesus rejects as the religion they suggest, that of exegetes and professors. He is affirming that one cannot depend on professors for knowledge of God. The final two verses are out of place in this context (cf. Mt 20:26).

What Jesus has in mind then in the passage is the hypocrisy of the Scribes and leaders of the synagogue. The essential characteristic of this attitude is deception of the other by means of religious gestures or usurped sacred prerogatives. The hypocrite will take to himself honors which suggest that he represents God (vv. 6-7), whom he seems to worship. But what he is really doing is setting himself up (v. 5). Accordingly, by his desire for notice (cf. Mt 6:2, 5, 16), he distorts the most religious practices from their true meaning. Moreover he uses his theological knowledge in the service of his own egoism, choosing by means of casuistry the precepts which suit himself, and imposing on others obligations from which he dispenses himself (v. 4; cf. Mt 23:24-25). Finally the hypocritical Scribe takes the place of God by arrogating a power to himself that he does not deserve (vv. 8-10; cf. Mt 15:3-14). Instead of bringing men to a personal encounter with God, at the deepest level of freedom and decision, he directs all attention to arguments, conclusions and regulations that are too human to be now signs of God.

TWENTY-FIRST WEEK

I. 1 Thessalonians 1:2-5; 8-10
1st reading
1st cycle
Monday

It seems certain that the first letter to the Thessalonians was compiled at Corinth in 51. Timothy had been sent by Paul to Thessalonica and has just returned. He has made a fairly favorable report on the faith, hope and charity of the Thessalonians (v. 3). The address and the first phrases of the letter are the direct echo of Timothy's good news.

a) Emphasizing the impressive progress of their faith (v. 3) and the marvelous nature of their evangelization (v. 5), Paul attributes this not to human eloquence, but to God's power (1 Co 2:4; 4:19-20). The word of the apostles derives its strength from the Spirit who has raised up Jesus with power (Rm 8:11; 1 Co 6:14). It carries on the miraculous word of Jesus.

b) It is charged with the power of Christ because it has Christ as object. This Christo-centrism is to be seen in the kerygma, which is accompanied by miracles comparable to those of Christ (v. 5), in catechesis and parainesis (v. 3), which kindle *faith, hope and charity,* and have Jesus as their single object.

In 1 Thessalonians faith indicates above all a man's fundamental attitude towards the revelation of salvation, which distinguishes him from pagans. It is made up of fidelity principally (1 Th 3:2-6; 5:24; 1:8) and adhesion to truths like the resurrection of Christ (1 Th 4:14) as well as that of all men (1 Th 4:13-18), and the unity of a history which is being directed towards fulfillment by the one God (subject of the whole letter).

God himself sends love into our hearts (2 Th 3:5), and if Paul does not speak of it especially in this letter, that is because his audience does not seem to need this (1 Th 4:9). He insists however that they are not to allow themselves to be shut in by the limits of the community, and must direct their attention to the world at large.

Hope is seen at three levels. It is the expectation of an extraordinary future (2 Th 3:16), confidence in God throughout the earthly pilgrimage (1 Th 2:9) and patience under trial (v. 3; 1 Th 5:8). But the object of hope is always the same: access to God's glory (1 Th 5:10; 1:11).

The triad faith, hope and charity seems to have been established among Christians prior to 1 Thessalonians. It was a formula readily resorted to by the Jew whenever he wished to describe something sacred. Probably Paul found it in use among Christian communities to describe the basic, harmonious Christian attitude *vis-a-vis* God and his Christ.

II. 2 Thessalonians 1:1-5, 11-19
1st reading
2nd cycle
Monday

Here we have the introduction to Paul's second letter to the Thessalonians. The structure is the normal one: a thanksgiving of complex structure, not all of which is reproduced in today's reading.

He praises the Thessalonians for their faith and charity. They should be congratulated for their hope too, but this he presents as endurance and patience, because the faithful were encountering trial. From this reflection comes the idea of retribution. Sooner or later God will punish the wicked and reward the patient. It is Paul's wish that the Thessalonians, with himself, will reach this day of judgment and glory.

a) The greatest consolation he offers Christians under trial is the *expectation of the Day* of judgment. He is preparing his readers for the eschatological teaching which will pervade the rest of the letter. The essential thing is that this day of trial and catastrophe will not be a threat to believers, but only to the wicked.

Paul may very well have deliberately substituted this appeal for patience for an invitation to hope. His audience, accustomed to endless discussion of the end of the world and speculation about its development, were in danger of forgetting the essential lesson about endurance under trial.

b) As a result of the spiritual progress of the Thessalonians Paul feels a certain *high spirit:* the word is almost synonymous with pride. He confesses to some pride, a pride that is based not on men, but on the fact that men are the instrument of God's work (Rm 5:11; Ph 3:3; Ga 6:14). There are many motives for this sentiment, the first still a somewhat human one, the success of his preaching at Thessalonia (v. 4). This is so striking that it cannot but be a work of God. Next, it has its roots in weakness and the cross (Ga 6:14; 2 Co 11:23-30), because it springs from the trying conditions in which the Thessalonian Christians find themselves. Finally, it has an eschatological dimension. Paul is elated in advance by the sentence in favor of the persecuted (v. 5), which will be given at God's judgment. This can be anticipated by reason of the high esteem in which Thessalonians are held by other Christian communities (v. 4, cf. 1 Th 1:7-8).

In this passage we get Paul's concept of the diffusion of faith. The Thessalonians live their human life with Christ, and invite others to adopt and imitate their style of life (cf. 1 Th 2:14). Faith is not a matter of argumentation: it is communication, and the sharing of a certain way of life. It was thus that the faith of the apostles came into being. It was not based on speculative knowledge of God or eschatology, but on the human life of Jesus lived with the Father and his brothers. If today we have so many problems in faith, could that not be because there is no longer a typically Christian way of life, and because the problems are too exclusively intellectual?

III. Matthew 23:13-22
Gospel
Monday

In chapters 21-22 Matthew had described the increasing tension between Jesus and the leaders of the people. This finds expression now in the picture drawn by Jesus of the leaders (Mt 23:1-12), then in a series of maledictions, and finally in a prophecy of extinction for the authorities (vv. 34-36).

Matthew's version seems to be the most original. He was in fact experiencing the developing tension between Christianity and Judaism, and had every reason to preserve a text so concerned with this issue. Mark (Mk 4:38-39; 12:37-40) and Luke (Lk 20:45-47) do not have the same perspective and consequently abridge the text considerably.

a) Of the seven *maledictions* pronounced against the leaders by Jesus our passage today gives us but three. Christ is now beginning the messianic judgment. That is why he exhorts no more and summons no more to conversion. The Kingdom is at hand and the Messiah takes up his function as judge.

Unlike Luke, Matthew omitted the maledictions of the sermon on the mount (Lk 6:24-26). That was because at this moment in his public life Jesus was presenting himself merely as a preacher or converter, not as a judge. Now, at this decisive moment, when the Messiah is beginning his task as judge, and when the reasons for condemnation of the world have become aggravated, he does not hesitate to introduce them. It is not indeed impossible that the early Christians gave their own interpretation of the condemnations. We know for instance that verse 14 is a later interpolation, taken from Mark 12:40 and Luke 20:47.

b) The first complaint of Jesus concerns the Scribes' and Pharisees' severity of doctrine (v. 13). The latter used precepts to exclude the faithful from the Kingdom, loading them with unnecessary guilt, whereas they themselves were careful not to put their own precepts in practice.

The Scribes displayed their *hypocrisy* by turning propagandist. They showed clearly that they were not interested in the genuine conversion of Gentile proselytes (v. 15) in that they made them separate from their spouses. Hypocrisy then describes the attitude of becoming lost in regulations, and disregarding the basic responsibility of a leader of having his followers enter the Kingdom.

c) The third malediction is the longest and most structured (vv. 16-21). It concerns two antithetical formulae current among the rabbis of the period (vv. 16b and 18). These are followed by two violent epithets (fools and blind). Jesus is affirming that *oaths,* whatever their form, ought to be kept, because an oath is made in the name of God, even if one avoids pronouncing it. If one respects the name of God, it is better not to make an oath (Mt 5:33-37) rather than use casuistry to evade its fulfillment.

We might well ask ourselves whether the invectives of Jesus have become obsolete, or whether they do not have a striking application now. Is not the behavior of certain Christians and Church leaders in contradiction with the very mystery of the Church? If hypocrisy is too strong a word in this context (only God can judge hearts), we can at least speak of illusion.

We have illusion on the part of those who believe in the mystery of poverty in the Church, but live according to the heritage of an outmoded imperial age that was characterized by grandeur and riches. We have illusion when people realize that the Church is not of this world, but use diplomacy and secular political pressure to spread the gospel. We have it when people believe in the Lord's humanity, but will not really listen to the human being, follow him in his quest, with full respect for his misgivings and hesitancy.

IV. 1 Thessalonians 2:1-8
1st reading
1st cycle
Tuesday

This is the first apologia of Saint Paul for his vocation and ministry. Its chief interest is the manner in which it expresses, according to the context of Jewish thought, that which Paul considers he has become.

a) As he sees it his *ministry* is first of all that of a suffering Servant (v. 1-3a). Thus his efforts have not been vain (v. 1) or, more exactly, "empty," a word which suggests plenitude (cf. 1 Th 3:5; 1 Co 15:58; Ph 2:16). The phrase is actually taken from the eulogy of the suffering Servant (Is 49:4). It is the more suitable now in that Paul has just undergone persecution at Philippi (v. 2; cf. Ac 16:20-24). His success at Thessalonica seemed to him like the recompense promised for the Servant's sufferings.

The second characteristic of his prophetic ministry is "confidence" or, better still, "assurance" (v. 2). It is the attitude before God of the persecuted just man (Wi 5:4; Jr 20: 7-8), something that Paul was often glad to experience in his ministry (2 Co 7:4; Ph 1:20; Ep 3:12).

Finally he describes his ministry as an "exhortation," or better, a "paraklesis" (v. 3a), the term probably taken also from Isaiah 49:10-13. It describes a ministry that shelters the "humble" from divine anger and eschatological punishment.

b) In verse 3 Paul discards different possible sources for his teaching to show that it can come from God only. In this context "error" is rejected. This doubtless is the error destined to be spread in the world by the Antichrist before the fulfillment of the final times (2 Tm 3:13; 2 Th 2:8-12). As the false prophets had hastened the downfall of Israel by their pseudo-oracles, so will the Antichrist and his associates hasten the final times by the confusion they will spread.

Paul also rejects "impurity," not in the fleshly sense, but all profanity that is incompatible with the Kingdom, all that lies outside the domain of salvation, self-sufficiency with its accompanying vices (cf. Is 52:1, 11).

Finally he rejects all association with "duplicity" as the suffering Servant had done before him (Is 53:9; cf. Wi 4:11). This is the fault *par excellence* of observers of the law.

In such fashion does he dissociate himself from Satan, from paganism and from Jewish sinners. God alone is the source and inspiration of his gospel. The divine inspiration manifests itself in many ways. He is first of all *invested* with the gospel (v. 4) by God who "fathoms hearts" and who "tests." Such language is taken now from Jeremiah 11:20; 20:12, not from Jeremiah 12:3;

6:27, where it sometimes describes the prophetic vocation. The apostle is immersed in the prophetic atmosphere of the Old Testament. His mission seems best represented by the figures of Jeremiah and the suffering Servant.

c) However, when he describes the actual operation of his ministry, his language changes immediately. He borrows from the vocabulary of Hellenism, and uses terms in their profane sense. Such are the phrases "to please men" (v. 4), "flattery" (v. 5), "cupidity" and "human glory." He rejoins the world in which he is living. In verse 7 he will state clearly that he is not alone a prophet in the Old Testament manner, but also the *apostle of the nations.*

Thus he does not hesitate to place himself in the tradition of prophecy and "service" of the Old Testament. He even compares himself to the suffering Servant, and this at a time when christology reserved the comparison for Christ. The Old Testament however does not exhaust the content of his apostolic ministry. He is Christ's apostle to the Gentiles. And so original is this particular mission that he has recourse to the idiom of his correspondents in order to describe it.

It is only on such principles that the essence of the Kingdom can be understood, and above all ministry in the Kingdom. No ready-made definition is ever quite adequate, because always we must be transcending what we have previously grasped. Things that have been touched by God are inexhaustible. The ministry is one of those things. That may very well be the reason for the great questioning concerning it that we now witness.

V. 2 Thessalonians 2:1-3, 13-16
1st reading
2nd cycle
Tuesday

This passage is an answer to the perplexities of early Christians concerning the time and manner of the Lord's coming.

a) Jewish Christians saw this event as a gathering of the nations in "assembly" with Christ (Mt 24:31; 23:37; 2 M 2:7). The Thessalonians however were troubled concerning it "by the Spirit, the word and a supposed letter" of Paul (v. 2), which proclaimed the imminence of the Kingdom (cf. 2 Th 3:17). Spirit in this context designates doubtless the ecstatic manifestations we know from 1 Co 12:8-11; 14. Just as he would require the Corinthians to exercise intelligence in controlling them, he now begs the Thessalonians not to lose their "good sense." They were disturbed and wanted to discern the "signs" which would herald the Lord's coming. Paul answers like Jesus. The coming and the assembly are not immediate: first must come defections and the Apostasy (v. 4; cf. Mt 24:9-13), then the "man of impiety" or the son "of perdition"* must appear in the temple (vv. 4-5; we recall the "abomination" of Mt 24:25). Paul's thought on the matter finds inspiration in Antiochus of Daniel 11:36, the Babylonian king of Isaiah 14:13-14, and the king of Tyre of Ezechiel 28:2. His perspective rather resembles that of Matthew 24: the Messiah's coming is delayed until after the profanation of the temple (vv. 4-5). Once the temple has been profaned however and its incapacity for reassembly demonstrated, then can come the veritable *reassembly* of men, and the Messiah's Lordship over the world will be realized (v. 8; cf. Mt 24:30-31; 26:64). We have the same lesson as in Matthew 24. Jerusalem must fall so that the reassembly of men under Christ's Lordship can take place.

He does not give any other details. He does not say clearly who the Antichrist is, or what is "retaining" him. One thing alone is clear. The mystery of Satan is already at work and the profanation of the temple will be the manifestation of this. And the lesson is clear: people should not be disturbed by the march of events. On the contrary they should continue to give thanks.

b) The reason for this thanks is the *history of the believer.* This begins in eternity by God's will to sanctify by the Spirit's action those who believe in truth (v. 13). It is pursued in the collaboration between the sanctifying Spirit (cf. 1 Th 4:3-8; Rm

* These two hebraisms are used in Christian apocalypse to give it a halo of mystery.

15:16; 1 Co 3:16-17) and the believer who is converted to the gospel (v. 14; cf. 1 Th 2:13; 4:7; 5:24; Rm 8:30). It is consummated in sharing the glory of Jesus Christ (v. 14; cf. 1 Co 15:23; Rm 8:17).

c) But the road between conversion and glory is a long one. It must be traversed in fidelity to the traditional teaching, which comprises first of all the gospel message itself (as in 1 Th 2:13; 1 Co 15:1-2; Ga 1:11-12; Co 2:6-8), and also characteristic usages of the Christian life (as in 1 Co 11:22-25; 2 Th 3:6; 1 Th 4:4-5). The essential *tradition* however is what Paul himself has received and transmitted: that Christ died and is risen (1 Co 15:1-5).

The theme of tradition received and transmitted is of Jewish origin. It suggests the Sinai scene when Moses received the law for transmission to the people, who transmitted it to generation after generation. This tradition is God's revelation, from which its witnesses desire their authority.

d) The believer's life then begins with the eternal design of God, and is consummated in sharing the glory of Christ. Between these two points come different stages in which tradition is received: the summons of the gospel and the response of faith, the teaching of tradition and the reaction of human fidelity. No one can respond without the *grace of God,* which provides comfort and constancy (vv. 16-17), because the believer's life is made up of struggle and challenge (cf. 1 Th 2:2, 16).

In the passage we have two concepts of history contrasted. The first causes unease because it does not discern the meaning of events, or have the key to their interpretation. The second involves thanksgiving because history is lived as the gift of God, an experience where man is constantly encountering the divine initiative.

Modern man has severed the religious link with nature, and he has also emancipated himself from the religious dimension of history. The idea of a history directed by God as a gesture of salvation no longer has much meaning. Any concept of predestination or previous divine plan is apt to irritate many of our contemporaries. This change does not make for respect for a past which is challenged, or dispose men to accept from God a future they propose themselves to mold. Thus modern man finds himself alien both to the thanksgiving proposed by Saint Paul, and the unease kindled by the false prophets.

Modern views of history do, it is true, ease the tension for the personal conscience. But Saint Paul's recommendations continue nevertheless to have validity: the perspective only is changed. Paul's view of history was for his time a liberating one. By giving it a meaning, he freed it from the cycles and the fatalism that paganism had evolved. We can only then be faithful to his thought when we evince an authentic freedom. Our witness will take the form that he proposes to the Thessalonians. We shall show in the first place that Christians are strangers to fear (vv. 1-3). In a world shaken by threats of catastrophe, we Christians shall remain basically optimist. We shall take the view that situations which seem devoid of meaning do nevertheless have human, and consequently divine, meaning. A Christian will not alone be fearless. He will boldly enter the new world that is being molded with thanksgiving in his heart (vv. 13-16). The human itinerary, whether it be historical or psychological, must always follow the path of Jesus' paschal mystery. The road to glory, and its necessary preliminary, must always be death.

VI. Matthew 23:23-26 *Gospel* *Tuesday*

Here we have a continuation of the discourse of malediction where Jesus takes on his responsibilities as judge, condemning the Jewish religious authorities. Today's passage gives two maledictions (vv. 23-24 and 25-26).

a) The first is made up of two verses which could have been separate (v. 23 is found in Lk 11:42, but v. 24 is new), but which were associated by Matthew for a very precise purpose. The *tithe* in the Old Testament was the Jew's way of acknowledging that his land was divine property. It was also the means of meeting the needs of the priests and furnishing the material of the temple sacrifices. So concerned however were the leaders of the people with administering the wealth accumulated in the temple (the Romans would find a fortune there) that they gave more weight to the actual money than to its religious significance. By concentrating on the tithe the authorities neglected "right" (the respect due to every human person), "fidelity" (the clauses of the covenant: Jr 5:1; Rm 3:3; Ga 5:22) and "mercy" (attention to particular and difficult cases).

Jesus is not saying that observance of minor precepts is valueless. He is merely condemning that perversion of observances which is designed for enrichment. It is thus that religion becomes mere administration, an abuse of the piety of the poor for the benefit of those in charge.

b) In the second malediction outward appearance and inward uncleanness are contrasted (Lk 11:39). We are shown the man who wants to purify himself by some ablutions, without thinking of the stains of intemperance (cf. Mt 15:11). Purifying the inside of the cup means sincerely obeying God's law, which cannot be done without a heart of the new covenant (Jr 31:31). One must undertake entry to the new covenant which Jesus proclaims and renders possible. That new covenant must take root in the heart (Jn 15:3; Rm 10:9-10; Mt 13:19; 12:34) before fruit can be borne. The mistake of the leaders of the people is refusal to do this. They cling to the external, empty observances of the old covenant, rejecting all circumcision of the heart.

VII. 1 Thessalonians 2:9-13
1st reading
1st cycle
Wednesday

Paul continues the description of his apostolic ministry. Having set himself in the line of Old Testament prophets (1 Th 2:1-6), he now describes the original characteristics of his ministry to the Gentiles.

a) His mission to the Thessalonians has been characterized by an unusual *tenderness*. He can hardly find words to express his feelings: the loving-kindness and sweetness of the benign superior (v. 7), the generosity of the mother (v. 7), the tenderness which goes the length of laying down life (v. 8), the concern of a father for his children (v. 11). Most of these images and terms are borrowed from hellenistic vocabulary, none from the Old Testament. There is a distinct cleavage between what is derived from Judaism, and what is original to this mission of God's love among the nations.

b) There is an eschatological dimension to the ministry: it leads to the *Kingdom* (v. 12). To begin with, it is a summons to conversion. Then it gives courage and patience under trial. Finally, it calls upon men to walk in such fashion that they reach the Kingdom of glory.

c) The most important concept in the passage however is that of Paul's *spiritual paternity.* This theme will become more explicit still in 1 Corinthians 4:14-21, though we have the principal lines laid down here. We should note that the apostle is not affirming fatherhood of the Thessalonians: he is using a figure only. He actually borrows the figure of the nurse as well from the Old Testament (vv. 7-8; cf. Ex 4:22; Ho 11:3-4; Is 49:15; Si 4:10). There is no intention of providing in this context a total definition of his mission, but rather of describing the nature of the Thessalonian mission. Seeing that he will not regard himself as fulfilling simply the role of a philosopher or publicist, and distinguishes his preaching from simple pedagogy (1 Co 4:14-21), claiming for it the function of transmitting life, the life to which God calls men, it is natural that his imagery be associated with the transmission of life.

He does however assimilate his person to his message. By his attitude, his sufferings, his zeal, he is himself a transmission of the gospel, a call to life. Consequently he does not hesitate to associate the concepts of father or mother with his own person, not literally, but in the sense that his person is dedicated to the propagation of the divine gift of life. There is no hint of assuming authority. His fatherhood is a manifestation of divine fatherhood:

it claims nothing for itself, but refers all to the unique source of life.

VIII. 2 Thessalonians 3:6-10, 16-18
1st reading
2nd cycle
Wednesday

Paul concludes the letter by dealing with a painful matter. Deceived by false eschatological expectations, many members of the community had turned to vain nonsense, refusing to work and depending on charity for subsistence (cf. previously 1 Th 4:10; 5:14). The treatment for such lazy members is summary. Christians cannot be further burdened with them (vv. 6 and 14). Subsistence will be cut off, in the hope that their laziness will disappear. Before executing this however, he invites the culprits once again to consider the value of work.

Christian charity cannot condone laziness. Each one should eat the fruit of his *toil.* Human dignity requires that one not be a charge on others. Paul does not develop any doctrinal arguments for this: he simply puts forward his own example. Is he not an apostle, and does he not by this title have normative authority (v. 7; cf. 1 Th 1:6)? He has never lived in disorderly fashion and has not eaten the bread of others, though he has had that right (v. 8). On the contrary, he has worked hard, night and day, in addition to his apostolic labors.

His toil has been due to a constant wish not to allow the spirit of gain to interfere where the spread of the gospel was concerned (v. 9; cf. 1 Co 9:12-18; 2 Co 11:7; 12:13). He puts this forward as an example to be followed. The Jews were devoted to work. Most of the rabbis known lived by their professional activity. The Greeks on the contrary would often leave manual labor to slaves and give themselves to leisure or philosophy. Good Jew that he is, Paul is reacting against this Greek attitude. Not only does he wish to avoid being a charge on anyone; he wants to change the Greek standards in this regard.

Jesus worked with his hands throughout the greatest part of his life, and his father was a carpenter. At the age of thirty he went to preach the Good News of the Kingdom, and does not seem to attach any importance to work in that he praises the birds of the air "who sow not, neither do they reap" (Mt 6:26). One thing only counts in his eyes, the Kingdom.

In fact the nature of the Kingdom he proclaimed was providing an unexpected answer to the grave questions raised in Israel concerning work. The Kingdom inaugurated in the person of Jesus must be constructed here below. It is not of this world. Yet in order to enter it and collaborate in its construction the terrestrial state was not to be avoided. It would be constructed by the way of obedience unto the death of the cross, an obedience which restored to suffering and death their true value.

Jesus did not, it is true, speak of work, but by inaugurating the Kingdom in this world, he revealed the true dignity of work which is based on evangelic obedience to the terrestrial state. To the extent to which man, fully accepting his creatural condition (which he does by means of the living link with Christ), confronts suffering and death and makes them the focus of the greatest love, love for God and love for men, he will give back to human values their true status. Passage by the way of death does not mean destruction for these, but purification and a real transfiguration. This applies to work. The circumstances under which work is performed on this earth, so far from turning men towards a quest for a new paradise, require them on the contrary to mobilize all energies so that work shall have its proper dignity here below. The child of God makes his contribution as partner to the building of the Kingdom by displaying his fidelity to the creatural state.

Christ is the new Adam and reminds men that their mission is to subdue the earth by toil. This can only be done however with proper objectivity, when they recognize that the one thing necessary is the Kingdom. In this perspective work acquires its proper inspiration and its due dignity. Moved by a love which goes the length of total self-giving, men can labor for the veritable humanization of the earth.

The apostolic writings do not put forward either a philosophy of work or a program for social reform. In the primitive communities were gathered people of every state in life. But in general they were of lower classes, including slaves. There was no question of preaching revolution to them; but when they were made free with the freedom acquired in Jesus Christ, a seed was sown in them which was gradually to change the face of the Graeco-Roman world.

So far as work was concerned, there were many circumstances that militated against this development. In the Graeco-Roman world Christianity found itself associated with a culture which had not much respect for manual labor, the province for the most part of slaves. It was a culture which professed a predilection for values of the spirit, and a disdain for anything connected with the body and matter. Contemplation was exalted above activity, speculation over the transformation of the world. Only in works of art was matter humanized. . . . Furthermore, from the moment that Christianity became the official religion of the Empire, instead of calling them constantly into question, it ran the risk of strengthening established social mores. Resignation began to be preached.

Yet the ferment of the Gospel at work little by little brought about an awareness of the distinction between religion as such, and the enterprise of civilization. Though they are closely articulated, it is essential to maintain a distinction between the two. The project of civilization began to assume its proper autonomy in the profane sphere. Out of this was to come the modern world where the concept of work would be transformed. It would no longer be just something necessary, but a value in itself governed by precise demands. If man, as a child of God, was to take part in building the Kingdom, he must contribute to the humanization of the earth and the transformation of relationships between all men. Things would be restored to a proper balance, and work to its proper dignity.

IX. Matthew 23:27-32 *Gospel Wednesday*

This is the conclusion of the condemnation of the leaders of the people by the Messiah-Judge. Verses 27-28 duplicate the theme of verses 25-26, and verses 29-32 return to the theme of hypocrisy.

The pious demeanor of the Pharisees could not conceal their basic infidelity to the law; an ornate tomb will not cancel the putrefaction within. But their *hypocrisy* goes even further. They take cover under the religious glory of ancestors (vv. 29-32; cf. Mt 13:17; 10:41), whereas in fact they are descendants of the murderers of prophets, and are actually now preparing the murder of Jesus (cf. Mt 21:33-43; Ac 7:51).

Nowadays hypocrisy has a wide range, because it is no longer an individual vice, but invests society itself. Political and religious structures maintain silence before injustice throughout the world. States and Churches tolerate social institutions that are alienating, or their condemnation is couched in such vague terms as to be innocuous. Consciences are lulled to rest by comfort provided from an economy that nourishes both state and church. Where are the prophets of today?

X. 1 Thessalonians 3:7-13 *1st reading 1st cycle Thursday*

The first part of this letter to the Thessalonians is concluded by a prayer. Previously Paul had recalled their evangelization and conversion (1:2-10), and stressed the difference between the behavior of the apostles and that of the false missionaries (2:1-16).

The time is the year 51, and Paul is far from

Thessalonica. He is apprehensive about the influence of false preaching, and the persecutions the Christians are undergoing. Not even the news brought by Timothy is sufficient to reassure him completely (2:17—3:10). Consequently he begs God that he may have the joy of seeing his own again, so that they will advance in faith.

His prayer has a precise structure. Verses 10-11 allude to the faith of the Thessalonians. Verse 12 recalls their charity and verse 13 their hope. The apostle's principal concern seems to be the theological virtues, the basis of the Christian life.

a) The *faith* of the community is frail: Timothy's report had probably revealed deficiencies. Probably Paul had had to quit the city before completing the necessary catechesis (Ac 17:1-10). He begs God to smooth out the obstacles which have so far prevented his return.

b) The second object of his prayer is increase in *charity* among the brethren, and in charity towards all men, even persecutors (Ga 6:10; Rm 12:10-21). He regards himself as responsible for the love the Thessalonians show one another. It is a reflection of the love he showed them (same sentiment in 2 Th 3:7-9; Ph 3:17; 4:9; 1 Co 4:16; 11:1).

A strengthened faith and charity will assure them holiness beyond reproach. This ought to be constantly intensified in the *hope* of the Lord's Parousia (1 Th 5:23; 1 Co 1:8). Paul thus shares the ideas of his time, the belief that the Parousia would come at the end of persecution. The troubles of his correspondents are but the prelude.

It would be unwise to distinguish the three theological virtues as if they were three distinct dynamisms in the soul of the Christian. Paul's distinction follows the literary genre of the triad. The Christian organism is a unity: one cannot have faith without love, or love without hope. This indeed is affirmed by the apostle whenever he describes the virtues. If one is a Christian it means that one gives a new meaning to reality in Jesus Christ. This is expressed in various ways, but some dimensions have an over-all significance. These are the meanings given to the life, death and resurrection of Jesus, to the life of men with one another, and to the whole destiny of humanity. Faith, charity and hope describe these meanings, and they are attitudes that can only be taken in the Lord's name.

XI. 1 Corinthians 1:1-9
1st reading
2nd cycle
Thursday

Compiled around 57, the first letter to the Corinthians confronts the great problems of Christian living in a pagan ambience, particularly in the decadent society of Corinth.

a) The opening sentences of the letter indicate at once the fundamental themes. He begins by stressing his role as *apostle* (v. 1). The authority by virtue of which he proposes to discipline the Corinthian Christians is not based on the fact that he is the founder of a religious sect or a philosophic school. It is based on the call of God. The words he is about to utter are not his own, but the Words of God, loyally transmitted.

b) Whatever be their faults however, the Corinth Christians do have their titles to nobility. They should remember these in solving their problems. The first title is *holiness* (v. 2). In this they are the successors of ancient Israel, which was set apart from pagan ways to become a holy assembly before God (Ex 19:6-15; cf. 1 Co 6:2—4:11). Their holiness obliges them to reject the amoralism of their society and become the representatives of divine transcendence in a pagan world.

c) The second title they should keep in mind is their *solidarity* with all those throughout the world who invoke the name of the Lord. Previously the cult of Yahweh was the privilege of Israel among the nations (Jr 10:25; cf. Is 43:7), and was Israel's way of saving the world. Now the responsibility for world salvation is that of Christians who invoke the name of Jesus. Their prayer and their behavior will ensure this salvation for themselves, and round about them.

d) As Paul sees it, the problems of the community can find solution in the *common union* of all in Christ (v. 9). One must be "of" Christ (vv. 6-7) and "in" Christ (v. 5; cf. 1 Co 1:10-30; 4:10, 15; 7:21-22, 39; 15:18-22, 31 . . .). Such union enables one to have the grace of God (vv. 1, 4, 7), a salvation that is given altogether gratuitously, and the divine riches (v. 5). These in particular are the Word and knowledge of God (under which he will classify the charisms of language and understanding to which the Corinthians were so given: 1 Co 12-14). By making this gratuitous gift of God the object of his thanksgiving, Paul is preparing the way for his diatribes against the wisdom of the world as a pretended means to salvation (1 Co 1-4).

e) The *witness* of Christ borne by him at Corinth has been partciularly solid, because he has not relied on the frail help of human wisdom (1 Co 3:12-15), but on the divine action itself (1 Co 2:4-5; 4:15; Ga 4:19) and on the power of the resurrection. This allusion to apostolic ministry in the transmission of divine graces has its point in the context. Paul will be concerned to place the charisms of which the Corinthians boasted under the control of the hierarchy (1 Co 12:27-30).

f) The gifts of God do not save automatically, once for all. On the contrary they are a ferment meant to "increase," "grow firm," "make irreproachable" (v. 8). They are the beginning of a pilgrimage that will be completed on the *Day* of judgment and resurrection (cf. 1 Co 5:5; 3:13; 11:26), the day of "revelation" (v. 7) and triumph as manifestation for Christ and his Church. Every grace then is a first fruit of glory and majesty, resurrection and plenitude of life in Christ (1 Co 15:24-28). Elsewhere Paul will speak at greater length of final resurrection (1 Co 15:35-53); but he affirms at this stage that one cannot share the revelation of

Christ in glory, if one is not already in him in faith, thanks to the gifts he distributes. God is faithful (v. 9): what he bestows now is the first fruit of Christ's life and glory.

g) The Corinthian Christians were acutely aware of the problem of Christian *dispersion* in the world. Where the Jews were able to endure dispersion in the hope of that Day when Jerusalem would be re-established as the center of nations, the Corinthians had no such concrete point around which to rally. Consequently they were tempted to rely on the wisdom of the surrounding world. Paul now reveals to them their veritable city, the very person of Jesus Christ, and the "Day," already present, of his glorification.

No longer does the Christian expect a divine intervention that will transport him to a marvelous Jerusalem. He knows that divine life is at work in him, and cooperates with this as he looks towards consummation in glory.

XII. Matthew 24:42-51 *Gospel Thursday*

Following the eschatological discourse in chapter 24:1-41, the evangelist groups three parables which stress the duties of vigilance during the period intervening between the Lord's Pasch and the definitive constitution of the Kingdom. The first is concerned with the duties of the community leaders (our passage), the others with those of Christians generally, women (Mt 25:1-13) and men (Mt 25:14-30). Actually, today's reading is made up of two different parables. The first (vv. 43-44) could be called the parable of the thief, the second (vv. 45-51) that of the servant.

a) The parable of the thief alludes doubtless to some burglary publicly known in the time of Jesus (aorist verb). He uses it to warn the crowd. Be careful that the coming catastrophe (the fall of Jerusalem probably, as in Mt 24:1-14) does not surprise you as the thief the householder (cf. 1 Th 5:2, 4; 2 P 3:10; Rev 3:3; 16:15).

Verse 44 was probably added by the primitive Church which made of the thief-parable an allegory of its own wait for the Parousia. The Son of Man takes on the characteristics of a burglar. A parable of moralizing import is made into an allegory concerning the delay of the Parousia and the coming of the Son of Man. The expectation of Jerusalem's fall becomes that of the Lord's return.

b) In the following parable (vv. 45-51) the *servant* has received a position of trust. The unexpected return of the master will show whether or not he deserved it. Originally, the scene of the parable was the earthly one of fulfilling responsibility. But the final words of verse 51 were added at a fairly late stage (cf. Mt 8:12) in order to make of the parable on allegory. The Son of Man is returning to judge his own, especially those to whom he has entrusted certain responsibilities (a theme more fully stressed in Lk 12:41-46). It is just possible that verses 48-51 received this allegorizing interpretation as a result of Judas' suicide.

In fact, in the servant figure Jesus probably saw those who bore this title at the time, the leaders and the Scribes that is, whose responsibility it was to interpret the events of the people's history. He was foretelling an unexpected trial, where their fidelity would be put to the test.

The entry of humanity into the Kingdom then must be the result of human effort (hence the concept of good service by the servant in the parable), an effort however that is perceived as a grace of God with all the gratuity this implies (hence the concept of the unexpected in the thief parable). There is then a possible continuity between the terrestrial world and the future one (something that is implied in 1 Th 4:11-18). But it can only be perceived and lived as the gratuitous gift of the divine initiative.

The conjunction of the two parables then is opportune. The quietism of inactivity is guarded against on the one hand, and absolute humanism on the other.

XIII. 1 Thessalonians 4:1-8
1st reading
1st cycle
Friday

Here we have a brief extract from what may have been a primitive catechesis. To begin with, Paul recalls that the Christian life is a "journey" (v. 1) towards the holiness that God wants to share with man (v. 3). His teaching is relevant in two domains, that of purity (vv. 4-8) and that of charity (vv. 9-12).

a) Like most Jews of the time Paul associated impurity with pagan life (Ac 15:20; Rm 1:24-31; cf. Ga 5:10; 1 Co 6:13-18; 7:2). He expected that pagans who became Christian should demonstrate their conversion by a life of sexual *purity*, thus exhibiting the holiness to which God was calling them. If God sanctifies man, his whole being, body and spirit, should radiate that holiness (v. 3; cf. Rm 6:19). He is specific with regard to three things.

One must abstain from all unchasteness (v. 3b). Doubtless he is referring to unnatural relations, prostitution sacred and otherwise, different orgies and bacchanalia.

One must possess one's body (vv. 4-5), transform it that is gradually into a spiritualized body "in holiness." This concept is all the more important in that paganism regarded the body as a corruptible element destined to disappear. Paul on the other hand dignifies it. Mastery of the senses is for him the sign of a vocation to share the new life of the resurrected.

One must reject adultery. In the context the recommendation of verse 6 about not wronging one's neighbor can only mean not taking his wife.

b) He provides a series of motives for such conduct. We must know God (v. 5) and realize that he punishes such faults (v. 6). We must remember that the Spirit of God already dwells in the Christian (v. 8). Sexual morality in other words is a religious attitude. Those who break the conjugal bond transgress God's plan for men and humanity's destiny for *spiritualization.*

Purity is not just a matter of will, but a sign that a man has been sanctified in the depths of his being by the presence, the active presence, of the Holy Spirit. It has nothing to do with flight, or fears or tabus. It is spiritualization and control in the service of love.

Too many Christians are inclined to reduce their faith to a moral ideal, and the gospel propounds a particularly elevated ideal. Bearing witness to Christ for such people means, more than anything else, living a life in conformity with the evangelic ideal. It is as if Jesus were no more than a master of wisdom, as if grace bestowed no more than a better adjustment of life and sexuality to his precepts.

Such a view of Christian morality is altogether too ill-adjusted and shortsighted, and has many inconvenient consequences. If we expect from grace direct results in an area not proper to it we deceive ourselves. From a missionary point of view the consequences can be even more serious. An exemplary moral life is not necessarily proclamation of the Good News. Balanced sexuality is not a monopoly of Christians. We find it among people who are totally irreligious.

It is worth noting that Paul speaks of sexual morality just before his treatment of the resurrection of the dead (1 Th 4:13-18). Not indeed that this resurrection is a reward given for a life of purity or balanced morality. For every man, as for Christ himself, it is the culmination of the earthly effort to spiritualize the body, to put it in service to the ideal and to love. Christian morality expects no reward; it is the intense living of a specific vocation.

The authentic basis of Christian sexuality is the event of Christ's death and resurrection. Our moral standard owes nothing to a theoretic wisdom, however elevated; it arises from existential association with Christ's Pasch. In the fullest sense it should be an "imitation of Jesus." "As I have loved you, love one another." We must always be discerning in events the will of the Father, who enables us to triumph over the weight of death they carry.

The Christian sexual life is a paschal life; apart from a lived faith it makes no sense.

In similar fashion it is life in the Spirit, who stamps on the awareness an interior law, a principle of action through all events. The Christian who obeys it finds himself gradually liberated. The law he obeys is no longer something exterior to him. Sometimes, true, it presents itself to him in objective form (in ecclesial prescriptions for instance); but the deeper reality which underlies this is the action of the Spirit which transforms hearts.

Let us remember finally that such "supernatural" sexuality does not withdraw man from his creatural condition. On the contrary it leads him to accept that with more lucidity. In other words the moral life of the Christian strikes the absolutely rational balance.

In the event of the Eucharist above all our moral life can be renewed. This is above all an event in salvation history which takes place in human history. The Word is proclaimed there, and the homily ought to make it fully actual. It is the business of the homily to show the link between the forces of death which Christ overcame and those presented by the world, both on the individual and the collective level. Over these latter, Christians, following Christ, can triumph in turn.

XIV. 1 Corinthians 1:17-25
1st reading
2nd cycle
Friday

Paul is convinced that the factions at Corinth are due to confused zeal for philosophy and the reduction of the gospel message to systems of human thought. Today's reading contrasts the pretensions of human wisdom with the wisdom of God, and show how incapable it is of expressing the ambit of faith.

In verse 18 we have the basic affirmation. The language of the cross is *foolishness* for human wisdom. It is however the only language that can lead to faith and thus to salvation. This is sustained by a series of arguments.

First, a scriptural argument. The quotation in verse 19 of Isaiah 29:14 is a reminder that Yahweh saved Jerusalem by his own power, without any reference to political systems.

Next, a challenge. The sage, the learned man and the Scribe were not converted. Very few such are to be found in the Church (v. 20; cf. 1 Co 1:26), a good indication that their wisdom is not that of God.

Finally, a diatribe (v. 21). Originally God had foreseen that man through wisdom would recognize him in creation. Man however had perverted this (cf. Rm 1:19-20). It only remained for God to speak outside the framework of human wisdom, through the cross that is, which is called foolishness because it stands apart from thought structures and philosophic definitions. As against the Jews then who sought God in miracles (Mt 12:38-40), and Greeks who sought to define him by philosophy, Paul points out that he is only accessible through the Gospel of the cross (vv. 22-24). Jews would have to see him as a suffering Messiah, a king who ascended the throne by the way of death. Greeks would have to recognize as the founder of a religion someone who was confused with a vulgar thief on the cross.

The progress of faith does not follow rational principles. It can be rationalized of course—it is in any case reasonable—but it appeals to elements in a man other than those of the intelligence. It is perhaps a malady of certain types of Western man, maladjusted in a conceptual and Cartesian culture, that they fail to comprehend if reminded that they possess faculties besides that of reason. A capacity for love and trust has been atrophied in them: they are closed to transcendence. Paul's message has more relevance than ever now in the twentieth century. In an atheist world the Christian must exhibit a firm equilibrium and develop those faculties that seem at first glance irrational. Paul would call them foolish. But they are nevertheless authentic means of human expansion.

XV. Matthew 25:1-13 *Gospel Friday* The parable of the ten virgins is not now in its original context. Verse 13 is not an adequate conclusion. The exhortation to watch does not take account of the total content, where all the virgins, wise as well as foolish, sleep (v. 5). The conclusion repeats Matthew 24:42, and seems to come from Mark 13:35. Our evangelist has indeed placed the parable in the context of the eschatological discourse (Mt 24); but the interpretation which associates it with the Parousia does not seem original. Jesus never compared himself to the spouse. No allegory seems necessary for the understanding of his similitude.

a) Probably Jesus recounted a real happening in order to remind his listeners of the *imminence* of the Kingdom, and spur them on to greater vigilance (cf. the suddenness of the deluge in Mt 24:39, the unexpected arrival of the thief in 1 Th 5:1-5 and Mt 24:42, the unexpected return of the master in Mt 24:48).

The sudden arrival of the spouse is taken from life. Dealings between the two families were prolonged in espousal, indicating the parents' interest in progeny. Almost always the bridegroom made his appearance when the guests began to grow weary. It was a custom well calculated to suggest the sudden manifestation of a Kingdom among people otherwise preoccupied.

b) The primitive Church however at an early stage transformed the parable into an allegory of the *wedding of Christ and his Church.* The bridegroom became a figure of Christ (cf. Mt 9:15; 2 Co 11:2; Ep 5:25), and his judgment was associated with the conditions for entry to the wedding banquet. This strains the meaning of the original similitude, where the bridegroom is not even mentioned. For the early Christians the ten virgins, foolish as well as wise stood for the Church-bride. Until the wedding is accomplished the Church is composed of good people and sinners, just as the fishing net gathers the good fish and the less good (Mt 13:48), as the just and unjust are assembled in the banquet hall (Mt 22:10), as the field produces good and bad grain (Mt 13:24-30). It is a cortege of human beings wending their way towards the Lord. Some keep in their hands the lamps of vigilance lit. Others are not careful to nourish their faith. Some do not dissipate their energies on a thousand and one futilities. They have chosen Christ and take the means necessary to be faithful to him. Others are content with a purely sociological membership of the Church. The difference will not be seen until the pilgrimage of the Church is over, on the day when Christ is wedded to those who have been faithful.

c) Matthew may very well personally have added another dimension still by following the eschatological discourse with this parable. He is actually answering the question about participation in the Kingdom. He distinguishes two broad categories. There are those who are openly of the people of God (Mt 24:45-25:30), and those who are unwittingly preparing themselves for the Kingdom (Mt 25:31-46). In the first category he has successively those responsible for the people of God (Mt 24:45-51), and the members, women (Mt 25:1-13) and men (Mt 25:14-30). The parable of the ten virgins would be addressed to Christian *women,* reminding them as a class of the duty of vigilance. He often follows this procedure, combining with a "masculine" parable a "feminine" one (cf. Mt 24:18-19; 9:18-26; 13:31-33). It shows how the first preachers were attentive to the diversity of their public.

XVI. 1 Thessalonians 4:9-12
1st reading
1st cycle
Saturday

Having recalled his apostolate at Thessalonica, Paul turns to parainetic counsels where, as frequently in such instances, he has recommendations to charity and purity.

a) Concerning *charity,* he insists above all that it comes from God. It is not a benevolence by command, but a true "communion" set up by sharing the same life. That is why it is "brotherhood" (v. 9): the Christian gradually purifies himself of sin, and consequently is more and more invested with the divine life.

b) He singles out one aspect of fraternal charity: the *delicacy* which leads a man to mind his own business and work with his own hands (v. 11), lest he be a burden on the community (v. 12). He is alluding to some poor of the time, who, like twentieth century hippies, refused to work, challenging the surrounding society in the name of an eschatological one. They proved inconvenient for the life of the community, and for private individuals as well.

XVII. 1 Corinthians 1:26-31 *1st reading 2nd cycle Saturday*

This is a continuation of the argument put forward by Paul in 1 Corinthians 1:18-25 to show that human wisdom by itself is incapable of Knowledge of God's person and his salvation plan. The proof is that God's manifestation and the fulfillment of his plan seem folly, because they are outside the purview of human intelligence.

a) He now turns to an argument *ad hominem.* God continues to act *foolishly* because, as a sign of his presence in the world, he chooses a community so little qualified as the Corinthian (vv. 26-28). Paul reminds the Corinthians that they would be better occupied in pursuing a vocation within their compass (bearing witness to God's foolishness) than in flirting with false philosophies which they are incapable of understanding.

b) Though men have no right to glory in the grace of God (v. 29), the Corinthians may do so provided they do so in Christ (vv. 30-31, taken from Jr 9:22-23). Their titles to glory are many, God's justice which has established them, the holiness that divinizes their nature, the redemption which delivers them from all alienation, including sin and death.

What human wisdom could bring such benefits? Living in Christ (v. 30) means finding glorification (v. 31) in him.

The intransigence of this piece could possibly embarrass modern Christians, who are anxious for dialogue with the world, and for adaptation of divine wisdom to human contexts. Nor are their misgivings likely to be allayed by pointing out that this is a particular literary genre, where reality is distorted by polemic and argument *ad hominem*.

The problem is deeper. In Paul's own text however we can find the hint of a solution, in that Christ is regarded as *Wisdom* (v. 30). He is so because he reveals the mystery of God (cf. Col 2:3; 1 Co 1:24) in unexpected fashion. He is the Wisdom which organizes the world and leads man back to God (1 Co 1:21; cf. Rm 1:18-22). He is the "foolish" revelation of the invisible God; but he is also the center of the cosmos, and the first-born of humanity (Col 1:15-16; cf. Jn 1:1-18). That is to say that man's effort to know the universe is under the aegis of Christ as Wisdom.

The gospel is a gratuitous revelation of God, a light for the world and for men, the key to proper balance. Man seeks that balance by means of all the "wisdoms," trying to know himself and the world better. The balance of the gospel however may not be appropriated by any single human system. It does not fit Marxist analysis for instance any more than it does capitalist. It must always be to some extent "folly" according to the measure of human systems.

Paul's main point can never be gainsaid. Human wisdom is neither the exclusive, nor the best, means of revealing Jesus Christ. He chooses to see in the relative inadequacy of Christians in this domain the sign *par excellence* of God's presence. God brings into being his Church from that which is not (cf. Mt 11:25).

And is this not also true of humanity today? Is it not the less fortunate, poor though they be, rather than the cultivated, who demonstrate that the human person is of greater worth than the bread given him? Are not our very weakness and our incapacity to conquer sin the signs of divine election?

We have nowadays in our eucharistic assemblies many "well-born," many wise and many powerful. But they do not cease to celebrate Him who came in weakness and in foolishness.

XVIII. Matthew 25:14-30 *Gospel Saturday*

Matthew's version of the parable of the talents is very different from that of Luke (Lk 19:12-27). He reproduces moral conclusion of Jesus' eschatological discourse (Mt 24), and describes Christian life in the period between the Lords glorification and Jerusalem's fall, and the final Parousia. The new assembly is substituted for the old Jewish one, its members indicating the coming Kingdom. Each class does so in its proper way, the leaders of the community (Mt 24:45-51) by their manner of service, the women (Mt 25:1-13) by their vigilance, Christians in general by the "stewardship" of the gifts they have received. Where the first part of the eschatological discourse shows us the realization of God's Kingdom by divine intervention, the second gives us man's part in the realization.

This context colors the whole version of the parable. Clearly Matthew has placed these parables where he does, to develop a theology of the time of the Church and the assembly. Luke's version is in a different context, and has a different emphasis.

a) One essential theme in Matthew's version is that of *delay* (v. 19), which is ignored by Luke, and reminds us of the Spouse who delays (Mt 25:5). Where Matthew thinks of the time of the Church, Luke contemplates merely the interval between Christ's death and the fall of Jerusalem (Lk 19:11). People believed in the imminence of the Kingdom. Jesus tells them that first they would experience a revolt against the King (his Passion), and the chastisement of the city (the fall of Sion). Doubtless Luke has in mind the example of Archelaus who went to Rome to seek the kingship. He was followed there by the Jews who intrigued against him. Luke's eyes are fixed on the present, where Matthew contemplates the "time of the Church."

b) Another difference between the versions is the character of the *servants* of the Master. Luke has Jesus give the parable to illustrate the attitude of the listeners. Some believe in him. Others show themselves indifferent or frankly hostile (Lk 19:9, 11). Once the Kingdom has come, each attitude will receive its recompense. Those who are wholehearted disciples will receive the power of jurisdiction (Lk 19:17-19). The Jews who are indifferent will see their privileges "withdrawn" (Mt 24:24; Lk 19:16). The hostile Jews will be destroyed (Lk 19:27).

Matthew's viewpoint is different. He contemplates the time of the Church which follows the fall of Jerusalem, and the extraordinary disproportion between the stewardship on earth and the promised reward (Mt 25:21, 23, 29). The Master distributes his riches (those of the Kingdom, that is) with due regard for the natural talents of each person. But a single talent at that time represented an immense fortune. It would be wrong then to understand the talents as natural abilities to be exploited. These are the interests of the Kingdom, the Lord's riches, of which the Christian has the stewardship, because the kingdom can only be advanced with his cooperation.

The Lucan interpretation must have seemed too narrow and immediate to Matthew. He gave the parable a new dimension by placing it in the context of a theology of the Church. The purpose, it seems to him, is to make the disciples aware of their obligation to make the riches of the Kingdom bear fruit during the time allotted to them, the time of the Church that is.

God confided his treasure to the high priests and Scribes, and they buried it in their Holy Office. As the financier risks his capital so he risked his word. Yet God does not hoard his Word: he entrusts it to our responsibility to be used. The last servant, pusillanimously refusing every form of risk, actually chooses a security that is deceptive. Riches that are not invested are in fact devalued. He who does not multiply, dissipates. He who "buries" his talent, through fear of compromising it, buries himself, and opts for death.

Jesus' harsh warning to the Jewish religious authorities of his time retains for us too its full force. How are we to share his treasure unless we are involved in the world? A Church which would refuse to risk its heritage, through involvement with the secular city, would already have lost everything.

XIX. Matthew 24:1-14 *Alternative Gospel Liturgy of the Word*

Matthew's eschatological discourse is undoubtedly made up of two distinct discourses, with some redactional additions. The basic discourse concerns the destruction of the temple (1-3, 4-8, 15-20, 32-35). The expressions "see" and "all this" are characteristic of it. It attempts to determine the preliminary signs of the destruction and its approaching date. Today's reading belongs to it. Matthew has added to it from another context (Mt 10:21-22, 35-36) verses 9-14. The second discourse (24:21-22, 29-31, 36, 23-25) is more eschatological in tone. The expressions "chosen" and "this day" are characteristic; they tend to give the temple's fall a pronounced eschatological significance. We do not have any of it in today's reading.

a) Good Jews that they were, the apostles showed that they were proud of the temple Herod had just constructed. They thought it capable of fulfilling the function of reassembling all nations, as foretold by Isaiah 60; 56:1-7; Ze 14:14. Now, Jesus was proclaiming *its destruction* before the function was realized (v. 2; cf. 21:12-16; 23:37-39). They understood that in this he was substituting himself for the temple (cf. Mt 23:38; 26:61-64); and they tended to believe that the destruction would coincide with the "coming" of Jesus (v. 3) and the end of the world, which was expected after the nations' reassembly. They were anxious to have preliminary signs of the end of the temple economy, and the Lord's coming.

Jesus' answer is in two stages. First: they are not to attach too much importance to certain facts. If Christ is announced everywhere, that does not necessarily mean he will be there (vv. 4-5). Nor, when things go badly (wars, famines, etc.) does it necessarily mean that the coming of the Lord is at hand (vv. 6-8). The decisive sign of the temple's destruction will be the presence of the emperor's statue in the sanctuary (Mt 24:15).

b) Everything finally depends on the manner of *"seeing" the "signs."* There are deceptive signs, when people think they discern the presence of the Messiah and the ominous harbingers of his coming (vv. 4-8). Then there are real signs: the apparent victory of evil (v. 15), suffering (vv. 17-22), trial of faith by false prophets (vv. 23-25) who proclaim peace while war is brewing (Jr 14:15; 23:3-40; Ez 13).

Fidelity throughout all this trial and denudation purifies the discernment of the believer, so that he can "see" the "sign" of the Son of man (cf. Ze 12:10; Jn 3:14; 19:37) coming on the clouds. Everything in events and things he will be able to relate to the Lordship of the Risen Christ. We should note that Matthew employs two different verbs for seeing the preliminary signs of the temple destruction (vv. 2, 5 *blepein;* v. 15 *idein*) and the sign of the Son of Man (v. 30 *orao*). Doubtless he wants to emphasize that the discernments are not the same. Carnal eyes can see certain things. But the understanding of these, in order to read there the sign of the Son of Man, is of the order of faith. The meaning of the whole passage then is clear. The disciples have to learn to see events with faith in the Risen Lord. They must be convinced that faith brings understanding of the progress of history and of life.

TABLE OF READINGS